Contents

We have lived in a time of change and corrosive skepticism and cynicism concerning the administration of justice. Nothing can more weaken the quality of life or more imperil the realization of those goals we all hold dear than our failures to make clear by word and deed that our law is not an instrument of partisan purpose, and it is not an instrument to be used in ways which are careless of the higher values which are within us all.

Mr. President, when you spoke to me two months ago you were eloquent and persuasive as to your high aspiration for this Department. And, speaking literally, you moved me.

I am sure that the able men and women of this Department will join with me in responding to your aspirations.

From Edward Levi's remarks at his swearing-in
ceremony as Attorney General, February 7, 1975

Foreword

Larry D. Kramer

Reading the speeches in this volume really made me miss Edward Levi. I don't mean miss him personally, though I did know him. Actually, I owe my career to Levi. You see, I went to law school grudgingly, mainly to allay my parents' anxiety about my career plans, or lack thereof. Secretly, I planned to stay for a short time only, maybe five or six weeks, after which I could tell them I had tried law and hated it and was dropping out to return to New York City, where I fantasized I would become a writer. (Looking back, I'm not sure what I was thinking, as I had no experience, nor any actual talent.) It was 1981, and Levi was still teaching Elements of the Law, a required first-year course he had created with Karl Llewellyn and had worked on steadily—for a time with Llewellyn, for a time with Soia Mentschikoff, but mostly on his own—for more than three decades.

A version of Elements is still part of the first-year curriculum at the University of Chicago. But with due respect to some very fine teachers, what's taught there today is a mere shadow of Levi's class—a ten-week forced march that began with the debate between Socrates and Thrasymachus about whether might makes right and ended 1,800 pages later with *Roe v. Wade*, while seeming to cover just about everything in between. It was brutal, but also surprising, exhilarating, and wildly challenging: a smorgasbord of materials from law, history, philosophy, classics, political science, and more. We read Augustine and Aquinas and Coke and Holt

Larry D. Kramer is president of the William and Flora Hewlett Foundation. He received his JD from the University of Chicago in 1984 and was dean of the Stanford Law School from 2004 to 2012.

and Blackstone and Austin and Rousseau and Hobbes and Hohfeld and
Holmes and a boatload of judicial opinions; we studied Nuremberg and
Rhodesia, the emergence of the jury, the relationship of law to morality,
and the nature of the common law compared to civil law and to statutory
and constitutional law. It was an eye-opening lesson in the unbounded
richness of legal studies—a demonstration of the way in which, as Levi
explained to the entering class of 1976, "law is pervasive throughout most
of human life" and "part of both the humanities and the social sciences."[1]
I was hooked. My skepticism about a career in law melted away, and I decided not only to remain at Chicago but to become Levi's research assistant, so I could work with him on the Elements materials. And everything
in my professional life has followed from there.

I never became close to Levi, though I worked for him all three years
I was a student at Chicago and think he even liked my work. I was still
too intimidated to ask for a letter of recommendation when I applied
for clerkships in my third year. And while Levi was genuinely witty and
could be immensely charming—qualities evident in the speeches that follow—he was somewhat gruff, perhaps drily disdainful is more accurate,
toward his students (and research assistants). My classmates and I were
absolutely convinced that it must have been Levi who supplied the real
inspiration behind *The Paper Chase*'s Professor Kingsfield, its Harvard
setting notwithstanding. Even after I returned to Chicago to join the faculty in 1986, I could never bring myself to call him "Edward."

So when I say that the contents of this book made me realize how
much I miss Edward Levi, I mean as an educator and public intellectual, as someone whose words and ideas could enlighten and inspire. I
miss him for what these speeches reveal about how people in positions
of authority used to talk to us. The records of Levi's tenure as Attorney
General remind us that we have had leaders who spoke to us like adults
and treated us as capable of grasping complex ideas. Obviously, Levi was
more erudite than most government officials, even in his time. But to read
his speeches is to be reminded that the level of political discourse in this
country was still quite high as recently as a generation ago. It is to feel
acutely how far we have lowered our expectations by embracing men
and women who compete for high office while wearing their ignorance
on their sleeves—indeed, while seeming almost proud of it—and by con-
straining even intelligent and educated leaders to reduce what they say to
kindergarten-level sound bites.

What makes these speeches so marvelous, so unlike political speeches today, is the extent to which they are filled with serious ideas presented in a serious manner. The utter absence of ideology, of simpleminded dogma and cant and false piety, is totally refreshing. Levi stakes out positions that frankly acknowledge the complexity of a problem, and he defends his positions with arguments that ask us to grapple with nuance and that assume we can do so. He does so, moreover, while effortlessly and unself-consciously drawing on history and literature and law and culture. As Attorney General, Levi was a political figure. Yet these do not feel like political speeches. They feel, rather, like the product of hard thinking by a responsible public official who, when faced with difficult choices, takes it upon himself to explain his decisions to a public he assumes is intelligent enough to understand and thoughtful enough to deserve nothing less. That's why I miss Edward Levi.

Levi's candor is particularly notable given the state of public affairs when he took office. After reaching a high point of prosperity and power in the mid-1960s, the country had endured one calamity after another: the souring of the civil rights movement and the devastating riots that followed, the catastrophically failed war in Vietnam, recession and inflation and our first energy crisis, rapid urban decay combined with steeply rising crime rates, and the abrupt rotting of a counterculture movement that changed seemingly overnight from the "Summer of Love" and Woodstock into the Manson family and Altamont.

But above all, there was Watergate. The passage of years may have softened the edges of the Watergate scandal, causing us to forget how truly demoralizing it was when it happened. In part, that's because we've seen even worse government misconduct since Nixon resigned, while his strengths have come to look better in retrospect. But at the time, Watergate was a shattering experience. It wasn't just the breadth and depth of Nixon's wrongdoing, though it did sometimes seem as if criminal misbehavior pervaded every part of his administration. It was also the petty and pedestrian nature of it all: the sordid, sleazy quality of White House "plumbers" and CREEP and all those "expletive deleteds."

These controversies were continually in the background—and sometimes the foreground—of Levi's public comments, and he did not hesitate to draw on them for lessons. A few examples should suffice to convey the flavor. We may have been mistaken to let "our ideals of justice in the world [overcome] our humility" in Vietnam, Levi cautioned, but we must take care lest "skepticism and doubt" lead us to "reject those ideals with

a fervor equal to that with which we held them before," or to lose "awareness of history and the understanding of current problems . . . in the energetic process of getting even."[2] And if Watergate taught us anything, it is
that we must not "assume that everything the government does is equivalent to law or the legal system."[3]

Concern for restoring public confidence in the Department of Justice and the FBI is a common theme—both agencies having lost credibility from involvement in assorted Watergate-related cover-ups and illegal investigations. "The institutions of law and the profession still have
the legacy of a skepticism which has grown over many years," Levi acknowledged at a meeting of the American Bar Association. But while
skepticism can be useful, "[m]istrust can be corrosive," and "[j]ustified
mistrust places the heaviest burden upon us."[4] Things needed to change:
"The Department has to be a special advocate, not only in defending governmental decisions at law, but in the attempt to infuse into them the
qualities and values which are of the utmost importance to our constitutional system. There must be a special concern for fair, orderly, efficient
procedures, for the balance of constitutional rights and for questions of
federalism and the proper regard for the separation of powers. It is sometimes said that, so far as the Department is concerned, courts alone have
this duty. I do not agree."[5]

Many of Levi's best-known acts as Attorney General—the guidelines
for electronic surveillance and for domestic security investigations being
only the most obvious examples—were motivated as much by the desire
to do something visible to restore the DOJ's reputation as they were by
the need to fix very real problems with the department's procedures and
controls.

Levi also tackled the related task of restoring departmental morale,
which likewise had been devastated by the scandals. "I know we all realize that in the past there have been grave abuses," Levi told the Senate Select Committee on Intelligence. "I am uncomfortable with a kind of
writing of history, however, which sees it only in terms of the abuses and
not in terms of past and present strength. . . . In spite of the abuses, there
is a proper place for pride. I take it our mutual work should be to nurture
that pride and the conditions which justify it."[6] In the final analysis, after
all, "[n]o procedures are fail-safe against abuse. The best protection remains the quality and professionalism of the members of the Bureau and
of the Department"—something Levi took pains to recognize and praise
on every possible occasion.[7]

Nor did Levi view the task of rebuilding morale as limited to the government's lawyers alone. He sought to do what he could to restore the faith of the American people as well and to do so in a comprehensive sense: to rebuild confidence not just in the particular agencies of government that had failed so badly but in our constitutional system generally. As he explained to the one hundredth graduating class of the FBI Academy, "We must never forget one essential truth": "Ultimately, enforcement must spring from the faith of citizens. In a free society there are essential values which would be destroyed were law enforcement to depend entirely on force of arms. Another kind of force must operate. That force is the willing acceptance by an overwhelming proportion of our people of the law's demands. People must believe, if not in the wisdom of a particular law, at least in the fairness and honesty of the enforcement process."[8]

The mere fact that Levi himself was the nation's top law enforcement officer probably went some distance toward restoring this belief, and for that reason among many, Levi was a brilliant choice to be the first post-Watergate Attorney General: a genuine intellectual, a gifted scholar and teacher, a former law school dean and university president, and an accomplished administrator of unimpeachable integrity who had experience in the Department of Justice but who had never been involved in politics. Few could match Levi's authority when it came to encouraging the American people to trust their system of government.

And encourage he did. "We have come through a crisis of legitimacy," he offered reassuringly:

> It is no doubt difficult for us to characterize objectively the nation's response to these events. We are left with uneven and see-sawing relations among the branches of government, with basic questions concerning parliamentary forms, the role of the executive and the courts, the nature of federalism. Of course we have much to think about. My guess is that history will not see our difficulties as great as we imagine them to be, that it will look with special favor, if not upon us, then upon the Founders who created a hope for mankind, and that indeed it will probably add a word of approval as that hope is renewed in our day.[9]

One could end here, having invited readers to enjoy these speeches for their historical value. But that would be to overlook other, equally significant aspects of Levi's writings. Levi was and always remained an academic at heart, after all, and while Attorney General he continued to follow—and comment upon—the legal intellectual movements of his day, including some that are still important but that were then just beginning to develop. Levi had absolutely no use for originalism, for example, seeing in the provisions of the Constitution "the expression of compromises that mirror the sort of adaptation and accommodation envisioned by the process the Constitution set into motion"—a process "intended as a confrontation with problems to be solved, and in its new form an invention for the future."[10] It was, in fact, "the special duty of the legal profession, and surely that of jurisprudence, to attempt to emphasize and explain the basic values of our legal order in the light of the problems of our time."[11]

Such sentiments are consistent with Levi's general pragmatism, a cast of mind very much at odds with the ideological reductionism embraced by originalists. This same intellectual disposition led Levi eventually to disparage both law and economics, of which he was a founder, and critical legal studies—two newly emerging schools of thought that presented themselves as polar opposites but that shared what Levi saw as a crude and simpleminded picture of law as nothing more than a tool of power used to manipulate or coerce. "While it is certainly possible to view all activities this way," he reflected, "it is only a partial truth. It elides important distinctions. It puts a gloss of politicization on all events, when in fact it is a question of more or less, and the designation sometimes hardly fits at all."[12] The incompleteness of a view that "describe[s] everything that goes on . . . in terms of power relationships or automatic reactions" was, in Levi's mind, not just misguided, but dangerous as well: "The position diminishes reason, disparages the ideal of the common or public good, adds legitimacy to the notion that law is only one more instrument among many to be manipulated. . . . I suppose it is not strange that our view of the struggle of self-interests, real or induced, is somewhat self-fulfilling. It builds easily upon the pragmatic strain among us with its inherent cynicism, even though events of the last thirty-five years indicate that one should not count on cynicism to combat passion."[13]

Levi's own intellectual proclivities ran rather strongly toward the movement that has come to be known as "law and society." The formal legal system of courts and lawyers is, in this view, only one institution among many that shape legal norms, and not necessarily the most important one. ("If we are to woo all the Muses and Graces," he teased, "let Humility be among them."[14]) Levi's description of how law functions reflects textbook law and society thinking:

Law is not only the product of lawyers. The whole society uses and interprets the law. And because of that, the law expresses something deep and important about the values we hold as a people. It expresses our strongest commitments and the highest aspirations. Law is not everything in society. The law is only one of a number of institutions through which we express ourselves and which in turn influence us, maintain our customs and change our habits. Thus law takes a place along with family structures, religious beliefs, the expressions of art and the explanations of science. Law embodies the values common to many of those institutions. Law, as the custodian of the historic rights mankind has developed for itself, must never be regarded as the tool of the power of the moment.

The public, the press, the academic community, the artists, all by their assertions and conduct inform and develop the law. As new human values and ideas make their way into common acceptance, they also make their way into the law which translates them into words by which common conduct may be governed. By guiding common conduct, by speaking in words, the law has its own power to educate, to alter commonly held views, to shape the thinking of the public whose thinking in turn shapes the law.[15]

While all this is genuinely interesting and important, ultimately, the real reward in reading these speeches is not what they show us about history, nor what they have to say about jurisprudence or legal theory. It is the opportunity to be exposed to the mind of Edward Levi: to hear his voice and experience his way of thinking. Levi was enormously learned, of course, and he had a genuinely penetrating intellect. But he combined these cerebral qualities with an uncommonly sensitive eye when it came to people and institutions and what made them tick, and it was the rare bringing together of these attributes that makes him stand out. Levi was, in a word, *wise* — and that wisdom is reflected on every page of this book. He is thought provoking and shrewd, occasionally eloquent, and always balanced and measured: a subtle critic who becomes all the more persuasive, because while he cares about his subjects and respects his audiences, he never takes himself too seriously.

It is, moreover, amazing to see how much of what Levi had to say remains directly relevant to our current situation. I will illustrate this with a single example, but the continuing pertinence of Levi's words will strike any reader pervasively in reading through the speeches. My example concerns the nature and quality of political discourse and public deliberation.

As diagnosed by Levi, post-Watergate America turns out to have had many of the same difficulties with this as America today—and for many of the same reasons. Speaking personally, I'm not sure whether I find this a relief ("things always seem this bad") or massively depressing ("they have just kept getting worse"), but the parallels are uncanny.

Political debate in the mid-1970s, like today, was acrimonious, tiresome, and utterly unproductive. Recalling George Washington's famous remark about the tendency of Americans to swing between extremes, Levi observed that "[w]e are in such a period of cyclical reaction today, justifying what we do now as a kind of getting even with the events of prior years."[16] This "energetic process of getting even" distressed Levi, who condemned the angry game of tit for tat for making politics simultaneously heated and empty—a destructive tendency that was being exacerbated by two new developments.[17] First, "the breakdown of so many supportive institutions"[18]: "I do not know whether the family, the church, volunteer religious orders, community organizations, the school, the university are less important than they once were. I suppose it could be argued that in some ways, contrary to popular belief, some of them have been strengthened. But in many ways they have removed themselves from a leadership of civility."[19]

The effect on public deliberation from the deterioration of these traditional institutions was worsened by a second change, the development of "new forms of communication," which produced "a veritable bombardment of capsulizing concepts and conclusions in a powerful and dramatic way."[20] It's hard to believe that Levi did not already have our twenty-four-hour news cycle and internet-based culture in mind:

> Modern communication emphasizes the immediate event which can be seen; it tends to make of discussion the declaration of opinions in a form to be quickly understood, suggesting that the complexity of a problem is always the result of inefficiency or bad motives. One can join to this the influence of widespread dissemination of the professional sampling of how people say they feel. At any time the ideal of reasoned discussion is hard to approximate. It seems harder now, even though there should be greater chance for it in spite of the obvious barriers which perhaps will turn out to be supportive in the long run. Voltaire once observed that the real scourge of mankind has not been ignorance but the pretense of knowledge. Today there may be more pretense of knowledge, a vice which most of us share, because there are more bits of knowledge widely distributed.[21]

The cumulative effect of such developments was ravaging American democracy by undermining the fundamental preconditions for its success: a reasonably informed citizenry made up of individuals willing to reconsider their positions or to compromise based on respectful discussion with people who believe differently. Each of these conditions seemed critical to Levi, as they should be to us today. Each also seemed to be failing, as they look to be doing today.

So, Levi noted, "[O]ver time a working society, with a broadened electorate and a representative government, cannot help but be elevated or depressed by the general level of knowledge and spirit of candor to inquire and to learn and to think and rethink possessed by the many."[22] Or, again, "Free inquiry means that we should put ourselves to the test of finding out what is wrong with what we think—an unsettling, a disconcerting, at times a most unwelcome pursuit of knowledge."[23] Or yet again, "A free society, a government by discussion, requires mutual respect. It requires mutual understanding. It requires a culture held in common—a culture not unitary but composed of many differences. The base for understanding must be built and rebuilt over time."[24] It is when our differences are greatest that "accommodation and compromise reflecting the exigencies of the matter at hand have been not only possible but a felt necessity. The essence of compromise is that there is no surrender of principle or power on either side, but there is respect for the responsibility of others and recognition of the need for flexibility and reconciliation of competing interests."[25] Nor, Levi notes in a particularly apt passage, are these concerns applicable to substance alone: "Andre Malraux has written, 'A civilization can be defined at once by the basic questions it asks and by those it does not ask.' I would add one more item to Malraux's comment: namely, the tone in which a society asks its questions. The tone itself may be even more important than the question or the answer."[26]

I said above that Levi was "occasionally eloquent." And it is true that the power of his writing usually comes less from rhetorical elegance than from intelligence and sense. But when considering problems like this— problems that cut to the heart of the democratic experiment, an experiment that looked in Levi's day, as it does in ours, to be seriously at risk— Levi's voice and pen could become exceedingly powerful. In a speech to the Fellows of the American Bar Foundation entitled "In the Service of the Republic," Levi offered his most heartfelt message to and for the American people, a lesson as necessary in 2013 as it was in 1976, and one no one today articulates as well:

The point which must be made, I think, is that behind the courts and behind the legislatures are the influential mechanisms of society which set or distort the debate, which enlighten, or by a delight in induced or assumed antagonism, cheapen every discussion so that the immediate reaction is never troubled by a later thought. These are harsh words, too harsh perhaps, but the freedom our society has given does place a responsibility upon the press and upon the professions, particularly our profession, to clarify the issues, not in a spirit of antagonists or adversaries—there are forums for that—but so an enlightened public will understand not the catch words, not the chosen disagreements, but the basic issues which are involved. If one believes in a government by reason or discussion, the victory comes when there is understanding. The problems we have are not easily solved, but the beginning is made when they are understood. This is of course much to ask. But it has a great deal to do with the role of our country if it is to continue to be the best hope in government for mankind.

I miss Edward Levi. The whole nation does.

Editor's Introduction

Two months before Attorney General Edward Levi turned over the position to his successor, Griffin Bell, he gave a speech to the Los Angeles County Bar Association. "In my view," he said, "one paramount concern must always guide our way. This is the keeping of the faith in the essential decency and evenhandedness in the law, a faith which is the strength of the law and which must be continually renewed or else it is lost. This has been a central principle which my colleagues and I have kept as our first concern."[1]

Levi touched on themes he had spoken about many times before in speeches included in this volume—particularly privacy, confidentiality, national security, and the need for serious thinking and rethinking in light of our values, all of which the Watergate scandal had brought to the fore. He told of an experience he had at the very beginning of his term:

> One area in which the process of rethinking began very early concerns the standards and procedures by which intelligence agencies should operate. I vividly recall that quite late in the afternoon on my first day as Attorney General this issue arose immediately. Just as I was settling into my chair and observing the handsome wood paneling of the office, an FBI agent appeared at my door without announcement. He put before me a piece of paper asking my authorization for the installation of a wiretap without court order and he waited for my approval. For close to 40 years the Department of Justice had been called upon to undertake electronic surveillance in certain cases without prior judicial approval. But I thought it was a bit unusual that I was expected to sign so automatically, if that really was the expectation. I asked the agent to leave the request with me—I think, perhaps, to his surprise—so that I could consult other officials in the Department.

This experience was one of many that led us to explore the question of how procedures could be perfected in this world of inevitable secrecy.[2]

I knew this anecdote well. Levi had told me a version of it the day that he asked me to join him as one of his special assistants. He was trying to explain the work he wanted me to help him with, but because it was all so highly classified he had to be vague. I barely understood what he was talking about. This problem of how to begin the discussion of matters that had been undiscussable was one of the great challenges of his Attorney Generalship.

Speaking in public became a vital instrument. Levi used his speeches to reassure people inside government and out that the Department of Justice was operating by the rule of law, that it was not partisan, and that it aspired to be wise. As is generally the case at this level of government, he often asked others to write early drafts of talks. When the subject concerned one particular part of the Justice Department, he would give that unit a chance to offer its ideas. At other times he would ask the public information office to try a draft. Or he would ask one of us on his personal staff. Usually the drafts did not even come close to what he had in his mind. In the end, he always thoroughly rewrote (or simply started over), which is why these talks are so distinctive both in content and in voice. He worked hard on his speeches, often for hours on end, sometimes at night or very early in the morning at his home, sometimes in a small, quiet study above his main office at the Justice Department where he worked curved over a typewriter like a parenthesis, testing every generalization and qualifying those that seemed to him overstated or reductive. This extraordinary care and commitment of time reflects the importance he gave his public addresses in accomplishing his goals for the department and the restoration of public faith in federal justice.

At times he spoke in public settings as a way of cutting through a cumbersome system and establishing a new direction, but most often he used his speeches to demonstrate the possibility of genuine conversation about the important and conflicting values in play and the choices to be made. He spoke often of his ideal of a "government by discussion," and he practiced it within the Department of Justice. It was a process that former Solicitor General Robert Bork, once Levi's student, described as being like a good seminar.[3]

At times Levi went beyond the leaders of the department and brought strong, sage voices from outside government into the discussion. At one

point he gathered a group of eminent constitutional scholars, including
Herbert Wechsler, director of the American Law Institute; Paul Freund,
Harvard constitutional law scholar and editor-in-chief of a multivolume
history of the Supreme Court;[4] Yale Kamisar, an important criminal law
and procedure scholar; and Gerald Gunther, a Stanford law professor and
author of his generation's standard textbook on constitutional law. They
met with Levi in his office to talk through the problem of electronic surveillance in national security cases: Should it continue to be used without
judicial warrants? Would a new kind of warrant give federal judges a role
beyond what the Constitution envisioned? To keep the conversation from
being abstract, Levi obtained security clearances for the law professors,
so that they would know what was at stake. Later, he retained as special
counsel Wechsler and Philip Kurland, University of Chicago law professor and editor of the *Supreme Court Review*, as he was deciding whether
to prosecute a number of Central Intelligence Agency employees who
had secretly opened mail addressed to or sent from the United States.[5]

Unlike a seminar, discourse was not an end in itself. It led to decision
and then to candid public disclosure. As Levi's former special assistant,
Ron Carr, wrote, "Perhaps the most remarkable quality about the process was the perfect congruence between the process itself and the way in
which Mr. Levi publicly described the consequences."[6]

Levi gave his talks before police officers graduating from the FBI
Academy, before people being sworn in as new United States citizens. He
often gave speeches to groups of leaders of the bar, because if they did
not believe federal justice was on the square, nobody else would either.
And he talked with academic groups, partly because they so often asked
him to, but also because they led opinion. And, of course, he testified before committees of Congress.

I have chosen for this volume talks that speak to what Levi called in his
Los Angeles County Bar Association speech his "central concern": dem-
onstrating his and the Department of Justice's commitment to the essential decency and evenhandedness of the law.[7] The first chapter includes
talks setting out Levi's view of the fundamental challenges he faced: the
corrosive skepticism of the times, the need to restore confidence by discussion and by demonstration, and the ideal of the executive branch "acting judicially." I also include a few brief anecdotes Levi told about life in
the Attorney General's office in this period. The second chapter includes
talks in which Levi located contemporary legal issues in a larger context.
He drew on classical and American political and intellectual history and

also liked to point out that law was only one of the institutions by which a society tries to do justice. The third chapter begins with a brief excerpt about the challenge of having genuine discussions. This is followed by several major addresses on key issues in which Levi engaged in government by discussion, deep public discussion. The talks deal with electronic surveillance, executive privilege, separation of powers, antitrust enforcement, and guidelines governing the FBI's domestic security activities.

Because 1976 was the year of the bicentennial of the Declaration of Independence, many of Levi's talks drew upon the early history of our nation, especially the ideas at play in the writing of the Constitution. It was characteristic of Levi to turn to history in considering the present. At one point a friend of mine interviewed Levi for an article he was writing for the *Atlantic Monthly*. When he finished the conversation, my friend came down the hall to my office and we talked. He said the interview had been remarkable. "In what way?" I asked. He answered with an example. Some way into the conversation, he had said to Levi, "You seem to be trying to make your decisions for history." Without a moment's hesitation Levi responded, "What else is there?"

In that spirit, a bit of Levi's own history and the country's as it emerged from the Watergate scandal that forced President Richard M. Nixon into retirement will help put the talks in this volume in context.

Born on June 26, 1911, Levi was the son and grandson of rabbis and a child of the institution with which he was identified most of his life, the University of Chicago. His grandfather, Emil Hirsch, was appointed one of the university's original faculty members in 1892. From his childhood at John Dewey's laboratory schools through the college and the law school, Levi received his education from the University of Chicago. At one point he contemplated a life as a writer and English professor, going so far as to write a radio drama and persuade a young Orson Welles to make an audition recording of it. But when the time came, Levi was drawn to the law.[8]

After the University of Chicago he went to Yale Law School as a Sterling Fellow (receiving his JSD in 1938). There he met a dynamic young professor who helped shape his later career. William O. Douglas was impressed with Levi, and when Franklin Roosevelt appointed Douglas to be chairman of the Securities and Exchange Commission, Douglas invited Levi to join him. Levi agreed. Then a faculty position came open at the University of Chicago. Douglas wrote the dean and told him he would be a fool not to hire Levi. When Levi received an offer and struggled with whether to take it or join Douglas in Washington, Douglas told him that positions on first-rate law faculties did not often present themselves to Jews. He would be a fool not to take it, Douglas said. The memory of this moment came back to Levi during the last, bitter days of Douglas's long service on the United States Supreme Court, facing the prospect of being replaced by Gerald Ford, a man who had tried to get him impeached. Levi played a key role in President Ford's selection of Douglas's successor, John Paul Stevens.[9]

When World War II came, Levi left the law faculty and finally went to Washington, serving as special assistant to Attorney General Francis Biddle, first assistant in the War Division, and first assistant in the Antitrust Division under Thurman Arnold. He returned to the University of Chicago law faculty in 1945 and married Kate Sulzberger Hecht in 1946, a remarkable bond that helped sustain him for more than fifty years. In 1949 he published *An Introduction to Legal Reasoning*, which has become a classic. He did further government service as counsel to the Subcommittee on Monopoly Power of the House Judiciary Committee and also served as counsel for the Federation of Atomic Scientists, where he was one of the authors of the Atomic Energy Control Act of 1946 that created the Atomic Energy Commission.[10]

Levi became dean of the law school at the University of Chicago in 1950 and held the job for twelve years, during which time he was summoned to testify before the Subcommittee on Internal Security of the Senate Judiciary Committee, which engaged in anticommunist investigations at the height of the Cold War. At issue in Levi's appearance was research into the American jury system by two law school faculty members. The research involved taping jury deliberations with the consent of the presiding judges but without the knowledge of the jurors. The chairman of the subcommittee was Sen. James O. Eastland (D-Miss.), who by the time Levi was nominated to be Attorney General had become chairman of the Senate Judiciary Committee, before whom Levi had to appear for confirmation hearings. Despite the hostility of their earlier encounter, Eastland and Levi developed a good working relationship.

In 1962 Levi was named the first provost of the university, and in 1968 he became president of the University of Chicago. It was not long before students took over the administration building. Levi's response was unlike that of many other university presidents at the time. He refused to call in the Chicago Police, then waited the protesters out. When they finally left, university disciplinary committees expelled or suspended more than a hundred of the students.

President Gerald Ford turned to Levi because he realized, as he wrote in his autobiography, that "nowhere did Watergate leave more lasting scars than at the Department of Justice. . . . It was important to select someone nonpolitical, and because the issues the department was considering were so very complex, it was essential that my nominee have a superior intellect."[11] Impressed by the way Levi had handled the takeover of the administration building, he felt that in Levi he had found a man who was "both firm and fair," an "excellent administrator," and also "unflappable."[12]

At the time of Levi's public swearing-in on February 7, 1975, the situation he faced was dire, a "crisis of legitimacy," he called it.[13] There was a deep-seated distrust of government and its officials, especially those charged with the enforcement of the law. He was the fifth Attorney General in six years. Two of his four predecessors ended up convicted of crimes relating to the Nixon White House's deployment of secret operatives against its political opponents and its effort to cover up this activity. The former acting head of the Federal Bureau of Investigation, L. Patrick Gray, had resigned when it was revealed that less than a week after the break-in at the offices of the Democratic National Headquarters in the Watergate Hotel he had received documents from the safe of the leader of the burglars. The White House counsel told him they should never see the light of day; Gray later burned them in a fireplace. The former head of the department's Internal Security Division (abolished in 1973) was under indictment for activities while serving in Nixon's reelection campaign.[14]

Though the FBI, despite Gray, had been instrumental in the investigation of the burglary, the scandal and its aftermath—as well as unreleated leaks of FBI documents—revealed information about a variety of the Bureau's previously secret programs to spy on and disrupt domestic political groups thought by the Bureau to be subversive. As Levi took office, Congressional investigations geared up to look into the FBI and other federal intelligence organizations. Electronic surveillance without a warrant, especially when agents had to break and enter in order to place a microphone, was under particular scrutiny, the Supreme Court in 1972 having ruled it unconstitutional in domestic security cases (those not involving spying, subversion, or terrorism by a foreign power).[15] Also deeply controversial were the FBI's so-called COINTELPRO operations in which agents tried various schemes to make life difficult for individuals and groups as varied as the Socialist Workers' Party, Dr. Martin Luther King, and anti–Vietnam War activists. (Levi said a number of times in speeches and testimony that some of these operations were outrageous, and the others were foolish.[16]) Within weeks of becoming Attorney General, Levi revealed to a committee of the House of Representatives a summary of the contents of the long-feared secret files of the late FBI Director J. Edgar Hoover. The files were mostly routine or administrative, but those that were salacious justified the fears, and in his disclosure Levi was careful not to put the unproven allegations in the secret files on public display.

As the Watergate scandals and their aftermath played out, the percentage of Americans who said they had a highly favorable view of the FBI fell from 84 to 37 percent.[17] And it was not only the FBI that was thrown into doubt. The press reported that the Central Intelligence Agency had for more than twenty years intercepted and opened mail between United States citizens and residents of the Soviet Union and that the National Security Agency (NSA) had a list of Americans whose international telecommunications it monitored. As Levi often said, it was as if the country were reliving decades of Cold War history all at once, without remembering the danger.

Still, it became clear to Levi that many of the government's intelligence activities had been undertaken without a thought to the law. Not long into his service as Attorney General, he and a few of his colleagues went to visit the NSA, the super-secret organization that monitors international communications and decrypts coded messages. After we were shown an array of dazzling ultra-secret technologies, the head of the agency gave a briefing. Levi asked to be provided with the memoranda in the files discussing the Fourth Amendment implications of the NSA's activities. When the NSA director asked his general counsel if he could think of any reason this could not be done, the lawyer paused for a moment and then said he couldn't provide them because there were none. The constitutional question had simply never been asked.

As the congressional investigations got underway, there were multiple demands for documents from the files of the intelligence agencies. Some of these documents carried the highest possible security classification, usually for good reason. There was intense resistance when Levi asserted that the decision whether and under what circumstances to disclose these matters belonged to the Justice Department, which might have to defend in court any decision to invoke executive privilege. Executive privilege, like many other legal doctrines, had been discredited by misuse by the Nixon administration, but a good number of people in the intelligence community had not yet appreciated its fragility. At one meeting of the deputy directors of the intelligence agencies, a senior CIA official bristled at the very idea of any disclosure of one particular spying operation. "That is something," he said, "that we can't even tell the President about."[18]

Levi prevailed, and many documents (though by no means all) were provided. Some were turned over to the committees' staffs, others given to the Senators and Representatives and not staffs, still others only shown or described to the committee chairmen. This did not satisfy everyone in Congress, of course, and there were calls to subpoena executive branch officials and hold them in contempt if they failed to provide the documents demanded. There was even a suggestion that a recalcitrant executive official might be seized and put in a jail in the Capitol building. Levi dealt with these subjects in his talks on confidentiality[19] and separation of powers.[20]

It was with the FBI that Levi felt the greatest responsibility both to reform and to defend. The Bureau was part of the Department of Justice, but it had learned during the J. Edgar Hoover years to resist the kind of direction and accountability that other parts of the department took for granted. The first order of business, then, was to begin a process of integration, and the key figure in this was FBI Director Clarence Kelley. A great bear of a man, Kelley had once been an FBI agent, then had moved on to become chief of police in Kansas City before being appointed by Richard Nixon to run an organization still churning in the wake of Hoover's death.

Not long after working with Kelley on disclosure of Hoover's secret files, Levi paid him a visit in his office, which was then still on the same floor as the Attorney General's in the main Justice Department building.[21] As Levi and a few others entered, Kelley greeted the Attorney General with a convivial slap on the back that almost sent him flying. Through the window we could see the dome of the Capitol lighted up for the night. Levi told Kelley that he knew they both understood that there would have to be changes at the Bureau. In making them, he said, "You can work with all those lions," pointing at the Capitol, "or this little mouse."

That meeting was the beginning of a process that would transform not only the relationship between the FBI and the Attorney General but the very manner in which the Bureau carried out its most sensitive investigations. Levi appointed a committee to draft investigative guidelines in a number of areas, most importantly domestic security and foreign intelligence and foreign counterintelligence. The application of the domestic security guidelines put an end to numerous investigations of political groups, including the Socialist Workers' Party, when the agents could find no evidence in the Bureau's voluminous files showing the groups had violated or were going to violate the law.[22]

The provisions of the guidelines have been revised numerous times over the years since, sometimes eviscerated, sometimes revived. In 2011 the FBI made public a new "Domestic Investigations and Operations Guide."[23] Though heavily redacted and extremely detailed, it seems to follow the basic structure of the original Levi guidelines. Significantly, it states that "rigorous obedience to constitutional principles and guarantees is more important than the outcome of any single interview, search for evidence, or investigation."[24]

The two most vexing FBI issues after Watergate were electronic surveillance (including the break-ins often required to install microphones) and what came to be known as preventive action. Whether FBI agents should take positive steps to prevent violent violations of law may seem to many people an easy question today. But at the time, the Bureau's COINTELPRO history[25] gave it a very different color than it has in a world on guard against terrorist attacks on a terrible, mass level. Under the rubric of COINTELPRO, too often the Bureau engaged in dirty tricks and worse, directed against domestic dissident political groups simply to make their dissent more difficult. Nonetheless, the committee drafting domestic security guidelines included a section severely restricting but providing for preventive action.[26] In the end Levi eliminated this section, probably for fear that it would undermine the acceptance of the rest of the guidelines by Congress and the public, which might lead to dangerous restrictions on the Bureau's other activities. The guidelines' purpose was not only to balance security and civil liberties but also to secure a degree of legislative and public confidence in the balance struck.

Electronic surveillance and other intrusive searches without warrants were even more complicated to deal with. The federal statutes authorizing judges to issue wiretap and microphone surveillance warrants had been drafted with a view to the investigation and prosecution of criminal cases.[27] They were unusable in cases involving the ongoing surveillance of, for example, Soviet spies, where the objective was to monitor clandestine activity in order to defend against it, not to arrest someone. Neither did the existing law fit cases in which surveillance was intended to gather information about a foreign government's plans and intentions (e.g., monitoring a Cold War adversary's communications from within the United States). Without a statute providing a warrant procedure suitable to the purpose, the government had to rely on the President's inherent power, which had been delegated to the Attorney General. Simply calling a final halt to foreign intelligence and counterintelligence surveillance was too dangerous to consider, despite the disrepute into which it had fallen.

It was not only Congress and a skeptical public that questioned the legitimacy of warrantless surveillance. Though the Supreme Court had been careful not to cast doubt on the President's authority when a foreign power was involved, four of nine judges of the U.S. Circuit Court of Appeals for the District of Columbia, sitting en banc, in 1975 suggested that all warrantless electronic surveillance and physically intrusive searches were unconstitutional.

Levi's response was to discuss the matter publicly and thoroughly, most notably in testimony before the Senate Select Committee on Intelligence.[28] It was, and remains, a remarkable performance, given that he was signing surveillance orders that critics, including some influential federal judges, said violated constitutional rights, which meant that signing them might have turned out to be a civil rights violation. He did not mount a full-throated defense of Presidential power, though he did defend it. Instead, he delivered a learned and nuanced examination of the development of the law of search and seizure in England and the United States, spoke of the important values in play on all sides, and explained the standards and procedures he applied in deciding whether to authorize surveillance without a warrant. I believe most fair-minded people would find this testimony extraordinary. Though complicated, the statement made clear the importance of *all* the conflicting national needs and values. The testimony, all sixty-one typescript pages of which Levi delivered orally, stands as an example of intellectual honesty under pressure. It is a valuable model to the present day.

Later, Levi designed a proposed statute creating a special court to issue national security surveillance warrants.[29] The Carter administration put forth a variant of this proposal, which passed in 1978.[30] It was the failure to use this procedure to provide judicial warrants for the National Security Agency's sweeping post-9/11 surveillance that ignited a new wave of controversy and led to the statute's amendment in 2007.

As Levi worked through the process of explaining, regularizing, and legitimizing warrantless electronic surveillances involving foreign powers and their agents, FBI investigators discovered in a safe in the Bureau's New York Field Office a file titled "Do Not File." It included documentation on numerous break-ins undertaken in domestic cases (such as the pursuit of Weather Underground fugitives) without a warrant or the approval of the Attorney General. Levi opened a criminal investigation into these break-ins. At one point the Bureau responded in kind by sending agents to question members of Levi's security detail about Levi's activities. The head of the detail, Floyd Clarke, was appalled at this act of attempted intimidation and ordered his men not to answer. A measure of how much the Bureau had changed, Clarke later became Deputy Director of the FBI and for a brief time its acting Director.[31]

Within the Ford administration Levi's interpretation of the President's delegation to the Attorney General of the power to authorize warrantless surveillance often came under intense pressure. At one point he refused to permit one very significant category of surveillance to continue. He did so because the procedures established by the President required that, with respect to that category, either the Secretary of State or the President's National Security Advisor had to certify that the intelligence being sought was important to the nation's security before the Attorney General could approve the surveillance. For whatever reason, Henry Kissinger, who held both positions, stopped certifying but at the same time demanded that Levi authorize the surveillance nonetheless. One day Levi was summoned to the White House to meet with the President and Kissinger. Kissinger attacked Levi's decision. Levi explained it. Ford asked Levi to stay behind as the meeting broke up. "Don't give an inch, Ed," the President said.[32] Ford's support was essential to Levi's work, and he gave it. He had hired Levi to make the changes necessary to end the crisis of legitimacy, and he never balked when Levi did just that.

Levi left the Justice Department at the end of Ford's term and returned to the University of Chicago, where he became the Glen A. Lloyd Distinguished Service Professor Emeritus in the law school. He also taught in the college, as he had done even when he was president of the university. He remained at Chicago, though for a brief period he was a visiting professor at Stanford University Law School. He also served as a trustee of the MacArthur Foundation and president of the American Academy of Arts and Sciences. In 1980 he delivered an important series of lectures, "Three Talks on American Jurisprudence," at the Salzburg Seminar. These examined the development of the idea of judicial review in England and the United States in search of insights into the question of how the rule of law and law of rules can be squared with the need always to change it in the direction of greater justice. Sadly, only one of these lectures has been published.[33]

Levi died in 2000. U.S. Supreme Court Justice John Paul Stevens called him "a national treasure."[34] At Levi's memorial service, Gerald Ford said, "It is no exaggeration to say that Attorney General Levi helped give us back our government."[35]

A Note on the Text

I have used the original texts—in the form of Department of Justice press releases.[1] These were often produced under severe time pressure, incompletely annotated, if at all, and inadequately proofread. As a consequence they include numerous typographical errors, slight misquotations of published material (none changing the meaning), and many, many quotations and other references without citation. I have corrected the quotations. I have been sparing in my correction of typos, changing the most obvious and making the book consistent with respect to such grammatical style matters as whether to use a comma before the final item in a series. (Levi seemed to prefer to leave the final comma out, but the texts are very inconsistent, one with another and even within a given press release.) Levi had some rather proud grammatical idiosyncrasies that I have preserved. When I have made any change that required any significant judgment, I have noted it.

There are other texts of some of these talks—a *Columbia Law Review* article based on a lecture on separation of powers, for example. I have referred to these alternative texts and occasionally found some useful guidance. But these were prepared after the fact, and some have textual issues of their own.

To avoid repetitiveness and remove matters that were of real interest only on the occasion on which the talk was given, I have abridged the original texts here and there, indicating this with ellipses.

Very few of the pieces in this volume originally had titles. I have given the others titles drawn from the words of the texts. I have also included, where it seemed useful, short introductions that provide some context.

I have also provided numerous citations not included in the original texts. These I have numbered. When the original text included a note, I have preserved it, correcting it when necessary.

All other things being equal, I have leaned toward books easily available in editions still in print (the Library of America collection has been invaluable) or free online. Occasionally I relied on translations or editions that Levi may not have used. My notes indicate, of course, which translation or edition I have used. The *Columbia Law Review* article proved quite helpful in identifying some of the sources for references in the separation of powers talk.

For the few speeches I have included that Levi gave when he was not Attorney General, I have included a reference to the text I relied on.

Acknowledgments

I am deeply grateful to Larry Kramer for writing the foreword to this book.

I also want to acknowledge here the group of mostly very young lawyers Levi recruited to work as his special assistants. They had a hand in many of these talks. Douglas Marvin later became counselor to the Attorney General, our leader. The others were Ron Carr,[1] Mark Wolf (now the Hon. Mark Wolf, of the U.S. District Court in Boston), and John Buckley. Later we were joined by Maurice Rosenberg (who took time from his duties as a professor at Columbia University Law School to work on the staff) and Walter Fiederowicz, a White House Fellow.

I also want to thank Levi's two attorney sons, John and David (his third son, Michael, is a nuclear physicist). They encouraged and helped me every step of the way. Judith Wright, associate dean for library and information services, and her colleagues at the D'Angelo Law Library at the University of Chicago were immensely helpful; the library's collection of Levi's work is compendious. Two members of the library staff were particularly helpful: Thomas Drueke was invaluable in checking citations and discovering the origin of some of the more obscure references, and Steve Coats did an enormous amount of careful gathering and scanning of documents as I prepared the manuscript and the library prepared the website of the original texts. Elisa Ho, associate archivist of the Jacob Rader Marcus Center of the American Jewish Archives, found the most authoritative text of a talk by Edward Levi's great-grandfather Rabbi David Einhorn, to which Levi referred in one of his speeches. Clair Ward provided careful work checking and correcting citations. John Tryneski, my editor at the

University of Chicago Press, guided me in my selections and helped me navigate the complexities of this kind of project. Kelly Finefrock-Creed did a careful job copyediting the manuscript. My wife, Debra Moskovits, has also been my editor. And that is the least of it.

Jack Fuller

CHAPTER ONE

A Crisis of Legitimacy

A Great Trust Waiting to be Reawakened

ONE HUNDREDTH GRADUATING CLASS OF THE
FBI NATIONAL ACADEMY

March 20, 1975

Edward Levi chose for one of his first speeches as Attorney General a graduation ceremony. The Federal Bureau of Investigation's National Academy provides professional training to law enforcement officials from the United States and abroad. Speaking there so early in his time as Attorney General emphasized the importance of all parts of the justice system—starting with the street police officer—in the restoration of confidence in the administration of justice. The theme of the expressive and symbolic impact of law in action often appeared in Levi's talks.

. . . As law enforcement officials, you, more than anyone else, represent the power and quality of the state. You hold a unique and difficult position of enormous responsibility to our society. It is by watching you that many of our citizens learn what kind of country this is. They learn what laws are to be enforced, what determination we have, what kindnesses and decencies we honor as a people. As government has grown larger— both at the state and federal level—as rules and regulations have grown more complicated, as rights and duties have proliferated, the government has come to be seen as an increasingly impersonal and remote force. Your action and direction bridge the gap between the government and the individual. By your conduct you represent the government as it affects people in their daily lives. Yours is a close relationship with the average citizen. And, I might add, where law enforcement is concerned, we are all average citizens because the law must act with a sense of fundamental equality.

Because you serve as the clearest intermediary between the government and the society, your role has a wide scope and your functions are not easily defined. Studies have shown that many policemen spend most of their working time on things other than crime control. One researcher found that only 17% of police service calls and responses in one major city related to crime. Detailed studies of another large city showed that police spent about two-thirds of their effort on social service and administrative work. I realize this kind of data might suggest there is something wrong with the way police and investigatory work is organized. I can imagine a flock of management control buzzards descending upon your profession to reorganize it, to narrow its objectives. But I venture to suggest the wider scope of the police functions not only reflects the fact that someone must perform the range of essential tasks police now perform, but it also reflects the judgment that these tasks are inherent and important to the intermediary and symbolic role of law enforcement. When people know that the purpose of police is to be helpful and to make the society work better for the individual, when people know that rules are to be guides and not traps, a trust arises within them that is very important. If it is any comfort to you, let me remind you that this wider aspect to an occupation is characteristic of most professions. Indeed, I am inclined to believe that the more important a profession is, the broader will be the field of duty surrounding its core of technical functions. In any event, that is most surely an attribute of the three learned professions of law, medicine and the ministry. Persons in those professions spend great amounts of time on matters far beyond the technical structure of their discipline. Most of what they do is to deal with people and to try to be helpful to them. So it is also with the police. What you do reaches the vast numbers of Americans who will never see the criminal justice system firsthand. When you act strictly as agents of the criminal justice system, the people with whom you deal will see in your conduct a mirror of the totality of government. Probably it is yours, as it is for no other groups in our country, to build or reinforce—or at times unfortunately to destroy—a basic trust in our system of law enforcement. . . .

You leave here to enforce the laws at a time when the very nature of law and its enforcement have been called into question, both by an increasing fear of crime that no one has yet been able to stem and by a deep want of belief in the fairness with which law is enforced. As police officials, you will bear the burden of that fear and of that lack of faith more than anyone else. You will also have more opportunity than anyone else to calm the fears and to restore the faith in American justice.

We must never forget one essential truth: Neither the law in general nor the criminal law in particular can be entirely enforced by the government. Ultimately, enforcement must spring from the faith of citizens. In a free society there are essential values which would be destroyed were law enforcement to depend entirely upon the force of arms. Another kind of force must operate. That force is the willing acceptance by an overwhelming proportion of our people of the law's demands. People must believe, if not in the wisdom of a particular law, at least in the fairness and honesty of the enforcement process. I am afraid that many Americans have come to believe that law is not evenly enforced, that the law is being used not for the sake of the social good but rather for the sake of the people who created it. I happen to believe that this kind of cynicism is wrong, but the fact is that it exists. And it has serious consequences for law enforcement in our system in which general belief in the law's fairness plays so important a role.

I don't believe it has been the rigor of enforcement that has caused people to lose faith in their laws. Rather it has been a failure to show in our actions as enforcers of the law an adherence to principle—really an adherence to the ideal of justice itself—a recognition that since laws exist for the common good, they must be enforced with fairness, evenhandedness and a proper and common concern for each individual.

As I have said, your profession is the agency which brings the criminal justice system to the people it serves. Your presence, your conduct, your basic decency and concern can make a great difference in the public's perception of the fairness of law. By your gentleness, civility and determination you can build or reinforce a basic trust in how our system of law operates. Another way of saying this, of course, is that you must have the discipline and proper goals of a profession which exists to serve society and protect the individual. For if law can be enforced only when there is a belief in the law, your job as policemen and our job in the Department of Justice must be in large part to strengthen that belief and to see it is a faith well-founded.

What I have suggested to you about the subtle way in which all of our conduct shapes the adherence to law in this country should give us all pause. How much easier it would be to believe that specific new laws, amazing new technological devices or vast expenditures of money would by themselves solve the crime problem in America. How much more difficult it is for us to realize that as enforcers of the law, everything we do has a deep and abiding effect. It is more difficult to worry about the whole range of our official conduct than to satisfy ourselves by drafting new statutes or buying new devices, but I believe it is also more sensible.

Your job as a profession is to cope with one of the greatest problems of our society. You stand where fear and cynicism now meet. But there is also a great trust waiting to be reawakened. By your conduct and skill—and I hope in part by virtue of what you have learned at this Academy—I am sure you will show the people of America that they may trust in the law and in you.

Security, Power and Equality

THE AMERICAN ASSEMBLY ON LAW AND A CHANGING SOCIETY

June 28, 1975

The American Assembly has set for itself a difficult, customary task—to look into the future so that our present institutions of law will be better prepared for what is to come, and to consider creating new institutions, if that is the part of wisdom. This is an optimistic adventure. We assert our ability to control our destiny somewhat. The discussion is for the purpose of informing action. We have sufficient faith in some statistical predictions to listen to them, although we realize such predictions sometimes have been in great error. We think, in short, it is possible and worthwhile to foresee future movements and requirements, and we are committed to social engineering. This attempt to fashion the new world seems a typical and very American enterprise.

But this probably does not describe our present mood or at least the attitude of our day. The buoyancy and conviction we once had—or think we had—are diminished. America once was the new world. The achievement was here. What was required was to permit it—or to encourage it—to work its ways. Now we are not so certain. We have no particular utopian dream to guide us, as older societies frequently had, either of the past or the future, although of course there is plenty of talk that things will be different. Utopian dreams—at least to the extent that they are elaborated and worked out—are always commentaries on the present. But we seem overwhelmed and puzzled by what has happened to us. Even as we assert the power to guide the future, we are conscious we have been taken over by a tidal wave of past and present events. Some of our guesses for the future, of course, may be satisfying because without more they may suggest some present irritants will diminish. But others gain meaning only as we see where we are today. It is our present condition, then, we must first try to understand. And as to our view of our present condition, I suspect we are compelled to welcome disagreement in good cheer.

In thinking of where we are today, three ideals or clusters of reactions, which summarize the events of the last half century, may suggest factors which have profoundly influenced us. The substance of the ideas could be put in many different ways and under different names. I have thought of them in terms of security, power and equality. The concepts are among the constellation of ideas which rule or are reflected in any society. They never can be seen only by themselves. They compete for dominance, not only among themselves, but with other sovereign constructs. Their meaning changes. It is because their meaning changes, and has been reactive in ways we recognize, that perhaps they help describe the commonplaces of our period. I certainly do not suggest them as insights but rather as ways to problems.

As to security, let me say we have not escaped the aftermath of the rise of an aggressive authoritarianism on an international scale, as to which it was widely thought the international community was slow in responding, and it gave the world an example of terror and destructiveness. The words of Churchill condemning Munich may not have been widely known or appreciated by a generation which died in Vietnam, but the connection was there. The international order, or the attempt to achieve security in the presence of old and new forms of hostility, inevitably gained a pre-eminence it never before had in American life. We were not prepared for this then. In some ways we are not prepared for it now. The domestic repercussions of reaction and counter-reaction were severe. We have not fully overcome or adapted to these reactions. Moreover, we are a society where many elements combine, including the freedoms we cherish most, to produce swings of reaction. In our bafflement as to how to reconcile the different requirements of international and domestic order or disorder, we have moved from one extreme to another, and perhaps the most constant theme is the refusal to face up to the differences between the in-

ternational and the domestic settings. But since the realms cannot be separated completely, and each realm tends to influence the other, the relationships require much more jurisprudential thought than has been given.
We have found it hard to come to terms with the measure of security required for our day and with the control of that security. Unfortunately the
ramifications are many.

The emphasis on problems of the international world has influenced
our views on the many forms of power. It has also, perhaps through the
convergence of particular movements, influenced ideas about the place of
law within the body politic. There is a paradox in this, since if the international community suffers from an absence of law and the absence of institutions of law, it is odd that this absence should be used to conclude that
law when it exists is but one more aspect of the many forms of power.
But other factors have contributed to this view, including, it must be said,
movements which have been willing to challenge the law on this very basis. Law is a normative subject. Its stated purpose and the stated purposes
of its institutions have special importance. Its commands are not simply descriptive of behavior, and indeed its orders are often violated. But
as countless examples show, even in times of great stress and objection,
these orders have meaning and influence conduct. The stated purposes
and their reflection in the orders given are influential with respect to the
conduct of citizen-rulers, for that is our concept of the rule of law. An explicit purpose in the rule is that it is not to be used as merely one more instrument in the hand of the strong against the weak. And it is a gross misuse of law if its special attributes of formality, legitimacy and fairness are
ignored, because then law is seen as only one more available means of influence. Law and legal institutions can be seen in that way, as can all human institutions, but it is a partial view, and the incompleteness so far as
law is concerned is particularly damaging because it can be self-fulfilling.

There are other reasons for the emphasis on power in our time. Wars
have produced social change. They have influenced demographic factors.
The shape of the American population is different than it was. This has
had a direct relationship for example on the problem of crime because of
the larger youth population. Other changes have occurred. While it is customary to cite Tocqueville—at least for something on occasions such as
this—and he did speak of the litigious spirit of the Americans as well as
their proclivity to form associations, one has the impression that groupism
has never been more prevalent than it has been in recent times. This is one
of those statements that may be over-reaching and may well be wrong. All

that need be said is that along with the claim that there is increased ano-
mie or perhaps just loneliness, there has also been a felt need to find identity in group membership. Frequently this is coupled with the claim that
injustice can be averted or corrected only through group action.

The phenomenon, in addition to involving an assertion of power or the
need for power, says something about the idea of representation. And it
is accompanied by skepticism or conviction about the sources of power
to control representatives. The demand is frequently that representatives
have a more abiding identity—through race, craft, sex, age or income—
with the group represented. Disclosure laws, open meetings, increased
standing to participate at all levels and dislike of neutrality suggest a variety of questions as to what is happening to the professions of representation and to the theory of delegation central to our government. In
a somewhat harrowing way this new approach questions the idea of the
good citizen or at least of public citizenship as separate from the manifestation solely of self-interest. It is an old debate, of course—one which interested Rousseau—and I do not know whether this new emphasis should
be taken in its own terms or rather as a reaction to the breakdown of so
many supportive institutions, a consequence also of the size and mobil-
ity of the population, and the effect of the communications media. These
items, along with the ramifications of the international order, are in any
event matters which we cannot forget.

The importance of special representation as an aspect of power has
naturally grown as this has been seen as the way to share, through governmental intervention, in increasing resources made possible through an
economy of abundance. Either the recognition that resources are limited,
with choices to be made, or the proliferation of overlapping interests may
save us, as the *Federalist Papers* hoped, from the worst forms of factionalism. Yet at the center of many demands for special powers and recognition is the insistence that the goal is equality. The concept is ambiguous,
limited and, perhaps inevitably, in its use contradictory. The traditional
constitutional problems of preventing discrimination, requiring affirmative action, denying or requiring that individuals be treated as members
of groups are well known. They press for definition and guidance and this
no doubt will come. Since society can be divided many ways, and population patterns will change, one can try to anticipate which groups in the
future may gain additional protection. But for long-term basic governmental policy, the frequent suggestions for a new bill of rights, requiring a
minimum standard of the requirements for everyone, seem to me to pose

interesting issues. The reason for the interest, I hasten to add, is because I think this is descriptive of the direction in which in fact we have been going. The large-scale federal intervention directly and indirectly at all levels and through local governments is largely for this purpose. We have travelled an enormous way from the time when only a most limited number of items were considered within the governmental power or appropriate for direct governmental action. Yet the proposals for a new charter seem to signify that this new direction has not worked sufficiently well. . . .

The concepts of security, power and equality, as I have used them, are merely suggestive of what I think are important trends, influences or problems. Security reminds us of the limitations and some of the influences on the open society of international conduct and pressures. Power describes the denigration of the idea of law and therefore the weakening of standards for official conduct. Equality marks an achievement and a direction, but also emphasizes the choices which must be made among resources, now seen as more limited, and among values. These concepts do not adequately carry the message of our malaise, which we know only too well. They are related to the events which have occurred, but there are other factors. There is a background of a lack of forthrightness, which history may or may not justify, but which takes its toll. It now permits a crescendo of recollection of past events, many of which were known in a different light at the time they occurred, but which we now permit ourselves to see, as though for the first time, in true cyclical fashion. I have always thought it was the special duty of the legal profession, and surely that of jurisprudence, to attempt to emphasize and explain the basic values of our legal order in the light of the problems of our time. It is one of the duties of the legal process to provide this explanation. The relationship between problems and values is reciprocal. The exploration of that relationship is particularly important in times of change.

We appear to be in such a period. The response of law is made more difficult and is conditioned by a transformation in basic units of order in our society. I do not know whether the family, the church, volunteer religious orders, community organizations, the school, the university are less important than they once were. I suppose it could be argued that in some ways, contrary to popular belief, some of them have been strengthened. But in many ways they have removed themselves from a leadership of civility. And law, recognizing this, has not only accepted but accentuated this trend. But a democratic society requires many kinds of institutions to hold it together and to give it governance. The individual citizen may be protected by the growing arm of procedural safeguards which the law now extends. But these safeguards, even though they may avoid some of the abuses of an older day, are most inadequate substitutes for the relationships of meaning, belonging and idealism. Many, although not all, of these basic units were willing to assume the role of reinforcing legitimacy and rules of conduct. For many centuries it was thought to be an obligation of law, even though it often regarded them as competitors, to be supportive of other basic units of societal organization. This is less true today; it is as though we were waiting for acts of creation to provide adequate substitutes. The consequence is that our legal system carries an overwhelming burden. The terrifying rate of crime is one of the results.

Even though the concept of legitimacy has not been in much favor in recent years, as though it were solely the protector of the power which corrupts, the concept of legitimacy is one upon which the law depends. So do our civil liberties protected by law. We have come through a crisis of legitimacy. It is no doubt difficult for us to characterize objectively the nation's response to these events. We are left with uneven and seesawing relationships among the branches of government, with basic questions asked concerning parliamentary forms, the role of the executive and the courts, the nature of federalism. Of course we have much to think about. My guess is that history will not see our difficulties as great as we imagine them to be, that it will look with special favor, if not upon us, then upon the Founders who created a hope for mankind, and that indeed it will probably add a word of approval as that hope is renewed in our day.

The Damaging Cycle

INAUGURATION CEREMONY OF BARD COLLEGE

October 11, 1975[1]

... It has become commonplace to complain that good leaders do not exist in the abundance we would like and that our society has few heroes. These observations should perhaps compel us to look at what we ask of leaders and what we regard as heroism.

Rather than asking how closely an individual approximates the wisdom, energy and persuasiveness of a fine leader, we usually ask what his new program will be. The continuous striving for the more material val-

ues for a better life, for more material goods, for a greater ease is part
of the human condition. But we have come to think, with a conceit of
which we should not be proud, that these desires can be satisfied only
by newness. So, to take as one example, foundations which rule the academic world, and government programs which do some ruling on their
own, always look for the innovative. The word is so misused it has become
a principal barrier to honesty and to thought. It has preempted the more
genuine and significant appreciation of excellence. It makes light of the
strivings of the past, and it is flippant about the purpose of our mission.

The expectation and demand for change lead to a view of the world as
a continuous round of dizzying cycles in which the new becomes quickly
old and must be replaced by something new which not long before was
the old that had been rejected. If we erred yesterday on the side of order,
then we think we must counteract that with an equal and opposite error
on the side of that kind of liberty which is sometimes called, to avoid argument, license. If our ideals of justice in the world overcame our humility, and we engaged in an undeclared war now covered with skepticism
and doubt, and with the tragedy of all wars, then we think we must reject
those ideals with a fervor equal to that with which we held them before.
Indeed we seem to welcome these reactions, believing them to be entirely
natural and necessary. Both the awareness of history and the understanding of current problems are lost in the energetic process of getting even.
We are distorting the process through which tradition and change, each
tempering the other, must be accommodated in the good society. We are
doing so without realizing that the persistent warning about democratic
governments, a warning which the Founders of our Republic well understood, is that this must be the temptation to be guarded against. The process which satisfies the need for change, while protecting fundamental
values and ideals, is of course extremely difficult. It may indeed, as Alexander Bickel described it, be a fragmented and complicated affair.[2] This
was the reason the Founders of our nation sought to moderate the process by creating a government of competing institutions. The Founders
thought about the problem. We seem to have put it out of our mind.

The cyclical process of choices and new endeavors is often called pragmatic, meaning it is experimental and tentative—that it favors ideas
having consequences in fact. If this experimental quality is taken as the
whole of the system, then the continuous swing of affairs from one error
to its opposite might seem inevitable. After all, we are trained to believe

that when an experiment produces consequences which do not verify the hypothesis, the hypothesis is quickly discarded and another experiment begins. That would justify our quest for newness. But it would be a misunderstanding of the system. It is much too kind in its acceptance of a justification. It misunderstands because pragmatism is a process of testing, which assumes some set of values by which the consequences of choices are to be measured. The appeal of the new has not only been an appeal for better devices better suited to the ends we seek but also for a shifting of the goals themselves. It is this combination which helps produce the damaging cycle. It is this which threatens the delicate balance between stability and change.

It is much too kind in its acceptance of a justification because it does not recognize the great emphasis placed upon public opinion, as it is understood to be, in our society. The emphasis is not a recent development. Tocqueville recognized it—and its hazards—in the early 19th century. He wrote:

> The nearer the people are drawn to the common level of an equal and similar position, the less prone does each man become to place implicit faith in a certain man or a certain class of men. But his readiness to believe the multitude increases, and opinion is more than ever mistress of the world. . . . At periods of equality, men have no faith in one another, by reason of their common resemblance; but this very resemblance gives them almost unbounded confidence in the judgment of the public; for it would not seem probable, as they are all endowed with equal means of judging, the greater truth should go with the greater number.[3]

I am quite sure all of us would reject this as a necessary consequence. If it were inevitably true, it would cut uncomfortably close to the heart of our faith. The reason we reject it is because we believe in education, whether formal or otherwise, and the freedom and individuality which education can bring. If so, education has let us down or, perhaps, we have let education down, not perceiving the enormous obstacles it must overcome in the modern world. The strength of a thought-reducing conformity compelling public opinion has grown steadily. In part this results because we not only have public opinion, a mysterious and changeable force, but we have produced, through the uses of scholarship, a one-dimensional version of opinion so that we may more easily make of it the star to guide us.

An opinion sample is like a photograph which captures the expression of uneasiness that sometimes occurs between laughter and a smile. The uneasiness is there, but only in passing. What is important is the humor.

I recall a moment—all of us have experienced them—in which opinion changed dramatically overnight. I was a member of a Congressional staff.[4] There was peace, but war in Korea threatened it. Had an opinion sampler visited that Congressional committee that day, he would have learned the unanimous feeling was that only a fool would enter the conflict. That night the United States entered the conflict. If the pollster had visited us the next day, he would have discovered that the belief was now as firmly fixed as the day before. But it was the opposite conviction. He would have found the opinion was that there was no choice but to enter. I do not say it is not worthwhile taking these soundings, but rather that the shift of the compass may result from the course of the vessel. But of course I really mean more. There is a vast difference between a government by discussion and as a result of discussion, and a fixation on opinion. The oracles of old, even though they could be manipulated, at least had the advantage of speaking ambiguously. Nor do I wish to overemphasize the role of the pollster. The role of the scholarly footnote is often much the same.

The problem of the importance of opinion is not only governmental. It pervades all our institutions, including our colleges. The assumption is that it is the right thing to go with the prevailing view, and so much easier to do it when the prevailing view is known. The source of the prevailing view is what we are told the prevailing view is. I recall being told by some entering students at the University of Chicago—an institution which rightly has a reputation for independence—what their views were on a variety of controversial subjects. When I pressed them as to whether these were really their own views, they assured me they were, and as a final irrefutable proof pointed out that *Life Magazine* had already said so. There is an accepted syndrome which connects the told prevailing view with popularity, and accepts the desire for popularity as a principal value. The syndrome is a problem for education. It is also a problem for representative government.

The growth of knowledge and the new methods of disseminating knowledge have heightened the problem. Powerful tools have been developed to tell us less about more, to simplify what is complex, to substitute immediate impressions for a deeper judgment. Students today are sure they know things which they do not know. Though this has always been the case—and it most surely is a phenomenon not at all limited to students, and we all share in it—it is more intense today. One side of an argument, one view of history, one theory of justice—these become accepted because there is no real discussion. There is a loss of the wisdom that to understand one side of an argument it is best to be able to state and to understand the other side. Discussion must overcome the statement of opinion and particularly the statement of opinion in the form of slogans.

The experts in advertising and public relations were not the first to discover slogans. They may have learned the value of the novelty of such epithets from the philosophers. The re-emergence of the slogan "God is dead" a few years ago is a reminder of this, as were the answering bumper stickers which replied, "God is alive and well and living in Hoboken." Much of scholarship develops and lives by slogans which expand until the concepts burst at their seams. The sovereignty of the disciplines as well as competition among and between them is at stake. This was the problem which worried Newman in his *The Idea of a University*.[5] It is a concern which every reflective institution of learning still has. It is sometimes hard for a scholar to realize that his discipline does not answer all the questions which are worthwhile answering, or that his way of answering, particularly as interpreted by disciples, may preempt more than was intended. The description, I regret to say, fairly well fits the course of theories about education.

There is a usefulness to the expansion of theories in the scholarly world. There is a sense in which discovery, knowledge and understanding must proceed through error. The magnifying glass distorts. The whole process of scholarly dialogue is to develop and then correct the distortion. The academic world recognizes that it is natural for each of us to wish to be medicine men or women with our own special nostrum. This recognition has not prevented frenetic desires to be first, or to claim to be first, or to place a personal stamp of a school on a whole train of thought. It has not prevented judgments to be made on what is at bottom a most partial view of things. But over time there is a discipline of correction which complements this process. For this reason the scholarly world has to cherish the opportunity of time, to see things not in the long run, but over the long run.

This happy view of the academic community to which I subscribe contains a dilemma. The dilemma is that scholars must have the freedom to be wrong so that they may be right. Indeed there is nothing that can be done about this because it is in the nature of discovery, or rediscovery, or understanding. And there is necessarily a protected long-run aspect to this. But it is nevertheless also true that there is an immediate and short-run aspect. Colleges do carry, along with other institutions in our society, and more than most, the responsibility for the training of the citizens and for the training—one might use the inept phrase—the basic training of the professions. If we are unduly ruled by swings of opinion, a demand for novelty, an acceptance of the idea that an error in the past justifies an opposite error in the present, that says something about the education of the citizen. If the expert advice our society receives is carelessly or determinedly partial, ignoring the scope of the problem, that says something about the training, and particularly the liberal arts component of the training, of the advising professions. For various reasons, including the comfort of ignorance, as well as the belief that I think there are many ways, my thought is not to tell you how to avoid this. It is rather to assure you that the matter is important.

Two problems in our society of major importance are examples of where there have been recurrent swings in approach with which the academic community has been involved. Both of them have been approached through the use of slogans. Both of them are enormously complicated. The first is the problem of crime. It is a national tragedy. It threatens the civility upon which a democratic society depends. One has to wonder how long the tolerance of it will continue and what measures intolerance of it might lead our society to adopt. The problem of dealing with crime has involved a variety of issues which taken together have made a solution almost impossible. But this certainly cannot be an acceptable result. The issues are only too familiar. Some of them are these: There is a fear that strict enforcement will treat unfairly those who are disadvantaged. But the chief victims of crime are the disadvantaged. There has been a belief that the growth of knowledge would lead us to the causes of crime and the eradication of the causes. But discoveries in this area, beyond common sense observations, have been disappointing. The treatment of the criminal has been analogized to the treatment of the ill. Individualized treatment was therefore indicated. This both had a special and unintended harshness in some cases and generally weakened the certainty, and therefore the effectiveness, of punishment. Competing schools developed around the concept of deterrence as the purpose of imprisonment, on the one hand, and rehabilitation as the more humane and constructive goal, on the other. Recent analyses of some of the inadequate statistics we now have show that rehabilitation does not so frequently occur. As a consequence many who favored rehabilitation as the sole or main objective, now disillusioned, would do away with prisons altogether, or would fail to upgrade into decency those which we now have. Others shrink from deterrence because it seems to hold out no hope to the unfortunate.

What is involved, I suppose, is the nature of humankind, as to which there cannot be expected to be startling new, even innovative, knowledge each decade. It must be recognized that the whole area of criminology has been a prime target of sociological and psychological research for many years. The discoveries have not come as quickly as an older day predicted. To recognize this may be itself a contribution of some wisdom. A long humanistic tradition would suggest that both deterrence and decency are important to the victim, the miscreant and the society as a whole.

The second is the problem of the use of resources. Just how this could have happened, I will never know, but those of us fortunate enough to be in universities during the sixties were assured from almost all quarters that this was the age of affluence where unbounded demands could be met with unbounded supply. It was hardly a question of choice; rather a matter of will. The notion of scarcity was gone; choice, other than that which might be involved in the avoidance of gluttony, because the individual could only take so much without individual harm, was regarded as irrelevant. For a while in this picture of the abounding universe, the problem posed to the colleges and the universities was how they could possibly strain themselves sufficiently to turn out all the Ph.D.s which the social scientists in that sector of expertness confidently predicted would be required. The only thing which helped some of us preserve our sanity during that period was our knowledge that with one exception all such studies had been uniformly wrong in the past. Today, of course, the picture is quite the opposite. The dismal science has once again come into its own. The bottom line, as it unfortunately has come to be called, is very important.

I have the uneasy feeling that I am calling for wisdom. I apologize for that, but what better place is there to make this plea. We need a wisdom which is possible when issues can be confronted with an awareness that the values at stake are old values or only partly new and that the ways of solution are old solutions or only partly new; when tradition and change will be recognized for the continuity they represent; when public opinion will be important because, of course, support is required, but education will enlighten opinion and give it leadership. . . .

A Burden of Mistrust

AMERICAN BAR ASSOCIATION CONVENTION

August 13, 1975

At one time I had thought to use this forum for a general presentation of the work of the Department of Justice. For reasons which I suppose are obvious, I soon realized this would not accomplish what I had in mind. The Department is accountable in many ways and to many groups. As Elliot Richardson frequently pointed out, lawyers are in a minority if one counts the total roster of the Department. Yet it is to the members of the bar I am most anxious to convey a sense of how the Department is approaching its problems and how it views the nature of some of its concerns. Your understanding is of the utmost importance, for we share responsibilities. In light of this I have thought it best to make some general comments and then to select four areas for this discussion. Each area is entitled to a much more detailed presentation. Yet the combination, I hope, will be of interest to you.

In preparing for this meeting, I recalled the timing of last year's gathering in Honolulu. The months preceding it were marked by a frenzy of activity and an expectation that there would soon be an historic trial in the United States. Then, only days before Chesterfield Smith officially opened your deliberations, the President of the United States resigned. The powers of the executive branch of the federal government passed to a new President. This year's meeting comes at a time when the business of law and government proceeds much more normally. The history of the transformation is a strong reaffirmation of the vitality of our institutions. The legal profession is free of some of the tensions of 1974. But the institutions of law and the profession still have the legacy of a skepticism which has grown over many years. Skepticism can be useful. Mistrust can be corrosive. Justified mistrust places the heaviest burden upon us.

Not long ago I conferred with members of your Special Committee to Study Law Enforcement Agencies. I was given the privilege then of seeing certain tentative recommendations—part of a work in progress and subject to change—aimed at protecting the stature of the Department of Justice and insulating it from partisan politics. I agree that among the functions of the Department—and perhaps its most important, for it summarizes all the others—is as a symbol of the administration of justice. There is no half-heartedness in our effort to achieve and maintain a Department of the highest professional competence and standards, free of partisan purpose. I choose to think my colleagues and I would not be at the Department if it were otherwise. . . .

I need not remind this gathering that the Department of Justice does not carry sole responsibility for the fair and effective administration of the laws of the United States. Much of it rests upon you. The nature of our laws; the procedure and judgments of the courts; the work of law enforcement officials; the wisdom, skill and zeal of the bar are all involved. In a larger but most important way, it is the combination and relationship among the executive and legislative leadership of government—in the context of federalism; the performance of units with specific professional responsibility for the law; and the mood, habits and ideals of our communities which determine the quality of justice. This larger picture—which is realistic—may seem to diminish the good which can be accomplished by any individual unit or segment. But the opposite is true. The system can change and be responsive. The recognition of interdependence is a necessary starting point, even as we insist, as we must, on the necessary independence which the discharge of specific duties requires. The Department of Justice must be seen in this setting.

The Department of Justice is an integral part of government. The oath of the President is to defend the Constitution, and the Constitution requires that he take care that the laws are faithfully executed. Because of the nature of the rule of law, the Department has a pervasive and particular role. If one looks at Article One, Section Eight of the Constitution, a lawyer, at least, will immediately recognize the point. The Department does not negotiate issues of conflict or trade with foreign nations, manage the national debt or coin money. It does not supervise the national programs for agriculture or for the regulated industries. It is not the administrator for systems of taxation and social welfare, nor for the protection of the environment and the sources of energy. But the Department over time has been concerned in greater or lesser degree in some way—and sometimes deeply—with all these activities. Indeed I am sure that one or more of my colleagues in the Cabinet may be pleased and surprised at this statement of partial renunciation. The Department has to be a special advocate, not only in defending governmental decisions at law, but in the attempt to infuse into them the qualities and values which are of the utmost importance to our constitutional system. Thus there must be a special concern for fair, orderly, efficient procedures, for the balance of constitutional rights and for questions of federalism and the proper regard for the separation of powers. It is sometimes said that, so far as the Department is concerned, courts alone have this duty. I do not agree.

The work of the Department inevitably frequently involves most directly the safety and well-being of the community and the protection of individual rights. This fact elevates the review which the Department must make of its performance and priorities to more than an exercise in efficiency, although that is important. The Department's work is likely to be at that central point where conflicting values meet. One traditional way for the law to meet such problems is to fashion a realm of ambiguity. Particularly where the government is involved, with its inherent coercive power, these cloudy areas invite suspicion and mistrust. Where the values are in conflict, the law is not as clear as it should be and the matter is of great importance to the safety of our country, the burden upon the Department is heavy.

I do not suggest ambiguities can be completely avoided. I know they cannot be. And the case by case approach of our law, which thrives on ambiguity—to say nothing of the lack of clarity in legislation—is part of the genius of government and no doubt is necessary. But a prime and useful function of the law as it operates is to help explain the conflict in values and often to bring to issue the problems which are involved. This is not always possible; discussion may be difficult. The central position and power of the Department are such that it ought to attempt to be articulate about these conflicts in values. The role is one of law revision, resolution or acceptance of dichotomies which in a democratic society ought to be set forth. There are other areas where change through legislation is much needed, but because emotions are high on both sides, no proposal is easy to advance. Again I think it is the duty of the Department, where the administration of justice is concerned, to encourage the discussion and to make suggestions. I do not regard these views as surprising. They are not always easy to follow.

The Federal Bureau of Investigation is established by statute in the Department of Justice. The basic jurisdiction for the Bureau's investigative work in the detection of crime derives from general legislation which gives the Attorney General the power to appoint officials "to detect and prosecute crime against the United States." Other statutes vest in the Bureau specific responsibilities to investigate particular types of violations. The same general legislation which gives criminal investigative authority also allows the Attorney General to appoint officials "to conduct such other investigations regarding official matters under the control of the Department of Justice and the Department of State as may be directed by the Attorney General." This provision and the authority of the President, exercised through executive orders, Presidential statements or directives, have been the foundation of certain investigative activities of the Bureau that do not necessarily relate, and frequently do not relate, to criminal prosecutions.

Shortly after I took office, I appointed a committee in the Department of Justice to study the practices of the Federal Bureau of Investigation and to develop a comprehensive set of guidelines to govern its future conduct. The committee of six attorneys, including one from the Bureau, has been meeting several times a week over the last five months. The mandate of the committee is broad: to reconsider the whole range of Bureau investigative practices from the use of organized crime informants to the use of warrantless electronic surveillance to collect foreign intelligence information. The committee has written detailed proposed guidelines in four areas: investigations requested by the White House, investigations for Congressional and judicial staff appointments, unsolicited mail, and investigations to obtain domestic intelligence. The committee is proceeding to draft guidelines for additional areas such as organized crime intelligence, criminal investigations, the federal security employee program, counterintelligence and foreign intelligence investigations, and background investigations for federal judicial appointments.[6]

Each of the guidelines has special problems and requires particular solutions. For example, some of the alleged instances of misuse of the FBI over previous periods have involved directions from the White House, often from low ranking officials, given orally, and couched in terms of law enforcement or national security. They involved such matters as surveillance at a political convention, investigation of a newsman unsympathetic to the administration cause or the collection of information on political opponents. The proposed guidelines require that the request be made or confirmed in writing, specify those who may make requests, require the official initiating the investigation to be identified, the purpose of the investigation stated among certain routine areas, and where a field investigation is initiated, include[7] an attestation that the subject has given consent.

During Congressional hearings, a great deal of concern was voiced about the FBI's retention in its files of unsolicited derogatory information about individuals—including Congressmen and Senators. The Bureau does receive a great deal of information which is unsolicited by the Bureau and does not bear upon matters within its jurisdiction. It is the repository of many complaints—some of which concern personal habits or incidents. As I commented at the hearings, there are policy considerations which argue in favor of retention of unsolicited allegations. A vitriolic accusation concerning a Congressman can become of substantial importance if there is a subsequent attempt at anonymous extortion or other threats. There are other examples not difficult to imagine in which the allegation, as part of a developing later picture, becomes significant. Moreover, the destruction of material which later might be thought to have been an alert to all kinds of serious problems can be seriously criticized. Nevertheless, I expressed the hope that a procedure could be devised to screen materials to be retained. The proposed guidelines would require that unsolicited information, not alleging serious criminal behavior that ought to be investigated by the FBI or reported to other law enforcement agencies, be destroyed—within ninety days of receipt. Other guidelines confront directly the question of the length of time other kinds of investigative materials should be retained.

Perhaps the most important guidelines the Department of Justice committee has yet drafted involve domestic intelligence inquiries. For decades the FBI has been conducting investigations of groups suspected by it or other government agencies of being involved in subversive activities. Unlike conventional criminal investigations, these investigations have no built-in, necessary, automatic conclusion. They continue as long as there is a perceived threat. They are not reviewed outside the FBI. They come close to first amendment rights.[8] ...

The proposed guidelines are far more detailed than the summary I have given. But the summary suggests the nature of the exercise. Despite the argument that to an investigative agency all information it comes across may be valuable—may even turn out to be crucial—the guidelines balance the argument against the interests of individuals in privacy. Despite arguments that domestic intelligence operations are essential to national security and must proceed unencumbered by detailed procedures of authentication, the guidelines recognize the effect that unfettered investigations of that kind might have on legitimate domestic political activity and propose tight controls. The guidelines ... are not in final form. Some might be most appropriate as statutes or executive orders. Others could be put into effect by regulation. Before any go into effect there will be more discussion, both within the Department and outside of it. They have not been adopted, although they frequently reflect current practice. Whatever the outcome, they do represent a necessary effort which undoubtedly, but for other concerns, would have been undertaken years ago.

The Department of Justice has had for many years, and now has, special responsibilities for warrantless electronic surveillance. . . . The Department has continued its efforts to perfect the standards and processes used, under the authorization of the President, when the Attorney General gives or denies his consent to a proposed electronic surveillance. . . . We have very much in mind the necessity to determine what procedures through legislation, court action or executive processes will best serve the national interest, including, of course, the protection of constitutional rights.[9]

The concern about FBI conduct and warrantless electronic surveillance are examples of the Department of Justice looking inward in its effort to confront important issues of civil liberty. The Civil Rights Division of the Department exemplifies the outward reach of this concern. In the late 1950s and 1960s it faced a situation in which many state and local governments enforced laws that blatantly discriminated. Discriminatory treatment in employment and public accommodations was the rule in large areas of the nation. Changing this situation was a long, difficult and painful endeavor. Even in 1968, sixty-eight percent of all black students in eleven Southern states went to all-black schools. The "dual school system" was still in effect. By 1972 that figure had declined to a little more than nine percent.

Today the Civil Rights Division's effort against race discrimination is a more subtle one. Often it is difficult now to show a history of *de jure* segregation, and more importantly, as the quest for equal opportunity becomes more successful, some of the demands of minority groups might, if met, involve unfair deprivations of others. A difficult balance is required. It is made more pressing today because a great number of private civil rights suits is being filed, which makes it even more important that basic legal concepts be clarified. This clarification is impeded in many respects by semantic breakdown. Words that could express the conundrums and conflicting values are taken to indicate broad opposition to civil rights. Euphemisms have been substituted for logic. Thus the metaphysics of the distinctions between quotas, which are taken to be bad, and goals, which are taken to be good. Now whatever these devices which seek a sort of numerical parity among racial and ethnic groups might be called, I think it could be agreed that they are appropriate when a specific showing is made about a specific institution that it has discriminated against minority groups in the past, and this form of relief is necessary. But the reach of affirmative action programs goes much further. Affirmative action would choose a parity figure and then impose it without regard to a specific showing of discrimination.

The Civil Rights Division has, of course, not solved the riddle of so-called "reverse discrimination." Neither has the Supreme Court. It had the opportunity in the *DeFunis* case,[10] but it withheld judgment. Perhaps that was wise. Perhaps it is not a moment ripe for the elucidation of a principle. Temporarily—and I hope briefly—we may be standing at a moment at which the internal conflict in our ideal of equality is seeking an equilibrium which is not yet obvious—nor even, perhaps, attainable—to us. But the problem is not insoluble, even though we might not immediately see how the resolution of competing interests can be accomplished. It is the duty of the legal profession—one we should welcome—to seek accommodations in difficult situations in such a way as to protect fundamental values.

Though its major work is still in the area of minority rights, the Civil Rights Division lately has begun to assert the rights of other disadvantaged groups within society. Beginning more than two years ago with an important test that involved the issue of a constitutional right to treatment for the institutionalized mentally ill, its work has extended into other sorts of institutions whose purpose require some limitation on individual liberty and whose residents are not in a position to assert their rights unaided. The aim is to ensure that every effort is made to minimize those limitations so that even the powerless and the infirm might enjoy some measure of freedom and obtain decent, civilized treatment. The Division has become involved in cases asserting a right of juvenile offenders to be treated during their incarceration, cases attacking negligent conduct by states in placing children who have become their wards and cases seeking to require state officials to bring nursing homes for the aged up to minimum health and safety standards.

It is well to recall in all these efforts on behalf of the disadvantaged among us, however, that our most benign efforts sometimes yield hurtful results. When society turned its gentle eye upon the young some decades ago, it produced the juvenile justice system which today is in many places a shambles. Likewise, the corrections reform movement of about a century ago insisted upon the humane ideal of rehabilitation, and that concept has lead to indeterminate sentences, dubious efforts and behavior modification, and despair so deep that the whole idea of helping those who are convicted of crime has been called into question. This is not to cast doubt upon the importance of the Civil Rights Division's efforts, of course, because they are aimed at righting some of the wrongs earlier reforms produced. But it is to suggest that as lawyers we must know the limits of the law and the fact that other social institutions are sometimes able to do that which the law cannot do.

I come now to the fourth area I wanted to discuss with you—the problem of crime. For some years the federal government acted as if its abilities in bringing crime under control were limitless. It created expectations in the public that could not be met. Public disappointment provoked, not a re-examination of the basic assumptions of the federal government's efficacy, but rather an increasing emphasis on toughness, even vindictiveness against those convicted of crime. This obscured a feature of the crime problem that it is now important to reconsider. Every success in reducing crime—especially street crime people fear most—is a victory for individual liberty so long as the success does not come at the expense of constitutional rights guaranteed criminal defendants. The sense of vindictiveness that intruded upon the discourse about crime led to the misapprehension that prosecuting criminals somehow infringes upon rights rather than protects them.

Serious crime rose 18 percent during the first three months of 1975 compared with the same period last year. In 1974 serious crime was up 17 percent, according to the FBI's Uniform Crime Statistics. Increases in the rate of violent street crime have paralleled the total increase. These sad figures do not begin to measure the effect on individual freedom increasing crime has had. It has affected not only the immediate victims of violence and theft; it has also embedded fear in the minds of countless Americans. Freedom of movement, freedom of association, even the freedom to rest secure in one's own house have been impaired.

Law enforcement is a central part of the protection of human rights. The sentiments that lead officials to believe it is better to minimize law enforcement in poor and minority group neighborhoods of our cities are at best misguided. A study by the Law Enforcement Assistance Administration of crime in five large cities showed that blacks were nearly twice as likely as whites to be the victims of robbery or burglary. In four of those cities blacks were also more likely than whites to be the victim of violent aggravated assault. Lack of adequate law enforcement, more so even than lack of other government services, deprives the poor of their right to live a decent life.

The President has recently delivered a message on crime which, while it admitted the limitations of the federal government's ability to solve the problem of crime, offered some reforms in the federal criminal justice system which might serve as models for states to follow. It set forth a program of gun control that offers the possibility of stemming some of the violence that besets our cities.[11] It emphasized the plight of the victims of crimes and thus began a process by which the problem of crime can be rescued from the rhetoric that has trapped it for years. It urged mandatory prison sentences, mainly for crimes of violence, leaving but limiting specific areas for judicial discretion. It strongly endorsed the recodification of the criminal code, but recognized the need for further consideration of some of the provisions of S.1.[12] ...

I have chosen these four areas for discussion because I believe they give some flavor of how the Department of Justice is approaching problems important to it and to the thrust of law in our society. I have chosen them as examples not only because they are important in themselves but also because they indicate ongoing work by the Department in areas involving the conflict of important social values. Our hope is that we can meet problems with candor and some depth of understanding, informed by the history of our discipline, conscious of the ideals to be maintained, vigilant for the welfare of our society and the protection of human rights; in short, in a way which fits the best traditions of our profession....

Acting Judicially

NINTH CIRCUIT JUDICIAL CONFERENCE

July 28, 1976

During the last year and a half, for various reasons, I have often recalled a statement made by Lord Devlin in his book which came out some years ago on *The Criminal Prosecution in England*.[13] In defending some lack of judicial control over pre-trial criminal investigations in England, Lord Devlin wrote: "What is beyond argument is that whatever the powers of the investigator may be, the ideal is that he should exercise them judicially." "It does not necessarily follow," he went on to say, "that the job should be handed over to the judiciary. For while it is desirable that the investigator should act judicially, it is essential for the safety of the realm and of its citizens that he should have at his disposal all the powers and resources of the executive arm." Then he added the axiom: "It would not be good for judges to act executively; it is better to expect executives to act judicially." And as to this he said, "It is not at all an impracticable ideal."

As a way of discussing a small segment of the Department of Justice's work, I would like to discuss three clusters of problems which in different ways concern the administration of justice and where the Department in the implementation of executive authority is attempting to "act judicially." The ideal is not impracticable. Of course, there are tensions.

The first cluster: The 1972 decision in *Branzburg v. Hayes*[14] held that newsmen had no absolute right under the First Amendment to refuse to testify before federal or state grand juries with respect to information given them in confidence or with respect to their confidential sources of information. The decision was by a 5–4 vote with Justices Douglas, Stewart, Brennan and Marshall dissenting.

In his majority opinion, Justice White began by distinguishing those situations where the confidential sources of the newsmen were themselves implicated in the crime from those instances where the source not so involved would refuse to talk to newsmen if the source feared his identity would later be revealed. But having made such a distinction, Justice White refused to recognize a privilege in either case. To recognize such a privilege, he pointed out, would involve the Court in defining categories of newsmen or writers, lecturers, academic researchers or dramatists who could be said to be eligible. If the privilege were to be a qualified one, as had been urged, this would in turn enmesh the Court in complicated considerations of what constituted a compelling governmental interest, suggesting a differential treatment among various criminal laws. He pointed out that newsmen were not helpless; they had powerful means of influencing public opinion to protect themselves from harassment or substantial harm. For this and perhaps other reasons, prosecutors might be expected to act with discretion. Indeed the Attorney General had already fashioned a set of rules for federal officials in connection with subpoenaing members of the press. These rules were a major step, and they might be sufficient to resolve the disagreements and controversies.

The tone of Justice Powell's concurring opinion was somewhat different. He emphasized the continuing role of the courts to quash a subpoena or to issue a protective order so that the asserted claim to privilege could be judged on its facts by striking a proper balance—the tried and traditional way of adjudicating such questions. So too the dissent recognized that if the privilege were conferred, the courts would have to make some delicate judgments, but that "after all," the dissenters said, "is the function of courts of law."[15]

Against this background the Department of Justice has operated on the basis of revised guidelines issued in 1973. The guidelines provide that no such subpoena may be issued without the approval of the Attorney General and state that if a subpoena is obtained without authorization, the Department will move to quash it. During my tenure we have construed the term "news media" broadly. For example, in a case in this circuit in which a group of documentary filmmakers were subpoenaed with respect to a film they were making about various fugitives, we had the subpoena, which had been obtained without approval, quashed.

The guidelines provide standards which call upon the Department itself to strike the balance Justice Powell's opinion in *Branzburg* discussed. They require that before the issuance of a subpoena to any newsman is authorized, all reasonable efforts to secure the information in question from non-media sources must first be exhausted and negotiations with the persons to be subpoenaed must be undertaken with a view toward securing voluntary compliance. If negotiations fail, subpoenas are issued to newsmen unwilling to appear only when the information sought is essential to the successful conduct of a criminal investigation, and every effort is made to limit the scope of the subpoena to that information which is necessary to verify the accuracy of published reports. The guidelines finally provide that "[e]ven subpoena authorization requests for publicly disclosed information should be treated with care to avoid claims of harassment."[16]

In the six years since the original guidelines were announced,[17] an average of fewer than 20 subpoenas per year have been issued to newsmen at the request of the Department of Justice. The majority of these subpoenas simply called for the production and authentication of photographs, films, tape recordings or other evidence of guilt or innocence in the possession of a news organization. In most cases, agreements with the newsmen were reached; the subpoenas were issued at the request of the newsmen as a matter of personal convenience or professional practice.

Difficult fact situations do arise, and when they do, we have given considerable weight to whether the information to be elicited by the subpoena was given to the newsman in confidence and whether the newsman would be asked to reveal confidential sources. Though these factors do not appear explicitly in the guidelines, they are, as the *Branzburg* case makes clear, properly the center of the press's First Amendment concerns.

Last year I was asked to issue a subpoena of a newsman who had written a series of articles purporting to expose misconduct on the part of government officials. There was some suspicion that a "source" quoted in the article was either mythical or was dissembling to the reporter. Despite these suspicions, I decided not to authorize the subpoena. My decision was reached in part because of the issue of confidentiality of sources. But I was concerned also that there would have been the appearance of harassment. The articles in question had gained considerable attention and had purported to uncover government wrongdoing. I should add that later the reporter agreed to testify voluntarily. I was about to say that my view is that our practice is working fairly well in this area, which is so close to constitutionally protected rights, and then go on to admit that I had not had to face the case where the compelling circumstance was that without the testimony a prosecution would not be possible. One reason the hard compelling circumstance issue has not had to be confronted is because the practical inhibitions which prosecutors feel have simply kept some cases from progressing to that point.

The second cluster: Another area close to the reach of . . . constitutional protection is the question of dual prosecutions by federal and state prosecutors.[18]

In 1959 in *Abbate v. United States*,[19] the Supreme Court reaffirmed its holding of more than three decades earlier in *United States v. Lanza*[20] that the Fifth Amendment's Double Jeopardy Clause does not bar federal prosecution of a defendant previously tried in state court for these same act or acts. In the *Abbate* case, the previous state court trial for conspiracy to destroy the property of telephone companies had resulted in a sentence of three months imprisonment. The Court reasoned that the federal and state governments are separate sovereigns; each can punish, independently of the other, offenses against its laws. Justice Black joined by Chief Justice Warren and Justice Douglas, dissented. Justice Black observed that the possibilities of unfairness to defendants, which the double jeopardy bar is intended to prevent, are implicated quite as much by seriatim prosecutions by different sovereigns as they are by such prosecutions by the same sovereign. "Most free countries," he wrote, "have accepted a prior conviction elsewhere as a bar to a second trial in their jurisdiction."[21] "It is just as much an affront to human dignity and just as dangerous to human freedom for a man to be punished twice for the same offense, once by the State and once by the United States, as it would be for one of these two governments to throw him in prison twice for the same offense."[22]

Shortly after the *Abbate* decision, Attorney General [William P.] Rogers issued a memorandum to the United States Attorneys concerning exercise of the dual prosecution power which *Abbate* had reaffirmed. The memorandum perhaps was the product in part of an apprehension, based on the forcefulness of Justice Black's dissent and warnings against abuses voiced in the majority opinion in *Abbate* and its companion case, *Bartkus v. Illinois*[23] (which involved a prior acquittal), that unless the power was exercised wisely and with restraint, the Court's decision might prove unstable. Undoubtedly also influential was Justice Brennan's dissenting opinion in *Bartkus*,[24] which charged the federal officers with having engineered the second—this time a state—prosecution.

In the memorandum Attorney General Rogers announced the Justice Department's policy that "there should be no federal trial for the same act or acts unless the reasons are compelling."[25] At the same time, however, Attorney General Rogers doubted it was "wise or practical to attempt to formulate detailed rules to deal" with the wide variety of situations that might arise. Instead, to ensure that the general policy was enforced, and enforced even-handedly, he required that no federal case should be tried when there has already been a state prosecution for the same act or acts without approval by the appropriate Assistant Attorney General with review by the Attorney General.

The requirement announced by Attorney General Rogers remains in effect.[26] Along the way, however, "compelling reasons" was changed in the U.S. Attorneys' Manual to read "compelling federal interests involved," which conceivably narrowed the focus. The application of the standard, at least in my tenure, has proved, both as to substance and procedure, to be difficult and puzzling. So far as one can tell, the Department does not have much of a memory on the cases which have gone through the process.

Very few of these dual prosecution problems come to the Attorney General's attention each year, in some years fewer than twenty—a very modest number compared to the volume of federal prosecutions. But they are important both as an effort to achieve fairness and also because of the necessity of adequately vindicating the federal interest.

Let me describe a few of the recent cases. In one case the complaining witness in a Mann Act prosecution was found murdered shortly before the federal defendant was to go to trial. The federal defendant was indicted for murder in the state court. On the same evidence, the defendant could have been tried in federal court for obstruction of justice. The federal prosecutor deferred to the state because of the greater penalties that would attach to a murder conviction. The defendant was then tried in state court and acquitted. There was no indication that the state prosecutors had been disabled from presenting all available evidence of defendant's guilt, or that the trial was anything but fair. There seemed to be no factual difference which would be relevant to the prosecution for obstruction of justice. There is of course a great federal interest in ensuring that a defendant guilty of obstruction of federal justice be punished, and moreover the federal interest is distinct from that of the state.

In another case a defendant was convicted in state court for embezzlement of funds, a portion of which he had transported in interstate commerce. The state court imposed what federal prosecutors regarded as an absurdly light sentence—a brief period of probation. Again, there was no indication of corruption or any unfairness in the state court proceeding.

In the third case, a man stopped by state police for a minor traffic offense was discovered in possession of a sawed-off shotgun—a federal crime carrying a possible ten-year penalty. He was taken by police to municipal court and arraigned. On advice of counsel, he entered a guilty plea to a state offense and received the maximum sentence: one month. Counsel in that case was quite astute. Counsel in other cases have shown a similar awareness of the Department's policy against dual prosecution to their client's great advantage. There apparently was an agreement between the federal and state authorities. State authorities had agreed to defer to federal prosecution, but had failed to inform the law enforcement officers involved.

As one struggles with these and other cases, one reaches for what meaning to give "compelling reasons" or "compelling federal interests." Overall one has to have a direction. Is it to be assumed that dual prosecutions are always suspect as unfair in the absence of compelling circumstances because inherently, if not technically, they involve double jeopardy? This could be taken as the warning of the dissent in *Abbate*. But there might be a different standard which would find unfairness presumptively only when there is reason to suspect that prosecutors who lost or were dissatisfied with their first attempt have in fact taken part in and brought about the second prosecution. Against these general alternative standards, one may then seek additional touchstones. An acquittal in the first case emphasizes the double jeopardy point. On the other hand, if the result of the state prosecution, no matter what its outcome, could not reach the federally mandated penalty, this suggests the possibility of an overriding reason or federal interest. Even absent such disparate maximum sentences, it is possible that the same circumstances may speak to a different federal concern. Overall there is the problem of how to go about getting effective reinforcement for an agreed upon division of labor between United States Attorneys and state and local prosecutors—each agreeing to defer prosecutorial responsibilities to the other where the law under which the other operates carries the greater sanction. Attorney General Rogers' 1959 memorandum stated:"Cooperation between federal and state prosecutive officers is essential if the gears of the federal and state systems are to mesh properly. We should continue to make every effort to cooperate with state and local authorities to the end that the trial occur in the jurisdiction, whether it be state or federal, where the public interest is best served. If this be determined accurately, and is followed by efficient and intelligent cooperation of state and federal law enforcement authorities, then consideration of a second prosecution very seldom should arise."[27]

In some jurisdictions, there are formal and informal cooperative arrangements to this effect; and in most jurisdictions, perhaps, *ad hoc* adjustments are made. The precise content of such arrangements and adjustments necessarily must vary from jurisdiction to jurisdiction, depending on the content of state law. The great virtue of such arrangements is that they deal with both sides of the problems—that is, state following federal prosecution, as well as federal following state—while the Department's policy, unilaterally enforced, can deal only with the latter. But such arrangements and adjustments have an inevitable instability over time, with changes in personnel, in prosecutorial emphasis—indeed, with changes in law. In addition, there is occasional laxity in application and the slip-ups common to law enforcement as to any human institution.

The Department of Justice is now engaged in an effort—an effort long past due—to bring some stability and coherence to the decisions as to dual prosecutions. One part of the effort, through revision and clear state-ment in the United States Attorneys' Manual, is simply to ensure that the United States Attorneys are clearly aware of Department policy and will act accordingly. In several cases the Solicitor General has moved the Su-preme Court for an order to vacate a court of appeals judgment affirming conviction and to remand to allow a motion to dismiss, where the United States Attorney has failed to obtain permission for dual prosecution and where permission would not have been granted had it been sought.

In one such case in 1975, *Watts v. United States*, Chief Justice Burger along with Justice White and Justice Rehnquist dissented from the Court's acceptance of the Solicitor General's recommendation. "[A]ssuming as I do," wrote Chief Justice Burger, "that *Abbate* and *Bartkus* remain good law, there is no reason for the Court to lend its aid to the implementa-tion of an internal prosecutorial policy applicable only by speculation on our part, and there are abundant reasons for not doing so."[28] This dissent-ing assertion of judicial independence, with which I have no doubt many of you have much sympathy, perhaps raises questions as to what kind of problems can be handled either by the guidelines approach or the case by case elaboration of prosecutorial discretion. The Solicitor General's mo-tion to vacate seems to us to be an indispensable tool if a consistent pol-icy within the Department and among the United States Attorneys is to be maintained.

The third cluster: Since at least 1940, the Department of Justice has had special responsibilities for the conduct of warrantless electronic sur-veillance. In 1965 there were 233 telephone wiretaps under this program and 67 microphones; in 1975 there were 122 telephones and 24 micro-phones. Lord Devlin in his book records that for England, where such in-terceptions are authorized by the Home Secretary, for the year 1956 the total number of interceptions for police, customs and security amounted to 159.[29] ...

Under the standards and procedures established by the President, the personal approval of the Attorney General is required before any non-consensual electronic surveillance may be instituted within the United States without a judicial warrant. All requests for surveillance must be made in writing by the Director of the FBI and must set for the relevant justifying circumstances. Both the agency and the Presidential appointee initiating the request must be identified. The requests come to the atten-tion of the Attorney General only after they have been extensively re-viewed by the FBI, by a designated Department official and by a special review group established within the Office of the Attorney General. Each request, before authorization or denial, receives my personal attention. Under no circumstances are warrantless wiretaps or electronic surveillance directed against any individual who is not a conscious agent or collaborator of a foreign power. A year ago I publicly stated that there were no outstanding instances of warrantless taps or electronic surveillance directed against American citizens. There are no such instances now.

Although there is a strong and essential legal basis for continuing warrantless telephone and microphone surveillance for foreign intelligence and foreign counterintelligence purposes, the President has proposed legislation providing a procedure for the issuance of warrants in these cases.[30] . . . We have not asked the judges to act executively. The warrant could be issued by any one of seven federal district judges, designated by the Chief Justice, only if, on the basis of the submitted facts, there is probable cause to believe that the target of the surveillance is a foreign power or an agent of a foreign power and the facilities or place at which the electronic surveillance is directed are being used, or about to be used, by a foreign power or an agent of a foreign power. The President's initiative in this matter was to the Congress and particularly to a bipartisan group of leaders in both houses. The bill has been reported out favorably with a vote of eleven to one by the Senate Judiciary Committee, and it is now before the new Intelligence Committee.[31]

While this initiative by the President, when seen in the context of the history of our country for the last thirty-six years, is a major move for the protection of both individual rights and for essential protection for the country, there has been opposition to the proposed measure. Part of that opposition comes from those who like Mr. [Tom] Wicker of the *New York Times*, believe the proposed legislation in full of loopholes, booby traps and provisions that extend rather than restrict the government's surveillance powers. Another part apparently, if one is to believe Mr. [Rowland] Evans and [Robert] Novak,[32] comes from those who believe the bill, on the contrary, will cripple our intelligence effort. It is said that in my advocacy of the bill I have been moved more by constitutional safeguards than demands of national security. That really is not a dichotomy I accept. I am concerned that a step long overdue, fashioned to protect constitutional rights and national interests, may be delayed and perhaps never put into place.

In the meantime, I trust the Department will try to act judicially, for this is an area of extreme importance.

Leading the Camel

*For Attorney General Levi restoring public confidence did not mean put-
ting up a magisterial front. Preceded by his reputation for erudition, he
sometimes surprised his audience with candid humor about the ways of
government. The following are a few brief examples. The first is from remarks he made after leaving the Department of Justice. The other two he
made while he was in office.*

During the earlier days of my second stay at the Department of Justice[33] I was repeatedly asked by reporters what I was going to do with
the Department. This really isn't very difficult to answer if one is willing
to play the game. Moreover the announcement of new directions—even
old ones—has some usefulness. It is quite a different thing, however, to
come up with solutions to some of the hardest problems which assault
our society. I had already said many times I intended the Department to
be non-partisan, that the administration of justice was to be non-political,
and that I hoped the Department would be thoughtful about some of the
very difficult problems which existed in the administration of justice, and
that we intended to face up to these problems. But this obviously was too
general. On one such occasion, for reasons unknown to me, but probably
moved by the unreality of the assumption of complete freedom, to say
nothing about adequate knowledge, and having reinvented the wheel several times that day, I responded, "I am like a camel tender. I suppose the
camel will do more or less what it pleases. But I will try to lead it." Since
then I have been in Egypt and I have seen a camel. I can only wonder at
the accuracy of my observation.

*From "Reminiscences," a speech to the Annual Dinner of the University of
Chicago Law School Alumni Association, April 21, 1977[34]*

If I may be allowed a personal reference, not long ago I outlined a talk
which I proposed to give on certain serious matters involving the administration of justice. The proposed draft was written for me somewhat differently than I had intended. A comment by the writer, which was perhaps left attached by mistake, explained the reason for the difference:
"You will . . . note that I did not incorporate all of the Attorney General's suggestions into the draft. . . . I am afraid that unless current de-

partmental policy is changed we can say only 'no.'" The commentator was sympathetic and offered to do a larger, objective study. As to one other suggestion I wished to make, his response was that I was committed by departmental policy to an opposite view.

From a speech to the Conference on the Place of Philosophy in the Life of the American Nation, October, 8, 1976

Since I assume I have been invited to speak at this solemn occasion because I am in temporary exile in a far off place, I thought it would not be amiss if I began by describing one of the amusing folkways I have encountered.

It occurred just last week as I began to prepare for a formal press conference.

Two days before I was scheduled to talk with the press, I received what is known in Washington as a "briefing book." This briefing book, prepared by the public information staff at the Department, in consultation with the various divisions, U.S. Attorneys and bureaus, includes questions that might be asked, with some proposed answers. In these days the briefing book is by no means brief. One peculiar thing is that the hardest questions often have no proposed answers. I suppose this is based on the theory that peril is a stimulant to wit.

In some ways the briefing book is a necessity, and it is a most valuable tool for the head of an agency. The Department is not a large department, as cabinet departments go, but it has about 52,000 employees. And while the Department has many aspects which go beyond those which might be expected in a large law office, the Department has enormous litigating, law advice-giving and related duties, which would qualify a part of the Department as a large, although segmented, law firm. The Department has about 3,600 lawyers, functioning as lawyers, handling a caseload of about 76,000 cases, of which more than one-third are criminal. . . . Suffice it to say that the briefing books, of which I have had many, are themselves valuable tools for keeping informed. As the Attorney General moves around the country, or even when he is in Washington, he is supposed to know or be able to say something—or look as though he could say something even if he says "no comment"—on every case, investigation or other matter in which the Department may be involved and as to which there is some curiosity. This convention of total knowledge is bothersome. But the briefing book is a legitimate help. The briefing book, however, goes beyond such questions.

Before an important press conference, the briefing book in the Department of Justice is supplemented with a session in which one goes over the questions and supposed answers with members of the Department's public information office. This session is, I suppose, a perquisite of office. I must admit that it has rather astonished me. This is one aspect of Department of Justice life which, before returning to the Department a year and a half ago, I would never have imagined would greet me.

So let me take you to this session which occurred last week. I apologize that this recounting inevitably involves an apparent preoccupation with myself. I like to think it would have happened to anyone. I just happened to be there. The book did not begin gently.

"Question: A recent article about you in one of your hometown newspapers suggested you regard the press as a rabble, unable to comprehend complex matters. Is this really your view?"

I remembered having been advised that the jocular style of the press has a glorious tradition, and that it has been best described in a Chicago setting by Ben Hecht and Charles MacArthur. I knew that it was not the better part of wisdom to make light of heritage. Of course when the revival of the play, *The Front Page*, opened in Washington this year, the *Post* piously observed that this play's bawdiness characterized a press era well past and an image of newsmen that had been eradicated by noble victories of reporting. Even so, I figured that as an outsider to the media I would only get into trouble commenting on style and tradition. Instead I mumbled weakly, as I was told this attack would be made upon me, that I might answer, "Some of my best friends are newsmen." "That answer won't do at all," I was told.

Then I moved on to the second question: "Columnists Evans and Novak recently described your performance with respect to the Boston busing case as 'hopelessly amateurish.' Notwithstanding the fact," the question went on, "that those who are aware of the background of this matter know differently, do you believe that unnamed White House aides are deprecating you in talks with reporters?" I suggested I might say that the busing decision perhaps seemed bad because it was not politically shrewd—indeed was not political—and in that sense was hopelessly amateurish. I was inwardly a little relieved by the kind suggestion that "those who are aware of the background of this matter know differently," but then I looked at the third question, and realized that he might have a reason other than just kindness for saying so.

The third question: "One characterization of you that has appeared in the press with some frequency is that you are thin-skinned and take strong umbrage to criticism. Is this a fair assessment?"

Frankly, that irritated me.

All of my attempts to answer this question before my colleagues failed as being hopelessly defensive, offensive or too lighthearted.

At this point, I was presented with the fourth question, concocted too late for inclusion in the book, but presented on an emergency basis.

The fourth question: "Various commentators in the press have characterized you as indecisive, vacillating and ineffective. Do you feel such comments are justified?" The suggested answer which was given to me began with the statement, "No, I don't," then proceeded to wobble along with a series of equivocating, indecisive, vacillating, ineffective and unpersuasive defenses. Realizing I couldn't use these, and by now feeling totally taunted and done in, I suggested I might answer the various commentators at different times had characterized foreign tyrants as great liberals, knaves as heroes and scholars as fools, and that a little indecision among commentators might have a salutary effect.

My colleagues were divided between those who though the answer was too flippant and those who considered it insulting.

Next I ventured I might reply that commentators have to say something in order to make a living and that is all right with me. One of my colleagues, playing the role of a newsman with a follow-up question, asked whether my answer didn't indicate the kind of grating arrogance that had been attributed to me. As to any answers to this, I was advised that I should be apologetic, but not so apologetic that anyone might think I was being thin-skinned. When I ventured a serious response as to how I thought reasoned decisions should be arrived at, the unanimous view was that I should not try anything so complicated and therefore evasive.

Now through all of this I felt what a student of Zen must feel when, asked by his master an unanswerable question, he tries to unriddle it and receives a blow on the head for his efforts. I suppose the genius in this Zen master approach is to thicken the skin by scarring it.

Anyway, the press conference came. I was livid with preparation for it. None of the questions was asked. It was all quite amicable. In fact it restored my spirits, which had been drenched by the hazing. But I was ready. I was ready.

From a talk before the Chicago Bar Association, June 24, 1976

The Constitution and the Idea of Law

An Approach to Law

DELIVERED TO THE ENTERING CLASS OF 1976 AT THE UNIVERSITY
OF CHICAGO LAW SCHOOL[1]

*Shortly before he became Attorney General, then University of Chicago
President Levi addressed the entering class at the law school he attended
and later served as professor and dean. His talk anticipated a number of
themes that characterized his work at the Department of Justice.*

. . . Law does not exist for or by itself. It operates for and with people, and in a society which, perhaps particularly in the United States, is
not homogeneous. It uses the tools of the intellect, and the insight and
craftsmanship required for an art. Even as you are fully absorbed, as you
must be, in the acquisition and perfection of skills, and as you gain for
yourself, as you should, an organizing view of the sovereign control of the
ends of the law, it is important to remember that law is not everything.
In more or less degree this is the advice which should be given for all
specialized study. Each major intellectual discipline seeks for itself a major dominating monopoly view of the world. But economics is not everything, nor are psychiatry, psychology or sociology. And not even public relations. Even in the natural sciences it is the preclusive boundaries which
must be pierced, not only to give renewed vitality to the disciplines, so
that questions and inquiry may find their own way, but also as a reminder
that enclosed structures give an imperfect view, and that while knowledge
is interrelated, the kinds of knowledge appropriate for different tasks and
perception vary with what must be done.

There are special reasons for emphasizing this with respect to law. Law builds upon and, I should like to claim, is one of the liberal arts. It uses words of persuasion and changing definition for practical ends. It has absorbed within itself a view of the nature of human beings, and of how their acts and the incidents which overtake them may be classified for favor or penalty, or for rights, permission or negation. Law, itself, is a mediating discipline, not only among the passions and needs of human beings, sometimes viewed severally and sometimes in groups or associations, but with respect to the craftsmanship which is useful, and to the relevance of what is perceived as current knowledge or opinion. As an instrument for practical action, law is responsive to the wisdom of its time, which may be wrong, but it carries forward, sometimes in opposition to this wisdom or passion, a memory for received values. . . .

At the heart of legal systems, as we know them, are rules normally accepted as obligatory, and the availability of sanctions or authenticating steps which may be imposed. A variety of organizations as well as active social customs have these characteristics. When Mr. Kimpton[2] was Chancellor, he was invited to dinner at Burton-Judson.[3] The Master of Burton-Judson requested that the male students wear suit coats for the occasion. They did so, but left off their trousers. I assume there are some institutions in which trousers could be required.

We might add as even more important attributes for the formal legal system (possibly assumed or inchoate in the two I have already stated), institutions or accepted ways for rule creation, interpretation and enforcement. Again, many social institutions have these attributes. Thus, life within the family, social, economic and religious enterprises might be included. To these requirements we might further join an insistence that definite procedures be followed, arising out of the conceptions created by the system itself, to enforce minimum standards of participation or representation and fairness. There is a temptation to think of the adversary system as merely a civilized adaptation of self-help or the feud, but obviously it is a great deal more.

It may be said that this recital of attributes, which at one time might have invited a belief that they marked the evolution of a legal system to maturity (I do not believe it is that simple), is flawed because it does not include the state as the moving power or authenticating force. I have left the state out to emphasize that if the state or government or sovereignty is decisive in our recognition of what is a system of law, we should realize that government action may be direct or quite remote, and only tangentially related. It may be implied or demanded, and thus bestowed after the fact, because the other attributes of law, or some of them, are present. The government, indeed, may insist, or others will insist, that if important rules are normally accepted as obligatory, these must be under the jurisdiction of the formal legal system. And yet if it is important to put the government in, it is also a mistake, as I suppose we have reason to know, to assume that everything the government does is equivalent to law or the legal system.

The first aspect of this relationship of law to other institutions of society or behavioral patterns, then, is to press upon you again that law is not everything, but it is a great deal, and sometimes it is too much. There is no evading this problem. It is a problem many generations of lawyers will have to meet. There, undoubtedly, are a variety of answers. But we must recognize that law is a powerful and frequently, perforce, crude instrument with which to regulate all human conduct. In modern Western society, law brings with it an increasing paraphernalia of structure, a public aspect, a determination—not always realized—to seek finality, an assumption that what has been done in one area should be done in another, a harshness, and an inevitable influence toward conformity. The quaint—to our eyes—older writing as to the sources of the law reminds us that the increased communication and centralization of our time have changed the quality of the law, and this must be taken into account.

There have been and are societies, China, for example, which are of ancient lineage and have developed so that vast areas of human conduct are controlled by social pressures outside of what we would call the formal legal system. To such a lesser degree as, of course, to mark a difference in kind, this is also true in the United States, although those areas where law is not intricately involved are diminishing. The example of China is appropriate because it reminds us that non-law systems can be authoritarian, and we like to believe, and there is truth in this, that the thrust of our legal system is for the protection of the individual. Yet it is a peculiar but natural arrogance, and I beg of you to think hard on this point, to believe that it is the system of law—one institution among many—which is always the best protector of human freedom. If we are to woo all the Muses and Graces, let Humility be among them. We still carry with us the thought that liberty is aided or protected if there are areas "which are not law's business." This phrase was the focus of an important debate between Lord [Patrick] Devlin and Professor H. L. A. Hart of Oxford, beginning about fifteen years ago. One of the notable addresses in that debate was given by Lord Devlin as the Ernst Freund Lecture ten years ago in this hall. The debate concerned the use of the criminal law to enforce morality, but the implications of that debate are broader. Of course the removal of matters of personal morality from the grasp of law is probably the easiest area in which to win approval from those who favor the extension of law for social action—and the reverse is probably sometimes true also. But I suggest the effects of intervention in a variety of areas need to be appraised and not taken for granted. Moreover, as our law develops, this is not necessarily a matter for public debate, but flows from accretions of constitutional interpretations, and further rides on the point that law is already present in the area and must be clothed with all its attributes.

Because I do not wish to be misunderstood, let me say explicitly that I think it is an urgent matter for governance and law to make effective a new or renewed charter of freedom for all citizens. But the challenge to statecraft is to achieve this with a minimum, not a maximum, of the structure of formal law.

The second aspect of the relationship between law and other institutions of society and to behavioral patterns is based on the unique characteristics and responsibilities which law carries. Thus, while it is important—and particularly for a lawyer—to observe the similarities in group behavior in the many areas of life where there are collective causes, there is a point in insisting that law is or ought to be different. There is a paradox in this, I realize. It is because law is seen as everywhere that the distinction between it and other activities is blurred. One can, of course, analyze society naively as though nothing more were involved than a series of pressure groups and devices. Roscoe Pound, who began his important work in the jurisprudence of interests at this university, powerfully influenced at that time by the work of sociology, saw the task of law as social engineering, mediating and responding to the various claims of society. But it is a far different conception which treats law as only another device for social pressure and leverage. The special responsibility for law is that its end is the common good. The values which it exemplifies in its treatment of individuals and groups must be conditioned to that end. Law does invoke sanctions which penetrate deeply and can be terrifying in their impact. The misuse of law as but another device for leverage is profoundly corrupting. Unfortunately we have many examples of this in our time. One would hope that the emergence of the lawyer as more than a scrivener or a clerk, and his acceptance as an officer of the court, would mean more than the duty to protect orderly procedures in that forum. Indeed, it has meant more. But to accomplish this, the profession carries an accountability to the system of justice it protects, and a duty to improve that system. If so, there really is a great deal for you to do.

I come now to the third aspect which deals more particularly with the relationship of law to other disciplines. You note I reject a view of law as being solely what a judge, as a judge, says it is. Such a view makes a valuable point, but it is seriously wrong. The judge may have the last word, even though sometimes for only a brief period. But one might as well say that for many matters and substantial periods, the law is what the practicing lawyer or commentator says or, in other areas, what the policeman does. Moreover, there is legislation; there are executive orders, administrative rules. There is obviously much more to law than the report of cases. And even if we tried to limit law to what the cases say, the social theories of the particular time will find their expression there. Witness the attention which has been paid to the so-called sociological footnote in *Brown v. Board of Education*,[4] and before that to the reference to the Brandeis brief in *Muller v. Oregon*,[5] considered enlightened for its time, and eloquent on the point that it is appropriate to restrict or qualify the conditions under which women should be permitted to work.

Law is part of both the humanities and the social sciences. . . . There has been an extraordinary growth in the social sciences, and surely law can be studied as a social phenomenon. Special aspects or problems can be looked at: the operations of the court system,[6] itself; the importance of guilty pleas or particular rules of evidence on some quantitative basis; the effect of evidentiary rules on police conduct; alternatives to ways of improving the penitentiary system. The list is long. But beyond these matters directly related to the legal system, itself, much modern social science research cannot help but have implications which may question the assumed results following from legal rules or the given reasons for the rules. Law is pervasive throughout most of human life. In his most famous speech on legal education, [Oliver Wendell] Holmes said, "The rational study of law is still to a large extent the study of history. History must be part of the study because without it we cannot know the precise rules which it is our business to know. It is part of the rational study, because it is the first step toward an enlightened skepticism." And then he went on to say, "[T]he man of the future is the man of statistics and the master of economics."[7] I assume he meant these specific subjects, but he also meant them to signify the growing substance and techniques of the social sciences. And I also suppose he meant you.

If law is a mediating discipline with respect to the craftsmanship which is useful and to the relevance of what is perceived as current knowledge or opinion, then it is important that the higher learning in law search out those techniques and theories of knowledge most relevant to the correction or direction of law. This law school has been one of the leaders in this research, not only in the relationship of law to other disciplines, but, as I think is necessary when such research is done, in the other disciplines directly. The point of this is that one cannot simply take the stated conclusions of another science and apply them. At some stage of the interrelationship, the question of law has to be reformulated, but the assumed impact and meaning of the external theory must also be reexamined. This is when the research really begins. This is the beginning of understanding.

Law is its own discipline, not to be captured by any other. It must keep fresh its relationships to other fields of knowledge and to the enlightened as well as the common thought of its time. But there is an integrity and cohesiveness of its own which must be maintained. Law has its own history which is part of its working process, the values it protects, the procedures which have been developed for change. It is a discipline to be studied. But it is much more. The problem for the lawyer, and for the legal scholar, is not just to know the law, but how to create within it. It is a world of artistry and craftsmanship and change. . . .

In the Service of the Republic

A SPEECH TO THE FELLOWS OF THE AMERICAN BAR FOUNDATION

February 14, 1976

It is a privilege to address this group of leaders of our Republic. There is no doubt that you are that, although you and I may be biased in favor of the bar. The shafts directed at your profession throughout the history of our society of advocates and scriveners can be treated either as a recognition of leadership or a warning of bias.

Edmund Burke, in describing the reasons for troubles with the colonies, gave some emphasis to the large number of lawyers "acute, inquisitive, dexterous, prompt in attack, ready in defense, and full of resources."[8] Later Burke was less complimentary in describing the role of lawyers in the French Revolution, but needless to say he found them no less troublesome. An anonymous essayist, opposing the adoption of the American Constitution and wickedly signing himself "A Federalist" when he was the opposite, complained that "lawyers in particular keep up an incessant declamation for its adoption; like greedy gudgeons they long to satiate their voracious stomachs with the golden bait."[9] I assume one day a research project for your foundation will list all these delightful sayings. It will make a big book.

I was surprised when I found in your program that the title of my talk tonight was "In the Service of the Republic." I do not recall, although it is possible that it happened in the rush of doing, that the title came from me. Somehow it has a pretentiousness to be properly reserved for law school deans or university presidents. I accept the title since, I hope it is not presumptuous for me to say, this is the way you should see yourselves, and I am certain you do. The idea of our Republic is that we are all in its service. As members of our profession we are all public citizens. We all take part in the effort to have the Republic serve and represent the citizenry and the common good. The responsibility and opportunity are not the sole possession of lawyers. The Periclean ideal of citizenship — no matter how impossible for us and for Pericles to achieve — is central to our society. Surely it is central to our profession. The responsibility and opportunity are certainly not reserved for those who happen to be in government where under some popular notions, which I trust are wrong, there may be even some loss of freedom and honor, which are after all essential ingredients for a serving leadership.

The lawyer's service is frequently regarded in the adversary model. I have been cautioned on several occasions during the last year that the office I now hold is supposed to be an adversary one. I was told this by some when the Department of Justice took the admittedly unusual step of not only filing a brief in the Supreme Court in defense of the Federal Elections Commission, for most, although not all of the provisions of the Act, but also filing an impartial amicus brief as well. I was told this also when I gave an Attorney General's opinion, as I am bound by statute to do, to the Secretary of Commerce. The opinion, it was said, need not be taken seriously because, coming from the executive branch, it was necessarily special pleading. The conceptions of the lawyer as agent or representative of the client or as servant of the rule and processes of law are, as we well know, not simple. The characterizations do not quite fit because the roles of the lawyer are many. The prosecutor, we are told, may strike hard blows but not foul ones, but this hardly adequately describes even the prosecutive function. Be that as it may, our entire legal system is sometimes described as an adversary one. The paradigm is the trial in which the arguments, the facts and the methods of presentation which will help win are advanced, and those which might help lose are subdued, or subdued to some extent, by both sides. The process is one which, when it works, has the merit of defining the issues and reaching a decision.

In spite of frequent criticisms, including those by judges of lawyers said to be ill-prepared for the task and others who find the process wasteful or not the best for truth finding, this kind of proceeding is, I think, much admired in our society. Indeed the modern form of public debate on policy issues sometimes assumes the style of a moot trial, which apparently is thought to enforce more discipline, perhaps drama, than the exchange of discourses of an older day. The decline of rhetoric and eloquence somehow has made the structure of a trial more appealing during the very period when science and its methods of research for its own purposes are claimed to go in the opposite direction. On entering my office, I am greeted every day by the slightly ambiguous inscription—ambiguous in part since the words are in a small rotunda, and one can begin the sentence in different places—"The United States wins its point whenever justice is done its citizens in the courts." I am also forced to take note of the fact that when one enters the Attorney General's office, one faces a rather large mural showing "Justice Liberated," but as one leaves one sees a large mural showing "Justice Enslaved." I wish it were otherwise. I take it both the murals and the inscriptions are admonitions to give care, quality and direction to the adversary process.

It is not strange, I suppose, that the modern view of our society is that it is, after all, composed of conflicting groups and their protagonists. Our form of government, with its checks and balances, was created in recognition of this and to curtail the power of factionalism. Roscoe Pound built a view of jurisprudence on the basis of interests pressing for recognition. The formation of our Constitution and its development have recognized not only this kind of interest, but the particular desire for power which governmental roles themselves induce. Nevertheless, our Constitution, with all the wariness it reflects concerning man's nature, came from the age of enlightenment with its hope—perhaps faith—in reason. But in our special kind of scientific period, which has tended to avoid the normative—and this creates a special problem for law, which, after all, is at least in part normative—there has been an inclination (I think this is changing) to describe everything that goes on, viewing the structure of affairs in action, in terms of power relationships or automatic reactions. It is, of course, possible to do this since it is one way, although, depending on what power means, an incomplete way, of looking at the world. The position diminishes reason, disparages the ideal of the common or public good, adds legitimacy to the notion that law is only one more instrument among many to be manipulated. Then, too, the products of our scientific age and their uses add greatly to the means for effective propaganda and to other techniques for gaining advantage. I suppose it is not strange that our view of the struggle of self-interests, real or induced, is somewhat self-fulfilling. It builds easily upon the pragmatic strain among us with its inherent cynicism, even though the events of the last thirty-five years indicate that one should not count on cynicism to combat passion. John Austin in his *The Province of Jurisprudence Determined* remarked that "[i]t was never contended or conceited by a sound orthodox utilitarian, that the lover should kiss his mistress with an eye to the common weal."[10] I suppose it is one of the tenets of the operators of the manipulative society that this result would not be and never has been beyond reach.

The events of the last twenty-five years—perhaps longer—culminating in the governmental crisis of a few years ago, greatly enhanced the view that no matter how things may appear, the struggle for power is what is truly and only genuine. The fact that there was a crisis might suggest an effective limitation upon that struggle as the sole standard and motivation for conduct. It is in any event an oversimplification, but the point is that it came to be believed. Today one has to argue that the appearance of conflict is not necessarily the whole story, or even that the absence of the appearance does not mean something is being concealed. One example is that almost every issue today at the federal government level is described as a conflict between the executive and the legislature. It may or it may not be. Another example is that the public press, clothed as it properly is in the mantle of the First Amendment, now so frequently sees itself totally committed to this adversary view of life. Since no institution is as sensitive to criticism as the press, I state this example with some trepidation, or perhaps assurance that I will be misunderstood. I do so only because, as I will say later, the responsibilities and powers of the press and other forms of communication are important and awesome. The point is not the role of the press as investigative reporter or essayist, or the constitutional mandate against abridgement. It is rather the choice of the role of adversary rather than as critic, because recent history is thought to have made the change necessary. Samuel Johnson, as one might expect, in his dictionary, said some unpleasant things about critics. He defined a critic as a "snarler or carper" but he also recognized a critic as an "examiner," or as "a judge," or even as "a man apt to find fault."[11] The adversary, on the other hand, in his dictionary, was "an opponent, an antagonist, an enemy, generally applied to those that have verbal or judicial quarrels." "It may sometimes imply an open profession of Enmity," he wrote, using as an example the sentence, "A secret enemy is worse than an open adversary."[12] The conception of the role of the press is, I think, a sign of these days, although I believe it is changing.

The laws of the United States, as they are in action, for reasons well understood, have furthered this sense of adversariness. A law against discrimination hovers on the edge of becoming a law for discrimination, not to correct past wrongs but because society is seen, not as composed of individuals with talents and rights, but as a series of groups vying for power. And this has come to be regarded as one of the uses of law, in litigation and otherwise, without, however, a legislative or constitutional confrontation of the values which are involved. In the interstices of the law are found the weapons to fight these battles of public policy, not just as to discrimination but also as to the allocation of resources and the determination of the forums for decision. Political theory sometimes argues for the formal representation of interest groups, chosen for them and exclusively by them in parliamentary assemblies. We have rejected this idea of corporate syndicalism for legislatures but recreated it for the law at large and particularly for the courts. The history of law can be written this way, but, in the cycle of history, the trend is accentuated in our time.

Popular governments are prone to cycles. It is one of their strengths as well as their weaknesses. In the confused days between the end of the Revolutionary War and the Constitutional Convention George Washington wrote, "We are apt to run from one extreme to another."[13] The Constitution was intended to form a government which recognized, moderated, but did not entirely do away with this tendency. We are in such a period of cyclical reaction today, justifying what we do now as a kind of getting even with the events of prior years. This in itself is another form of the game of victims and losers. We are adversaries not only with ourselves, but also with the past.

This seems some distance away from the spirit of the Founders of the Republic, who did not overestimate the nature of man, or minimize the difficulties in which they found themselves, who had many disagreements but were thoughtful about their attempts at resolution. "We have probably had too good an opinion of human nature in forming our confederation," George Washington wrote.[14] In the midst of the Constitutional Convention, Benjamin Franklin was moved to say, "We indeed seem to *feel* our want of political wisdom, since we have been running around in search of it. We have gone back to ancient history . . . ; we have viewed modern states . . . , but find none of their constitutions suitable to our circumstances. . . . [G]roping, as it were, in the dark."[15] But from this assemblage which knew it had a serious task to perform, and which could write about the problems with explicitness and eloquence, there came, as Charles Beard wrote, more than a bundle of compromises. It was "a mosaic of second choices accepted in the interest of union and the substantial benefits to flow from union."[16] It was a convention in which necessity and discussion made a difference.

At the time of the Convention and for many years thereafter, as has been noted, there was a special quality to American law. Because of the method of training, or, we might say, non-training of lawyers, there was an emphasis on general principles, both of law and of government, and on the practical necessities and the customs which had been developed and were changing. There was the guidance also of a sense of history and a feeling of destiny. I have taken advantage—and beg your indulgence on this point—of this bicentennial year to give some impression, quite unnecessary in this group, of the thought and words of that period. In a country which for some reason not clear to me knows so little history as we do, a recollection of that period represents an opportunity, but we may end up with echoes from that time and the impressions of the present, without much conception of what happened in between, even ten, twenty, or thirty years ago. We are the captives of, and are only learning to master, forms of communication which impose upon us a kind of existentialism, an immediacy which does not have the reality of discussion or the wider historical sense. That this should happen in a country which has more formal education widely distributed than has ever been the case is not as odd as it sounds. Education never ends or it dies; it is not easy to achieve, and half education, like half truths, represents at least the same challenge today and probably more so, as did the necessity for an educated citizenry in the much smaller country of four million people two hundred years ago.

History, like law and economics, is not everything. But one may pause to consider the oddity of the one-dimensional character of much present discussion. The abuses of investigatory agencies over at least the last two decades, while real and cause for alarm, are viewed as if they existed out-

side of time or as if they had all occurred today, thus removing from critical scrutiny the most important factor: namely, the environment in which
they took place—an environment which, it must be said, has a habit of reappearing at various intervals in the life of the Republic, starting, perhaps,
with the Alien and Sedition Laws of 1789, but really before. One only has
to think of Madison's letter to Jefferson in March 1786, secretly planning
the Constitutional Convention and expressing his concern: "I saw enough
during the late assembly of the influence of the desperate circumstances
of individuals on their public conduct, to admonish me of the possibility
of finding in the council of some one of the states fit instruments of foreign machinations."[17]

    Or think of the problem of secrecy. The Congress of the Articles of
Confederation met in private. It was called a "dark and secret conclave."[18]
So did the Constitutional Convention, which required a pledge of confidentiality as to its proceedings, and which, in order to prevent leaks,
watched Franklin with particular care. Jefferson, who was not present,
complained in a letter to Adams: "I am sorry they began their deliberations by so abominable a precedent as that of tying up the tongues of their
members. Nothing can justify this example but the innocence of their intentions, and ignorance of the value of public discussion."[19] But there is at
least some reason to believe, sunshine laws to the contrary, that the new
Constitution could not have been created under any other circumstances.
There are many other examples of footnotes on subjects now current, including the covert action by France, which perhaps made this Republic
possible, and the refusal of Washington, noted in his diary, to consult with
the Senate on the "places to which it would be necessary to send persons in the Diplomatic line" because "they have no Constitutional right
to interfere" and "it might be impolitic to draw it into precedent,"[20] or the
better-known example of refusing to provide the House with the background papers on Jay's treaty with Britain. This is not to say that history
should repeat itself but rather that it might save us from the surprise that
dulls reflection.

    There is no hidden agenda in this discourse. Rather I seek to emphasize
one attribute of the kind of government, republic and society it was hoped
we could be. It was to be a government and society which moved by reason. The Revolutionary War, it was thought, had itself spread among the
Americans a greater knowledge of the science of government. We should
not relegate to extinct Fourth of July addresses the brash affirmation of
Joel Barlow, American poet and statesman who later settled not too glo-

riously the matter of payments for trade on the Barbary Coast, when he proclaimed in 1787, "[T]he present is an age of philosophy; and America the empire of reason."[21] The *Federalist Papers* reflect the view that there was a new science of government. The belief came at a fortunate time so that it could be later reaffirmed by other examples of the progress made through the miracle of evolution and the discovery of new principles. The ability, the willingness, the freedom to exchange ideas and to discuss were extremely important. So Mill wrote in *On Liberty*: "Where there is a tacit convention that principles are not to be disputed; where the discussion of the greatest questions which can occupy humanity is considered to be closed, we cannot hope to find that generally high scale of mental activity which had made some periods of history so remarkable."[22] So Bagehot, the English Economist,[23] applying Darwin's theory of evolution, wrote that it was "government by discussion" which would break the bonds of ages.[24] I don't think we need to be reminded of the American dream in this area, but rather to take heed of what it requires.

There is a sense, of course, in which it cannot be fulfilled. Frank Knight, the great American economist and, I would say, philosopher, took grim pleasure in pointing out how few real discussions ever took place. The understanding and exchange of ideas, to learn and to change what one knows — all this is extremely difficult. In a purist sense it hardly ever happens. Yet the measure of the excellence which is reached is of concern to all of us, and particularly to the nation's laws, which are bound to be in considerable part a reflection of the nation's thought and confusion. "Representative bodies," John Jay wrote Washington, "will ever be faithful copies of their originals, and generally exhibit a checkered assemblage of virtue and vice, of abilities and weakness."[25] He was wrong, of course, in his despondent prediction. The Constitutional Convention did better than that. But over time a working society, with a broadened electorate and a representative government, cannot help but be elevated or depressed by the general level of knowledge and spirit of candor to inquire and to learn and to think and rethink possessed by the many.

The great experiment which the *Federalist Papers* proclaimed was not so much representative government or checks and balances within the general or central government. The *Papers* recognized these were borrowed ideas. Even the creation of the executive, which was the greatest necessity to which the Constitution responded, was not the distinctive contribution. Even Jefferson, who was often doubtful about the need for a strong executive until he became President, was urging the importance of separating the executive and legislative powers. Again Washington records in his diary the closing interview between the new President and the French Minister. The French Minister, according to Washington, said that "[h]itherto he observed that the Government of this Country had been of so fluctuating a nature, no dependence could be placed on its proceedings; which caused foreign nations to be cautious of entering into treaties, etc., with the United States. But under the present government there is a head to look up to—and power being put into the hands of its officers, stability will be derived from its doings."[26] The originality which the *Federalist Papers* claimed was in the application of the principle of representation through federalism to make possible an extended republic of great territorial size with a national authority and many subordinate—that was the word used—governments with their own legislatures and councils and "their due authority and activity."[27]

Writing about the American republic at the turn of the century, Barrett Wendell of Harvard described the strategic and complicated position which law occupied in this extended republic. "It is a happy legal notion," he wrote, "honestly believed by most Americans from the beginning to this day, that no question can arise which the law does not cover." Then he went on to portray the unprecedented complexity of legislation, each state with its constitution, its legislature, almost every town subject to a legislative body. "This state of affairs has combined with the somewhat superstitious confidence of Americans in legal forms, to cover the face of the continent with an intricate network of often conflicting statute law, varying in force from Acts of Congress to resolutions of aldermanic boards." He thought a hasty glance at the incredible confusion of American legislation might mislead a stranger into a belief "that any country thus fettered must be virtually paralyzed." But the solution, he said, is in the system that, as with the constitutions, confides in the courts the power of interpretation. The courts have been animated "by a conviction that their duty is to keep the machinery of society in working order. . . . In brief, what has saved America from the benumbing result of excessive legislation has . . . been the swift and luxuriant overgrowth of unwritten law." "If the working of carelessly drawn, preposterous or conflicting statutes can be stretched into practical consistency, the Courts may usually be trusted to stretch it. If statutes prove utterly unpracticable, the Courts will commonly make this fact so clear as to induce repeal or amendment."[28] The least dangerous branch was fulfilling the role of linchpin, but more than that, in the government of the United States.

Considerable progress has been made in the last century to clarify the network of law. Codes, uniform laws and the restatements have helped greatly. Studies coming from the American Bar Foundation and from other associations have provided important background material and recommendations. The course of legislation in some areas has been helped. The growth of administrative law and procedures has added to the intricate pattern. But in matters of important social policy, legislation is most apt to be incomplete, hortatory, evasive and irresponsible. The role of the courts has not diminished. It has been magnified. The federal Constitution has been treated in part as legislative enactment, or in lieu of legislation, and the federal courts have become the mechanism for the federal presence in state and local governments. The opening up of the courts through changes in rules of standing and class actions has[29] enabled the courts to play a much more active role in the conflict between interest groups. That which cannot be decided in the legislature moves to the courts under the rubric of constitutional doctrine where the adversary proceeding will be fought out, followed, perhaps, by a period of court management of local institutions. The system no doubt responds to important needs and no doubt is a spur to progress, but it also works a delay, as elected officials can wait for the time when the blame for action can be placed upon the intruder. When the council of revision, which would have included the judges, was debated in the Constitutional Convention, it was argued that putting the courts in this position would lose them the confidence of the people. But the present situation frequently places a burden much heavier upon the courts, sometimes acting on the basis of legislation, sometimes without it, navigating most difficult areas where a society, which must husband its resources and which in fact wants to find a new charter for human rights, has difficult decisions to make.

The point which must be made, I think, is that behind the courts and behind the legislatures are the influential mechanisms of society which set or distort the debate, which enlighten, or by a delight in induced or assumed antagonism, cheapen every discussion so that the immediate reaction is never troubled by a later thought. These are harsh words, too harsh perhaps, but the freedom our society has given does place a responsibility upon the press and upon the professions, particularly our profession, to clarify the issues, not in a spirit of antagonists or adversaries—there are forums for that—but so that an enlightened public will understand not the catch words, not the chosen disagreements, but the basic issues which are involved. If one believes in a government by reason or discussion, the victory comes when there is understanding. The problems we have are not easily solved, but the beginning is made when they are understood. This is of course much to ask. But it has a great deal to do with the role of our country if it is to continue to be the best hope in government for mankind.

A Lawyer among Humanists

DINNER IN HONOR OF PAUL FREUND ON THE OCCASION OF HIS
JEFFERSON LECTURE

April 30, 1975

It is a strange but customary question to ask—and believing wisdom may follow this compulsion I put the question to you—"What is a lawyer doing among humanists?"

It was the son of a lawyer, naturally, who contributed greatly, although his help was hardly required, to the literature of derision descriptive of the learning and doings of the legal profession. It was Rabelais who provided in the library of St. Victor such titles on law and judges as I would not dare to recite.

Yet, among the books, I can safely report, was one on the "Flimflams of the Law." This was a natural title for the inventor of Judge Bridlegoose, who decided cases, as you all recall, by the toss of large and small dice—an efficient method—but only after tomes of pleading and paper had been provided and intricate procedures followed.

The question which is put is not why the use of the dice—since the sense of that, being statistical and also final, is obvious—but why the prior flimflam?

Bridlegoose gives four answers concealed among three. First, the formality is essential for the credibility of the result. Along with this is the obvious point that sometimes the formalities are able to destroy the substance. Then second, engaging in the procedures and formalities is fun, diverting in itself, like the game of muss. It can be taken, like so much of learning or doing, for its own sake. Third, all this procedure delays matters so that sifting, searching and examining creates a ripeness and maturity which win acceptance when the dice are eventually thrown.

Surely, any editor of one of your editions, if he lives that long and gets that far, will understand the point.

One might think the case for the humanism of the law has been made. But there is more to come. Rabelais has his principal character assure us that "laws are excerpted out of the middle of moral and natural philosophy." But then, distinguishing between law and lawyers, he completely does away with the latter "since they have studied less in philosophy than [a] mule."[30] Surely the analogy between law and the humanities has now been completed. But the action is threatening.

This forerunner of sociological surveys should give us pause. Should we impose a similar disqualification on humanists who have not studied philosophy? How many would be left? Law as a craft has often been deserted by those who, like John Donne, while ostensibly studying law in Lincoln's Inn spent their time reading divines, philosophers, chroniclers and poets. Let us hope we can call them humanists rather than merely subjects for humanists despite the age of specialization which is ours. And let us hope that some we can call lawyers.

We might think for a moment of the development of law as a craft, created to write for others, and thus to speak for them, when few could write. Thus the servant for the soldier, or the servant for the man of affairs, until the servant becomes the action maker himself.

How does one give meaning and order to a world which has both regularity and unpredictability? So form becomes substance trying to get to the essence and to make use of the mysteries which surround us. Order is never completely possible, but order is sought, because order is the explanation, and when order seems right, we call it justice.

The basic tool for the lawyer is the word—the inherited word, the changing word which reflects, as Jefferson noted, the operations of the workshop of society in which language is formed and elaborated. The lawyer uses the word ultimately to explain that which, to some degree, as every lawyer must know, escapes complete explanation. "Like art," Paul Freund has written, "the law seeks to impose a measure of order on the disorder of experience, while respecting and drawing vitality from the underlying spontaneity, diversity, and disarray. Like science, the law seeks to find uniformities and interconnections, to build more general formulations that are simpler, more faithful to experience, and more serviceable; and then, if necessary, to break down the generalization into new particulars at the higher level of insight."[31] The process is never-ending. If it were to end, it would cease to be understood. And not ending, it must probe the mysteries.[32]

Archibald MacLeish, sharing the platform with Paul Freund on a previous occasion, explained how his poetic art and his legal education were joined. "The business of law," he said, "is to make sense of the confusion of what we call human life — to reduce it to order but at the same time to give it possibility, scope, even dignity. But what, then, is the business of poetry? Precisely to make sense of the chaos of our lives. To create the understanding of our lives. To compose an order which the bewildered angry heart can recognize. To imagine man."[33]

The occasion of the Jefferson Lecture this year celebrates not the return of law to its proper goals but a continuity of discipline and endeavor which law has always shared with other humanistic efforts. The sought-for achievement is to know mankind with its strengths, weaknesses and aspirations, and to help create and give vitality to that order which gives guidance to a community.

Robert Penn Warren last year in his Jefferson Lecture said, "If we conceive democracy as involved in our notions of civilization, then we must realize that democracy cannot exist in a society that is merely mechanical, that is not, in a deep sense, also a community of individual selves with common feelings, ideals, and conceptions of responsibility."[34]

Those who would give this guidance must be interpreters. They carry a heavy burden. They had better be humanists.

For those of us who claim to be of the lawyer's craft and who care deeply about the role of the humanities, we are proud Paul Freund has spoken for us. Grace, wit and learning are his possessions, not only for the feast of the Jefferson Lecture, but even when it becomes necessary, as it sometimes does in the everyday, in the tossing of the dice. But that is the stuff out of which poetry and law are made.

The Rule of Law

LAW DAY DINNER

May 1, 1975

This is a special day for law and for the legal profession. The day has added meaning for the Nebraska bar and the University of Nebraska–

Lincoln College of Law. You have dedicated a new law school building to the service of the profession, a building where new attorneys will be introduced to what Sir Edward Coke called "the artificial Reason and Judgment of the Law."[35] And as they master it, they will become members of a proud and great profession.

But Law Day is not solely a celebration of the legal profession. It is intended for our entire society because law by its virtues and by its defects affects all of us—the powerful and the weak, the learned and the unlearned. We recognize this universality of the law when we speak of the sovereignty of the rule of law under which we all live.

The law which is sovereign is not complete, and it is not perfect. If we measure law by justice, we find it wanting, for we know there are many injustices. Also there is great cynicism about the law now, as there has been at other times. Some see it merely as an instrument in the hands of the powerful for accomplishing their personal aims. Even if we think of law as a noble instrument of society for maintaining civility, we must pause at its[36] lack of success. . . .

Of course, the law is imperfect. It is made by man. It reflects his failings, his human weaknesses. But it also reflects his powers and wisdom. It is made by man, and it must contend with the forces man sets against it. It must contend with our conflicting desires and ambitions for power and material goods. It exists in a human society where each man does not necessarily judge correctly in his own cause, where resources for which men compete cannot satisfy them all, where factionalism is probably the inevitable price of diversity.

It is not necessarily a reproach that our society has not fulfilled all its aspirations. In many ways we have progressed far beyond the dreams of the Founders who set our law into motion—in our size and numbers, in the distribution of material advantages, in the access to education and in the cultivation of the arts. In many ways our aspirations have changed and will continue to change. Even the good society—perhaps because it is good—cannot ever be wholly satisfied. Indeed the good society must have ideals beyond its attainment. A vital society inevitably has problems which must be solved. It is the responsibility and the joy of the lawyer to try to solve them.

Our society and its law have difficult problems to face today. Not the least of the problems is the increasing resort to the law to settle differences among individuals and organizations once resolved by informal relations of trust and comity. The courts clog with lawsuits brought either because people don't believe they can make their grievance known any other way or because they don't want to give up a single chip in the process of bargaining for an advantageous settlement of their claim. The lawsuit is no longer the last resort. For those who think they are powerless in the face of impersonal and indifferent institutions, the lawsuit is the only resort. And for those who are well-schooled in the resolution of disputes, the lawsuit is a method, not so much of having a tribunal resolve an issue as for forcing a resolution out of court.

As the system of civil justice has become cluttered, the criminal justice system has fallen into incredible disrepair. The burden of increasing crime has put pressures upon the system which it is incapable of supporting. Criminals have learned to use the inefficiency of the system to their own advantage and the result is grave. An unpublished study conducted in one major American city showed that only 4 percent of the persons arrested for a felony were actually convicted of that felony. Even fewer ever went to prison. FBI statistics show that there are only 19 arrests for every 100 serious crimes reported. The lesson for potential criminals in this is clear: that they can use the law's weakness to avoid being punished. The deterrent force of the law falters upon that lesson. The crime problem spirals upon itself. If the criminal justice system weakens the deterrent force of the law, then there is more crime. And that extra crime puts its burden directly back on the already overwhelmed system.

The law has also outgrown many of its traditional categories as we have called upon it to solve complex, technological problems. For example, while once the law of nuisance served as the bulwark of environmental protection, today its easy maxims are not nearly enough. The law is now called upon to discover what may harm us, strike a subtle balance of harms and benefits and recognize that the conduct of any one of us may be trivial individually but devastating in the aggregate. The law must concern itself with events so great as an accidental burn-out at a nuclear power plant and so small as the tiny bursts of vapor from the nozzles of aerosol cans. Of course, the law has always been general, has always applied to the great and the small. But the burden put upon our law by scientific knowledge about the consequences of our acts and the technological advances that raise ever more complicated questions of control cause some to yearn for the return of innocence. They might wish for the return of an era in which the threat to our environment might again be as obvious as a chimney belching black smoke now seems to us. But that era will not return. Rather what we must now reach for is a much more delicate balance of interest.

There are problems, indeed, and it is because of these problems, not in spite of them, that the rule of law is so central in maintaining progress. For the rule of law requires that we meet these problems by applying to them our deepest human values. What then is the rule of law?

It is often said upon solemn occasions such as this that ours is a system of laws and not of men. The idea of the rule of law developed in the Middle Ages in an otherworldly context that could distinguish laws from men. In the 13th century in England Bracton argued that since a universal law rules the world, even kings and rulers were subject to the law. British history gave content to Bracton's abstract argument, and by the 16th century the medieval idea that a universal law governed the world supported the growing belief in the supremacy of the common law.

That belief is really quite extraordinary. Its development was hardly irresistible. Lord Coke himself resisted it while Attorney General only to advance it powerfully when he became a judge. On a Sunday late in 1608 in Whitehall Palace Coke, then Chief Justice of Common Pleas, stood before King James I as the King assured him that the King would "ever protect the common law." But Coke replied, you will recall, "The common law protecteth the King," and James flew into a rage, calling Coke's argument traitorous for it set law above the monarch. By Coke's own report, the King proclaimed that since the law was founded upon reason, the King's reason could be the final source of law. To that Coke replied that the King had natural reason as well as any man but that "his Majesty was not learned in the Laws of his Realm of England; and abuses which concern the Life, or Inheritance, or Goods, or Fortunes of his Subjects are not to be decided by natural Reason but by the artificial Reason and Judgment of the Law, which requires long Study and Experience before that a man can attain to the cognizance of it."

The King's reply was explosive. He threatened to strike the Chief Justice, and Coke fell prostrate before the King's majestic wrath.

But the next day, from the Bench, Lord Coke issued an order under his seal which again asserted the supremacy of the common law.[37]

Over time Coke's view as to the supremacy of law prevailed and even the Crown's prerogatives became so circumscribed by parliamentary and judicial limitation that those which remained could only be described as existing as an aspect of the common law, exercised by the Crown only because the law allowed it. What does the rule of law mean today? It cannot mean that the law operates independently of men. It must mean that there is some common center of agreement that informs the conduct of all men who work with the law. Sometimes the rule of law is taken to prohibit discretion in the application of government power. But the law works through words, and words themselves invite discretion in their application. The rule of law, if it means anything in this regard, refers to the disciplined application of words or ideas to the situations they are called upon to influence. No rule is automatic in its application. To a greater or lesser degree the step of determination is always required.

As I said at the outset, the idea of the sovereignty of the rule of law recognizes the universality of the law's effect. It also recognizes the universality of the manner in which law develops. Law is not only the product of lawyers. The whole society uses and interprets the law. And because of that, the law expresses something deep and important about the values we hold as a people. It expresses our strongest commitment and the highest aspirations. Law is not everything in society. The law is only one of a number of institutions through which we express ourselves and which in turn influence us, maintain our customs and change our habits. Thus law takes a place along with family structures, religious beliefs, the expressions of art and the explanations of science. Law embodies the values common to many of those institutions. Law, as the custodian of the historic rights mankind has developed for itself, must never be regarded as the tool of the power of the moment.

The public, the press, the academic community, the artists, all by their assertions and conduct inform and develop the law. As new human values and ideas make their way into common acceptance, they also make their way into the law which translates them into words by which common conduct may be governed. By guiding common conduct, by speaking in words, the law has its own power to educate, to alter commonly held views, to shape the thinking of the public whose thinking in turn shapes the law.

As the law is the custodian of historical value, the legal profession has a special role as the trustee of the law. But what is the nature of the legal profession? It has many different roles.

If one reaches back into legal history, the difference between courts and legislatures was much less marked than it is today. Parliament still functions as a high court, a reminder of the time when the distinct functions of legislatures and courts were seen as one. Today the courts and legislatures operate quite differently, representing separate aspects of the legal system. Nevertheless, the distinction between judging and legislating is quite old. Even though legislatures do sometimes merely restate the law and even though judges sometimes change it, there is a central difference between applying the law as a judge and changing it in the public interest as a legislator. The legislators are guided, of course, by their vision of the Constitution's meaning and by a sense of duty to lead and speak for their constituents as the constituents would speak were they present to be informed by debate in the public forum. The question of change is before the legislators[38] and the fashioning of the public will must be their goal. Legislatures in large part are the forum for public involvement in its most immediate, changing and diverse form.

Courts recently have on occasion been places of high public drama, and modern procedures allow great diversity of interest to be represented in cases which would at one time have included only the two primary parties in dispute. Still the courts have a different goal than legislatures. Theirs is not primarily to shape the public will although they do this somewhat. And they must display a different sort of reasoning to support their judgment. The power of judges to resolve disputes and speak the law depends in large part upon the unique tone in which they render their judgments. More than any other lawgivers, they derive their power from the acquiescence of others in their judgments. Confronted with the duty of resolving a particular dispute based upon a particular set of facts, the judges must meet the duty by applying resonant rules of general and lasting application so that their decisions will be seen as legitimate. Thus they determine finally the rule of law as it applies among the parties before them,[39] but they state the law knowing that their statement will bear heavily in resolution of future disputes. Though the courts use the language of principle, principles change over time as society reassesses its values and comes to accept new ways of looking at its problems.

Because they phrase their judgments in terms of the reasoned application of principle, too often what courts say has been mistaken for the single voice of the law. Lately the practice has been to go to the judges when legislators and officials of the executive branch fail to live up to their responsibilities. The apportionment of legislatures, the operation of public schools, even the conduct of the war in Vietnam have all been brought to courts by those who would have the judges state the single rule of law. Sometimes the judges have wisely declined to comment. Sometimes they have not. In any case, the appeal to the judges as the only spokesmen of justice results from a failure to recognize the more subtle nature of the rule of law in this nation.

Throughout the history of Anglo-American law there has been a debate over the meaning of justice and its relationship with the law. The two have been seen as, in some ways, distinct. Justice has many forms. Justice is one of the virtues, to be sure, but in some sense it is all of the human virtues viewed collectively. Justice is the name we give our values, and as such it is the source all members of the legal profession must draw upon.

The lawyer's job is to translate these values into rules. It is to make those rules consistent one with the other in a craftsmanlike manner. It is to try to clarify the ambiguity of words, to use language in the service of values. . . .

It is an enormous responsibility a lawyer bears—to face the most complex and demanding problems that our society faces, to treat them dispassionately but not without feeling, to work with words which demand constant interpretation. Yet it is also his pleasure to do so. It is what distinguishes him from others in the system of law he shares with everyone.

The purpose of this day is to honor the law, and the purpose of the law is to try to create the conditions for the just society, for the continual reexamination of our values and the way they are reflected in our actions. It is to the aspirations of the law that, whatever its inevitable current failings and weakness, we may rightly and unhesitatingly pay tribute today.

A Period of Agony and Triumph

DEDICATION OF THE TEXAS LAW CENTER

July 4, 1976

. . . The American Revolution and the years of political creativity that followed it were suffused with a spirit of the law. It was a period in which human liberties were dearly won. It was also a period in which knowledge of the workings of the political institutions of a republic was widely learned by a considerable portion of the population. That period of agony and triumph and intensive learning during the difficult years between the Declaration of Independence and the making of the Constitution provided a strong tutelage for our country. As David Ramsay wrote in 1789: "The science of government has been more generally diffused among the

Americans by means of the Revolution. The policy of Great Britain, in throwing them out of her protection, induced a necessity of establishing independent constitutions. This led to reading and reasoning on the subject. The many errors that were at first committed by unexperienced [*sic*] statesmen, have been a practical comment on the folly of unbalanced constitutions, and injudicious laws. The discussion concerning the new Constitution, gave birth to much reasoning on the subject of government."[40] But much as we find pride in the ultimate attainment of that period in the formation of our Constitution, it would be a mistake not to acknowledge the efforts of the long prior history which marks Western civilization's progress through the creation of institutions to protect human rights. Because of that tradition of which our revolutionary period was a part, we were established from the beginning as a nation of law.

A nation of law—the phrase commends itself to us as an antidote to tyranny, not only the tyranny of men but also the tyranny of the moment. In James Wilson's inaugural lecture in 1789 as the first professor of law at the College of Philadelphia, given before an audience which included George Washington, Wilson coupled, as descriptive of the American character, the interlinked love of liberty and the love of law. And because of this he argued that "the science of law should in some measure and in some degree, be the study of every free citizen and of every free man."[41] This was a recognition that, if we are a nation of law, it is because the law is in some sense an independent force. It cannot be subjugated to other forces without great peril. The fundamental independence of the law and its existence for the people as a whole were ideas that informed the early development of our nation. When the colonists revolted, as historian Gordon Wood has written, they revolted "not against the English constitution but on behalf of it."[42] They carried as a banner the rule of law, a rule given meaning because it stood for values long and deeply held, and these values and that vision contributed greatly to the success in building a new government.

The system of government created in 1789 included many features not directly or solely attributable to the English heritage. The written Constitution, the Bill of Rights, the federal system and the special embodiment of popular sovereignty in the three separate branches of government,[43] these achievements reflected the Founder's belief, as Hamilton stated in the *Federalist Papers*, that "[t]he science of politics . . . , like most other sciences has received great improvement. The efficacy of various principles is now well understood, which were either not known at all, or imper-

fectly known to the ancients."[44] At the same time the insistence upon the
rule of law, the protection of the individual and the independence of law
from the power of men and from the compelling circumstances of the moment, these were part of the Founder's inheritance. They passed them on
as a legacy for the future. They gave to us also their belief that the science
of government, like other sciences, was amenable to mankind's reach, and
that the government they had created would itself be a continuing experiment in the craft of governance.

The principles and the craft of governance—not only the art of advocacy—have always been in this country a part of the study of law. The bar
is often said to have a unique and overwhelmingly influential role in the
governance of our country. While sometimes the share is said to be too
large, it is difficult to see how, in the earlier days of our nation, communities so widely separated could have been governed in common without
this shared background, just as it is now difficult to see how our complex
society could operate without it. Perhaps this diversity and complexity explain the phenomenon which Tocqueville noticed, and which surely per-
sists today, that most questions of importance in American society end
up as legal issues before the courts. Jack Greenberg, in a recent Cardozo
Lecture, said, rather gleefully, I think, that "[l]awyers still love the judicial forum."[45] As we acknowledge this, we should perhaps take it also as
a warning. The training of a lawyer, whether this is made explicit or not,
has to be a training in the ways of our society and in the needs of our society. The cases he or she reads are filled with the concepts and categories
which mark recurring problems and recurring acts. They tell us a great
deal about the life and problems and coherence of our communities. But
the material is in cases, and a court is always at the center of a case. There
are other instrumentalities, I hardly need to say, but it appears to require
emphasis, which explicate, expound and make the law. Those who create
the legal forms used in the lawyer's office are among the most influential.
And then, after all, there is the legislature, and there are boards and local councils. While the courts have served an essential purpose in the governance of this diverse and complicated society by law, their central position at times has altered the strength of other political processes—not the
least because when courts assume responsibility this sometimes encour-
ages other political institutions to hold back from making the difficult decisions or taking the unpopular steps which are required of elected officials in a democracy. Of course we must also recognize that courts have
often stepped in because other institutions have not assumed their right-

ful burden. To recognize this is not for the purpose of giving praise or blame but rather to say that we must benefit from the experiences we have had.

The bar has had a special role in the judicial forum, and this role has increased in importance, breadth and challenge as the legal process has been made available to more and more people. But the role of the lawyer must be seen in a wider horizon. As every lawyer knows, the shape and meaning of the law are created and nurtured in the lawyer's office in the process of advice giving. Without the lawyer as the intermediary our complex society could not function. I realize that this very complexity is sometimes thought caused by the lawyers. This danger is another mark of the lawyer's great responsibility, for simplification and understanding are greatly required, and much of this, if it is to be accomplished, must be undertaken by the bar. Thus the bar becomes the interpreter of the requirements of the citizens; it becomes the interpreter of the rules and regulations of governance. Thus the bar and its members play the role of public citizens, whether they are in or out of government, and the very ability of lawyers to move in and out of government is a welcome reminder of the purpose of government, which is to protect and perfect the liberties and rights of all.

It is the lawyer's genius for the practical that the bar brings to the nation's governance, because we do have a government which always has an element of change and of experiment. The science of government calls for an art—the art of reconciling principle and the practical, or of giving life to principles in their application. The art becomes more difficult and more necessary when values which are generally accepted seem more indeterminate and changing. There once was a time when, as Tocqueville wrote, in America "moral principle [was] regarded as fixed while the political process [was] left open to debate."[46] Today the debate has to be about the values themselves, as well as their application. To understand the values, to expound them, to see the relationships among values have to be part of the lawyer's task. The task is a heavy one and one searches for points of guidance.

One basic theme—and it is a commonplace which always needs to be kept fresh—is that a political society exists for the good of its members. The simplicity is, in a complex society and perhaps in any society, deceptive. The members of a society will always have different and competing interests. The constitutional government established in 1789 in this country was designed to mediate these differences and to minimize the corrosive effect of faction upon liberty. The result of the constitutional system of accommodation and compromise, with its division of powers and its theory of popular sovereignty, has not always been a steady progression. Our history is marked by cycles in which the interests of one group—along with the institution of government in which it holds greatest power and the values that favor it—have gained ascendency for a time only later to decline. The use of the governmental system by one group to "get even" with another is a kind of vindictiveness that has no place in our constitutional system. It is the role of the bar, and of the law, to mediate the effect of these cycles by insisting upon a due regard for the importance of other institutions and for the protection of other fundamental values. This is what the Constitution and the rule of law require.

We are now in a period in which many legal and political institutions have come under intense scrutiny. Coming at a time in which nongovernmental social institutions that give us stability have gone into decline, this puts a heavy burden on the law. The burden is in part to support those institutions and in part to reinforce its own strength which inheres in the faith people have in it.

Another theme, which relates to the first, is that a government of law requires some separation of powers. The constitutional doctrine of separation of powers developed out of a healthy skepticism for the effect of power upon the men who hold it. It was Montesquieu's vision. Madison wrote in *Federalist* 47 that "his meaning . . . can amount to no more than this, that where the *whole* power of one department is exercised by the same hands which possess the *whole* power of another department, the fundamental principles of a free constitution, are subverted."[47] In *Federalist* 51, Madison elucidated the point by reference to the proposed new American Constitution. He wrote that the branches had both independence and interdependence so that "ambition [could] be made to counteract ambition."[48]

Separation of powers is a fundamental principle of a free constitution because without it there is no guarantee of deference to the limitation of government power and protection of individual liberty that the Constitution was established to maintain. From time to time elected representatives may seek to give certain rights greater emphasis than others or to favor certain groups. But if power is divided, this may only be done within the values embodied in the Constitution. Other engines of government are free to check power at its edges, to refer back to the central precepts the society holds, to counteract ambition or malice or a surfeit of good intentions. This is a part of the meaning of the independence of law.

The administration of government must always be non-partisan. It is often forgotten that separation of powers makes this possible. Though it has become something of a fashion now to think of justice as an arena of power and politics, there is nothing more destructive than the belief that justice is to be used by those in power to reward their friends or punish their enemies. As Lawrence Friedman recently put it, "Without faith in authority, the formal law can look like a wheel of fortune for the average man."[49] If faith in the law is shaken, so too is the law's efficacy, since its greatest strength lies in voluntary compliance. Yet despite the fashion of cynicism, I think that the shock we feel so profoundly when we see the law used in a manipulative way for personal or partisan purposes indicates that independence of law is part of our central beliefs as a people. We hold this to be without doubt, that the law must not be made to order for any man or any faction.

The bar has a great responsibility for seeking solutions to our social problems, for mediating the cycles of reaction, for enunciating the values we cherish and approximating them in practice. I need hardly say the law does not exist entirely for lawyers. An attorney can neither properly be solely an advocate of his clients' cause to the exclusion of all other concerns nor completely his own man using his clients to serve his own ends. It is a complicated duty lawyers have; it looks both to the individual client's interest and also to the interests of society, which are the law's. This requires a special honesty and objectivity. Cicero said that if you couldn't state your opponent's case, you didn't know your own. Beyond that, as every lawyer knows, arguments can be stated in such a way as to mislead or inflame. This is not the road to problem-solving, which is at the center of the bar's responsibility.

The law in the United States has been under a severe strain. The bar must attempt to make clear to the public, with an eloquence that suits the importance and subtlety of the matter, the nature and importance of its special role. This need for eloquence and clarity is generally required of us, particularly in this period, to persuade the society of what we know is true: that the law deserves people's faith and that without this faith the law fails.

The complications of life in our society grow. The rules increase in scope and complexity. Interpretation and explanation of these rules by the bar are required. So too is the willingness to explore hard problems, to find them before they explode upon us, to reach for solutions as part of the science and art of government. Finally, it is essential that the bar hold first to what we have that is good and strong and wise and valuable — not to be afraid to be alone in asserting that the value abides — for that is what the American vision 200 years ago was about. . . .

Giving Bigotry No Sanction

BICENTENNIAL OBSERVANCE OF THE SOCIETY OF FRIENDS OF
TOURO SYNAGOGUE

September 12, 1976

I am honored to join you in commemorating the 200th anniversary of our Declaration of Independence and President George Washington's historic message to the Hebrew Congregation of Newport shortly following the founding of the Republic. It is fitting that we choose to remember these events in this place.

The religious impulse in America is strong indeed. Those who first came here were seeking an opportunity to worship freely. This hope has motivated millions of their successors.

America was a metaphorical reliving of the Old Testament — some would say it was more than that — a new land, a chosen people, a vision of the future. In 1630 John Winthrop described his Massachusetts Bay Colony, as Israel of old — a "city on a hill" with the "eyes of all people . . . upon us."[50] After the American Revolution, Ezra Stiles, once a minister in Newport with a special interest in this congregation, looked forward to the day when "the Lord shall have made his American Israel high above all nations."[51] And in the nineteenth century, Herman Melville proclaimed, "We Americans are the peculiar, chosen people — the Israel of our own time; we bear the ark of the liberties of the world."[52]

The messianic tradition can be one of exclusivity. Exclusivity can lead to intolerance. Indeed, it was this attitude which prompted the expulsion of Roger Williams from Massachusetts and the genesis of Rhode Island's special place in our history.

The Founding Fathers — George Washington, Thomas Jefferson, James

Madison and their colleagues—were deeply religious men. They shared a sense of America's mission. Yet they were in the tradition of Roger Williams. Their commitment to religious and political liberty for all was, in part, attributable to their unhappy experience with state-established religion. It also reflected a politically pragmatic recognition that America's diversity demanded religious tolerance if a nation of nations was to be established.

Most important, however, they considered religious and political liberty essential because of a shared conviction that God had indeed created all men equal and endowed them with certain rights which no civil government could properly grant or restrict. In 1878, my great-grandfather, Rabbi David Einhorn, described the Founders of the Republic as "men of deep and profound inner reverence for the unfathomable Universal spirit, in whose name they undertook their immortal great deeds."[53] It was a recognition of the unknowable nature of the Divine that required tolerance and created a sense that, in Jefferson's words, the "integrity of views more than their soundness, is the basis" of respect among men.[54]

In this conception, to the equality and sovereignty of the people there was joined the ultimate accountability. Thus, Madison's Memorial and Remonstration for religious freedom spoke of the duty to the Creator "precedent, both in order of time and in degree of obligation, to the claims of civil society."[55]

It is these values which are eloquently expressed in Washington's message to the Hebrew Congregation of Newport. He spoke of a government which "gives bigotry no sanction, to persecution no assistance" as an example to mankind, "a policy worthy of imitation." He described a government in which "[a]ll possess alike liberty of conscience and immunities of citizenship" and, most significantly, rejected scornfully the idea that toleration could be regarded as an indulgence bestowed by one class upon another, rather than a recognition of inherent natural rights.[56]

Washington's words are particularly impressive when recalled in perspective. Tolerance and mutual understanding then as now could not be taken for granted. During the War of Independence, in order to facilitate the raising of troops, England eliminated the required oath to the Anglican Church, which, in effect, prohibited Catholics from serving the King. But the controversy this provoked culminated in a march in London of 50,000 protesters, led by Lord George Gordon, a member of Parliament, who alternated between addressing the House of Commons and haranguing the crowd outside. This march was soon transformed into what would become a five-day riot resulting in hundreds of deaths, the destruction of many Catholic chapels and the emptying of the city's jail.

The First Amendment of the United States Constitution, which was ratified within a year of Washington's visit to Newport, expressly prohibited the federal government from making any "law respecting an establishment of religion, or prohibiting the free exercise thereof." But at the same time, more than half of the states, including all in New England except Rhode Island, had state-supported religions. As late as 1820, the voters of Massachusetts rejected by almost 2 to 1 an amendment to the state constitution which would have extended public support to non-Protestant religious teachers and terminated compulsory attendance and public worship.

Although the United States Constitution prohibited religious tests for holding office, some of the older states retained disqualifications regarding Roman Catholics, Jews and other minorities. In 1809, the North Carolina legislature unsuccessfully tried to exclude Jacob Henry, who, as a Jew, did not subscribe to the Divine authority of the New Testament as required by the state constitution.

In 1819, Henry Brackenridge rose in the Maryland House of Delegates to put the question, "Have the Jews a right to be placed on a footing with other citizens?"[57] It was not for six years that a law was enacted permitting Jews to hold office, serve on juries and practice law. The disqualifications against them were not removed from the North Carolina constitution until 1868.

Equality before the law, of course, does not signify an end to intolerance. Washington rightly assumed persistent prejudice when he announced the new government would give it no sanction or assistance. His echoing words are in no way disparaged, indeed they are given added meaning, because they have charted a course, and not an easy one, for fulfillment.

My great-grandfather, David Einhorn, occupies a certain position in the growth of American Judaism: author of one of the outstanding prayer books, abolitionist, defender of human rights. It is perhaps inappropriate for me to speak of him, but it also would be odd for me not to recognize—as others have done—the historic centennial address which he delivered in 1876. He spoke then of the vision of the Founders of the Republic—the religious spirit of Washington, the Jeffersonian rejection of the concept of the racial sanctity of any class of men, the wisdom of

Franklin, who was able to direct the lightning flashes of his spirit to destroy the chains of servitude. His message was perhaps commonplace. He recognized the power and the greatness of our Republic which had been achieved within one hundred years. The country had become a giant, but its strength was not in possessions, but, because of its Founders, and its people, it had become a messenger of redemption with a deep and profound inner reverence for the unfathomable Universal spirit. And so the country had survived with its message through a veritable multitude of dangers. He asked then, at that centennial: Are the words and thought and examples of the Founding Fathers "still today the guiding stars which determine our people's thoughts and feelings, our actions and failures to act?"[58] If the past is to have meaning now, as we desire it to have, this question always must be asked, and it is not to be obscured because the light of history makes the noble qualities more apparent by recognizing imperfections as well. The question comes to us now laden with events of subsequent cruelty in the world which I dare to say would have been unimaginable in my great-grandfather's time. When we have doubts, as often we must, we still must recognize, particularly in this bicentennial year, that we have had and still have these guiding stars which have helped to create the world's best hope.

In 1852, Henry Wadsworth Longfellow visited the Jewish cemetery at Newport. This synagogue was then closed and the Jewish community was virtually extinct. Viewing the graves of immigrants, Longfellow wondered, "How came they here?" And he then recounted a remarkable journey of "pride and humiliation" in words which you know full well:[59]

> In the background figures vague and vast
>   Of patriarchs and prophets rose sublime
> And all the great traditions of the past
>   They saw reflected in the coming time.

Surveying the cemetery, Longfellow suggested that the Jewish people had expired because they let "life become a legend of the dead." Longfellow was wrong.

He was wrong about the Jewish people. In 1854 Judah Touro remembered his father, who ministered to this congregation. Like his brother before him, he substantially contributed to the restoration of this building—not as a monument to the past, but as a living memorial, a part and symbol of the revival of the Jewish community here.

Longfellow was wrong also if he failed to understand that the American dream is itself a biblical dream, a response and reawakening of an ancient tradition which lives in many ways. It lives in us and it lives in others.

Today we remember Washington and Jefferson and Franklin and that inspired message of loyalty and hope expressed by this congregation to the federal union and to its leaders. That message and its response are treasures for all mankind.

It remains for each of us to keep strong our sentiments with the past so that we may perfect the life of today and tomorrow, to keep strong the varied traditions of different groups which make our country great. In doing so, we shall be rededicated to giving bigotry no sanction, and to recognizing, guarding and helping to perfect the dignity of each individual among us.

The Tone of Our Asking

THE O. V. W. HAWKINS LECTURE AT BUCKNELL UNIVERSITY

October 28, 1976

... In this university setting I thought it might be appropriate to reflect upon some of the conditions of public life in our times and in our country. There is, I believe, a continuing obligation for those in government and in academic institutions to exchange what may be errors but which we hope are insights on problems of leadership, representation and participation which so clearly have an effect upon the quality of life. I shall attempt, therefore, to discuss some of the aspects of public service in the United States. Public service is not limited to government service. In our kind of community of communities the responsibility is great upon institutions of higher learning, and on many other groups, and in some genuine sense upon each of us.

Briefly the points I would make are these: First, reiterating what I have just said, it is a mistake, particularly with our form of representative government in its present setting, as it has developed, to think of governmental office as the primary road for public service. Both forms of service, governmental and non-governmental, in many different aspects, can be public. In addition, the flow of ideas and influences are reciprocal and more intense than they have ever been. This does not mean that obligations and ways of doing things do not differ—of course they do; the measures of control should not be the same. It does not mean that the conditions for representation are markedly different from what they were in the past.

Second, the most basic change influencing our society has occurred because of the enormously increased availability of higher education to so large a proportion of our population. Resulting from this are the emphasis, under new conditions, on the continuing importance of that recognition in practice which many and differing institutions of higher learning now give to basic values and the creation of a new pressure of ideas, and openness to them, within the society where there is a constant necessity to explore ideas and their effects.

Third, this openness in the society does not by itself make ideas easier to comprehend; it may have the opposite effect. New forms of communication, which in the long run may be most helpful to an enlarged discussion, now may diminish understanding through an emphasis on popular beliefs as the primary standard, and upon immediacy and repetition.

Fourth, even in an open society there still is the continuing necessity for the recognition of authority, its limitations and legitimacy. Popular views about power and coercion tend to distort both the process of discussion and the primary institutions of government.

Fifth, even—or perhaps particularly—an open society requires the recognition of common values which are accepted in the midst of diversity, and this recognition requires the help of many institutions. That help is for the common good; it is in the public service.

Sixth, there is a built-in tension in our society which becomes visible in cycles of reaction. Governmental arrangements cannot alone deal with this, although they were purposely designed to diminish the danger of factionalism. The underpinning of a society which believes in free and robust discussion also requires a certain tolerance and grace. These qualities cannot be assumed; they must be sought.

Our view of public service through governmental position has alternated between what might be loosely termed a kind of Periclean vision and a counterview of extreme cynicism. The Periclean vision, while it is not all that precise, has many facets, including the claims it makes for the achievement of excellence and virtue and the relationships which it sees between public and private life. "There is no exclusiveness in our public life, and in our private intercourse we are not suspicious of one another, nor angry with our neighbor if he does what he likes," Pericles is written to have said. "[A] spirit of reverence pervades our public acts. . . . We rely not upon management or trickery, but upon our hearts and hands."[60] "[T]he individual Athenian in his own person seems to have the power of adapting himself to the most varied forms of action with the utmost versatility and grace."[61] Pericles evokes the image of an entire citizenry educated to take part in public affairs. The eulogy for those who died in the first stages of the Peloponnesian war is a glorification of the kind of society as a whole, memorializing the final sacrifice which the city requires in wartime by stressing the shared responsibility in Athens in times of peace. The model blurs the lines between governmental office and the public acts of individuals. An Athenian citizen did not neglect the state because he took care of his household, and even those of us who are engaged in business have a very fair idea of politics. Governmental policy arose out of a process of discussion among the citizenry preparatory to action. The man who took no part in public affairs was regarded as a useless character. In this setting the holding of government office did not arise out of special privilege. Pericles even dared to say it was conferred because of merit.

The vision does not deny that there might[62] be burdens or special risks to office holding. Good men, Socrates argued, took public office only because of necessity. Money and honor would not attract them. They had to be made to serve by the fear of punishment. The punishment was that he who refuses to rule is liable to be ruled by one who is worse than himself. A mild cynic might note that the fear of this punishment was not sufficient in Socrates's own career. He was deterred by his inner spirit from becoming a politician, and rightly so, he said, for he would have perished long ago "and done no good to either you or myself."[63] A mild cynic might take note also of Tocqueville's comment as to why salaries for public office did not attract talent to government in the United States in the first part of the 19th century. It was because "those who fix the amount of the salaries, being very numerous, have but little chance of obtaining office so as to be in receipt of those salaries."[64] The passion play of Socrates is its own puzzling commentary on Athenian life and sometimes our own. But surely Socrates was engaged in a public task, and, as has been said, Athens spoke through him.

The Founders of our Republic, who saw their work in the continuum of history, were, of course, familiar with the Periclean vision. There are echoes of it in many of the documents which form the American testament. Pericles, while he understood full well the nature of leadership and the important effect of government itself, chose to emphasize the overwhelming force of the quality of the particular society. In the gloom between the Revolution and the Constitution, John Jay wrote to Washington, "Representative bodies will ever be faithful copies of their originals."[65] And Washington responded, "We have probably had too good an opinion of human nature in forming our confederation. . . . We are apt to run from one extreme to another. . . . Retired as I am from the world, I frankly acknowledge I cannot feel myself an unconcerned spectator." Like the story of Cincinnatus, which is part of the same classical tradition—the access to public life, the withdrawal and the return—Washington considered himself as having no claim to public attention; it was not his business to embark again on a sea of troubles, but "[w]ould to God that wise measures may be taken in time to avert the consequences we have but too much reason to apprehend."[66]

I have given perhaps too much emphasis to this classical tradition of concern for excellence, virtue, representation and responsibility which could be shared among the citizenry, but I do so because it was influential in the formation of our Republic, is imbedded in our Constitution and remains with us as a powerful factor today. The American experiment was a self-conscious one. Of course it began with the determination to make available to American citizens the rights which Englishmen enjoyed. But it also built upon a view of the triumphs and troubles of the republics of the classical period. It involved basic conceptions about the nature of individuals and a belief in the power of reason and in a benevolent Providence. I think we are inclined to take too much for granted this inherent optimism, tempered as it was by the doubts of the days between the first confederation and the Constitution. We could have a society, given slightly different circumstances, because this tradition also existed, based much more on a belief in the necessary catastrophe, and in the ferocity of tempers and manners which would not have been hard to find.

The experiment was to begin, as the great seal of the United States said, "a new cycle of centuries." It was to be a government by discussion which would break "the bonds of ages and set free the originality of mankind."[67] "Whenever," John Adams wrote, "a general knowledge and sensibility have prevailed among the people, arbitrary government and every kind of oppression have lessened and disappeared in proportion."[68]

The settlement of America was to be seen as "the opening of a grand scene and design in Providence for the illumination of the ignorant, and the emancipation of the slavish parts of mankind all over the earth."[69] It was to be a time of new knowledge, science and invention. The Constitution itself reflected the new invention of federalism as applied to a republic, as the *Federalist Papers* claimed. But there would be other discoveries and other truths which would be found out.

Professor Wendell in his concluding chapter of the volume on the United States in the *Cambridge Modern History* was undoubtedly correct in 1903 in stating that the educational leaders in America "may be taken . . . as among the most characteristic figures whom the country has as yet produced. For, however they differ concerning all manner of detail, they are agreed in faith that education should be a fearless search for truth; that the truth, honestly proclaimed, will make life on earth better and better; and that the best way to discover and proclaim truth is to open to all who can use them the fullest resources of learning. In which buoyant faith," he went on to write, "though often obscured by the superstitious errors of the moment, there glows a deep belief in the ultimate excellence of human nature."[70] I think one can say today that our educational institutions, recognizing there are differences among them over a wide range, reflect what is still this characteristic American spirit. The result is that there is a sharing in the work of this ideal to the extent never before known in the history of the world. It is not just that we take for granted what is rejected in large portions of the world, that education is intended to liberate the mind, and not just to capture and control it, and that our society is committed to the change which this introduces, but also that the proportionate number of those attending colleges and universities is more than twice that of France—more than four times that of England.

There is no reason to deny that this expansion carries with it certain difficulties. Such a customary absorption of the time of so many people raises more sharply the question of the different purposes of education. It is, for example, one thing to say that education is a good in itself, for it provides an enlargement of the understanding of the humanities and the sciences and that it will help us attain some unity of conception of the world and ourselves which should elevate the quality of life. It is another thing to think of education in a more vocational way and thus to have to wonder whether the craft trained is the craft needed. Indeed, as you know, it is sometimes urged that the education is disabling. One thinks of Benjamin Franklin's report on the answer given by the Indians at Williamsburg in 1774 to proposals to provide education for their children: "We have had some experience of it," they said, ". . . but when they came back to us, they were bad runners, ignorant of every means of living in the woods, unable to bear either cold or hunger, knew neither how to build a cabin, take a deer, nor kill an enemy, spoke our language imperfectly; were therefore neither fit for hunters, warriors, nor counselors."[71] Somehow I don't particularly like this story; I am not sure the Indians ever said this. But they may have, and the story has a more generalized point.

But there are other consequences. The places for investigation and research have been vastly multiplied. There are more participants in the discussion of the meaning and effect of particular ideas and solutions to problems. The conversation is much more extensive, more immediate, the volume is greater. The learning society always has been an ideal, but with that much learning afoot it becomes more of a necessity. The reason is that the self-correction of education is an integral part of the process. It may be true that correct or better ideas win out eventually in the marketplace of ideas, wherever that is, over incorrect or inferior ones, but only if there is an active response. Today education can no longer be regarded as only preparatory. It never should have been regarded that way. It has to be viewed now as continuing and life-long, both for the sake of the individual and the well-being of the society. Moreover, because of new forms of communication, centralized and regional, the society daily receives a veritable bombardment of capsulizing concepts and conclusions in a powerful and dramatic way. In this setting, the practice if not the theory of representative government changes. There is a new accessibility and vulnerability to ideas and movements. It was one thing for Sir Robert Walpole in the 18th century to insist that the people, influential as they were, had no right to instruct the members of Parliament on how they should vote. It is different when the voices of instruction can be heard all over the land, and access to the media is so important. Again this may be highly desirable, but not always. There can be a play-acting, or manipulative, air about it. Richard Crossman in his recently published book, *Diaries of a Cabinet Minister*,[72] wrote that from the point of view of the bureaucracy one of the functions of a Minister is to sell himself to the public with announcements and pronouncements which, though they are not making any new policy, give the public a sense that he is doing something. In contrast I as-

sume that the convention which formulated the original Articles of Confederation and that which drafted the American Constitution could not
have been held, as they were, in secret conclave. They would have been
regarded as conspiratorial, as they were then, but now one has to suppose the criticism would be sufficiently powerful or persuasive to prevent
this privacy, or that the privacy in any event would have been shattered
by piecemeal accounts instantly reported to the outside world. I think it
is fair to assume that at least the latter document could not have been
drawn up under the circumstances we would now require.

For many reasons, not the least of which is the sense of injustice itself, it became popular in recent years to see all relationships within and
between societies in terms of power, manipulation or coercion. While it
is certainly possible to view all activities in this way, it is only a partial
truth. It elides important distinctions. It puts a gloss of politicization on
all events, when in fact it is a question of more or less, and the designation sometimes hardly fits at all. In doing so it becomes false both norma-
tively and descriptively, for many institutions, arising out of human needs,
have as their very purpose, and actually can fulfill the function, of sup-
plying some correction to such tendencies. For example, Reinhold Nie-
buhr, whose book *Moral Man and Immoral Society*[73] was strongly influential in projecting such a view of omnipresent coercion, found that the
corrective of an impartial tribunal to check society's power would have to
be viewed as similarly disfigured. It is not enough to say that such a view,
which places all institutions in a simple category of power structures, is
motivated by a desire for greater egalitarianism. If so, the central questions is, as it always has been, what is justice and how can it be implemented, and this involves the coalescence of many values.

There is an undoubted attractiveness, when people want to get things
done, to the thought that all the institutions of government and society
can be treated much the same as power mechanisms. But the history of
the implementation of justice—the central concept of due process itself—belies this kind of carelessness. Due process cannot protect anyone
if there is no recognition of both legitimacy to and restrictions on the uses
of authority. Equality before the law, and therefore the rights of individuals, including particularly the most disfavored, are greatly weakened if
the moral prestige of impartiality is to be denied to the judges. The re-
sponsiveness and accountability of the legislative function are diminished
if the most controversial issues are too often seen as beyond the reach

of legislative action, because constitutionally determined, or as too easily dealt with by legislative action by placing the changing solutions in the
hands of some other department. The relationship among the branches
of government becomes unfortunate if there is insufficient recognition
of their differences and separate functions. The same point can be made
about federal-state relationships. The safeguarding of the integrity of non-
governmental institutions otherwise vulnerable to governmental direction is necessary if rights of association and the very concept of a learning
society are to be maintained. But no one of these issues can be properly
handled if the rubric is to be simply a version of "strategic politics." There
are problems of crises management, and our society has not been in want
of these. Such events test the maturity of a society not only to handle the
matter at hand but to return to its central values.

In a much-quoted statement Matthew Arnold once wrote:

> The difficulty for democracy is how to find and keep high ideals. The indi-
> viduals who compose it are, the bulk of them, persons who need to follow an
> ideal, not to set one; and one ideal of greatness, high feeling and fine culture,
> which an aristocracy once supplied to them, they lose by the very fact of ceas-
> ing to be a lower order and becoming a democracy. Nations are not truly great
> solely because the individuals composing them are numerous, free and active,
> but they are great when these numbers, this freedom and this activity are em-
> ployed in the service of an ideal higher than that of an ordinary man, taken by
> himself.[74]

I think we can reject the explicit language and overtones of this passage
which questions the attainment of excellence among us, but we cannot reject the importance of a value structure and high ideals to hold a community together and to elevate it. Universities contribute greatly to our life
through the inventiveness and discoveries of their members. They contribute more, however, through the values they exemplify. This is true
within an institution where the mood and attitudes reflecting the qualities which are honored are the most decisive determinants of its future.
One has to believe this is true of our academic institutions as a whole
with respect to their influence on our national life. Other institutions—
the family, churches, the professions, the companies and private associations—have their influence as well. But if it is true that we have become,
or are required to become, a truly learning society, then the responsibil-

ity upon the universities is truly enormous. "The very techniques and con-
ventions of scholarship," Sir Eric Ashby once wrote, "carry their own rep-
ertoire of moral principles: reverence for truth, which requires humility
and courage, equality for any scholar, however junior, . . . international-
ism, for whether a theory is upset by a black man or white, Christian or
Muslim, communist or capitalist, the theory is upset all the same."[75] This
respect both for individuals and ideas is much needed in a democratic society which charts its own way. I would add also a remembrance for the
past so that we may perfect and continue the better part of the traditions
we have inherited. This, also, is in the special keeping of the universities.

André Malraux has written, "A civilization can be defined at once by
the basic questions it asks and by those it does not ask."[76] I would add
one more item to Malraux's comment: namely, the tone in which a society
asks its questions. The tone itself may be even more important than the
question or the answer.

A Constitution Born in Doubt

CITIZENSHIP DAY CEREMONY

September 17, 1975

On this anniversary of its signing, we honor those who wrote and
achieved agreement in our basic charter of government and liberty. The
debates of the Constitutional Convention were secret. But we now know
from Madison's notes and other sources that nearly every provision of the
document survived or was shaped by extended, often passionate debate.
The document reflects many compromises. At the end, few delegates, perhaps none, were completely satisfied. But they signed, as Franklin said, because each "doubt[ed] a little of his own infallibility."[77] Ratification, too,
was neither immediate nor, in many instances, enthusiastic. It required
strenuous persuasion, most remarkably in the *Federalist Papers*. But there
were innumerable other efforts. They succeeded, but the success was not
easy and many doubted that it could last.

The Founders were driven by their awareness of the necessities of their
time and by a belief in their mission for the future. They were faced, as
the *Federalist Papers* argue, by the natural death of the confederacy. They
fashioned their hope in the context of history. They were the inheritors

of the best in Western political thought. They had experienced much. As has been written, many of them knew exactly what they were doing. They had a decent regard for the opinions of former times and the customs of other nations, but they relied upon "their own good sense, the knowledge of their own situation, and the lessons of their own experience."[78] They intended to perfect and extend the principle of representation as the key to a viable union of republics—a union which would be the bulwark against foreign danger, the conservator of peace among ourselves, the guardian of commerce and other common interests and the proper antidote for the diseases of factions. They consciously created a government of separate departments, each to be strong in its own domain, each to be checked and balanced by the others. They intended to create—and they succeeded—a structure for ordered liberty.

The Constitution was born with many doubts. It was not claimed to be perfection. Unlike the Articles of Confederation, it provided for a process of amendment. The Constitution arose out of a view of life, of society and private associations, of political action. That view recognizes that individuals and groups will disagree, in accordance with the diversity among them. The Constitution sought to protect, while moderating, that diversity. The Constitution, perforce, created a governmental structure, but its object was not government as such. It was the well-being of "We the People of the United States." It was from the ability of the people, their own actions, their thoughts, their difference of view, their individuality and originality, their own institutions, that progress would come. Not everything was known, and progress would make for change. Thus the government to be created was one to be responsive to continuing discussion and resolution. As Mr. Justice Holmes put it, the Constitution "is an experiment, as all life is an experiment."[79] It has sometimes been said that our Constitution because of its underlying belief in the need for discussion, diversity and checks and balances, with the dispersion of responsibility, has created an inefficient system. But to say that is to ignore the power, which our Constitution protects, of a society of many parts, which learns and grows as it works out its differences.

Our Constitution has passed through many difficult times. And time, as Mr. Justice Holmes said, "has upset many fighting faiths."[80] The conception of the Founders anticipated this. It is right that we should pay homage to those who created a charter for government to protect the differences among us, the continuity of representation, and the ordered liberty of "We the People."

The Infinite Task

September 28, 1975,

. . . Universities have a particular role when a national bicentennial celebration attempts to evoke the past. In our day the writing and thus the rediscovery of history is largely the keepsake and the captive of institutions of higher learning and scholarship. The chronology naturally has been written many ways. The words and events then come to us with a gloss of cycles of interpretation. There is a richness in our history—an articulate call to a shared culture, which is an extraordinary inheritance. From the beginning the American nation was seen as an experiment in education. Education was the way of progress, and education was thought of broadly. Society was to engage—and indeed was to govern itself—by a process in which judgments would be formed through the continued discussion and inquiry. Out of this, new discoveries of the mind and of government would come. An anniversary such as ours gives the incentive to look again at what was said at important times in our past, a useful venture, not because these words are timeless, if that is to mean they were not in reaction to particular events, but because our own are time-bound, and the more so, apparently, because of the gross ease of communication which is both the achievement and the burden of our day. These words, theirs and ours, are part of a dialogue which began long ago.

In this dialogue we need not give way to indifference because all the words have been spoken and all ideas set forth. It is in the understanding of them, as well as through reflection on the experience of the events which come to us, that we will continue the tradition of a government consciously fashioned to safeguard the rights of "We the People of the United States." This was the great attribute of the young Founders of this republic of republics. The Founders were well acquainted with the writings of Western political thought. Thus they related what they did, as any university must, to the best in a long tradition which preceded them. They put within this tradition the innovations which their own experience and necessity suggested to them. Since they were conscious of being engaged in a unique experiment of self-government, they looked ahead. Their writings discussed fundamental questions.

It is correct that toward the beginning of the 200 years, they described themselves somewhat differently than we would describe ourselves. "Providence," Jay wrote, in words frequently echoed, "has been pleased to give this one connected country to one united people; a people descended from the same ancestors, speaking the same language, professing the same religion, attached to the same principles of government, very similar in their manners and customs."[81] Today we would be more apt to emphasize our differences. But the Founders expected diversity of interests; they were concerned about factions. They intended to create a structure which would be responsive, would mediate, and would be effective. Mankind, they knew, could easily be inflamed with mutual animosity. But the science of politics, they thought, had received great improvement. Among the new inventions were the idea of a confederacy of republics, yet one nation, the regular distribution of powers into distinct departments, the introduction of legislative balances and checks. These do not now carry for us the ring of "wholly new discoveries,"[82] which Hamilton claimed for them. Here we approach the words with a background Hamilton did not have.

But some of the words still carry an interesting edge. They add a different voice. Writing for the *Federalist Papers*, that collection of serious essays which helped to win the ratification of the Constitution, and from which I have just quoted, Hamilton asks: "To what purpose separate the executive, or the judiciary, from the legislature, if both are so constituted to be at the absolute devotion of the legislative?" "The representatives of the people, in a popular assembly," Hamilton goes on to comment, "seem sometimes to fancy that they are the people themselves; and betray strong symptoms of impatience and disgust at the least sign of opposition from any other quarter; as if the exercise of its rights by either the executive or judiciary, were a breach of their privilege and an outrage to their dignity."[83] As for the executive, Hamilton finds that "decision, activity, secrecy, and dispatch"[84] are necessary attributes for that energy required for good government. The language leaves no doubt as to the vigor of Hamilton's position and reminds us, first, that he really did mean the separation of powers, and checks and balances, and second, that the dialogue is not closed, as it never will be.

If it is our condition that we are condemned to repeat history, or perhaps our good fortune to be able to do so, then the reading of history is likely to have this double aspect—no matter how much we try to avoid it or criticize the mixture—of being a look not only at the other times but at ourselves. I am prepared to assume that this violates the principles of this most professionally minded of the scholarly professions. But then let it to be said, if this assuages—as I fear it will not—that perhaps I am speaking less of history, and more particularly of those documents which are intended to speak to the human spirit, out of the conditions of their time, and beyond.

The task of giving these documents a central place in the conscious learning of our culture is not an easy one, although it has been done better than we do it now. Most of us, although not all, remain foreigners in our own tradition. One thinks of the irritation expressed by James Joyce's character, Stephen Dedalus, bridling at an English heritage we share with him, commenting on a conversation with an Englishman this way: "The language in which we are speaking is his before it is mine. How different are the words *home, Christ, ale, master*, on his lips and mine! . . . His language, so familiar and so foreign, will always be for me an acquired speech. I have not made or accepted its words. . . . My soul frets in the shadow of his language."[85] But this is true in some degree for all of us.

In our time, the heritage of government by discussion places great importance upon the university. This is the role which universities have always fulfilled. To some degree, they are the creators of it. The responsibility is greater and more difficult today for several reasons. The change might be thought to mark the singular success of our institutions of higher learning, as well as the fruits of technological advancement. I do not doubt that more people can be heard to take part in the discussion than ever before, although to many of them it may not appear that way. One reason making for and resulting from the difference is that the universities and colleges have preempted more time of more people than ever before. The role of the amateur or the self-taught has been reduced, or changed in direction, or has tended to be linked to the work of the universities. Then, the environment for teaching has changed, particularly the teaching of commonalities, because other institutions whose guidance is important have changed. Modern communication emphasizes the immediate event which can be seen; it tends to make of discussion the declaration of opinions in a form to be quickly understood, suggesting that the complexity of a problem is always the result of inefficiency or bad motives. One can join to this the influence of widespread dissemination of the professional sampling of how people say they feel. At any time the ideal of reasoned discussion is hard to approximate. It seems to be harder now, even though there should be a greater chance for it in spite of the obvious barriers which perhaps will turn out to be supportive in the long run. Voltaire once observed that the real scourge of mankind has not been ignorance but the pretense of knowledge. Today there may be more pretense of knowledge, a vice which most of us share, because there are more bits of knowledge widely distributed.

The idea of a bicentennial assumes a shared actual or vicarious experience. We are a country of many heritages. Jay spoke of those "who, by their joint counsels, arms and efforts, fighting side by side throughout a long and bloody war, have nobly established their general liberty and independence."[86] Washington in his farewell address repeated this theme to his friends and fellow citizens. "You have in a common cause fought and triumphed together. The independence and liberty you possess are the work of joint councils, and joint efforts; of common dangers, sufferings and successes."[87] A larger, older nation perhaps can never relive the excitement of its birth. Yet the unity of our diversity is perhaps just as extraordinary and just as difficult to achieve. A free society, a government by discussion, requires mutual respect. It requires mutual understanding. It requires a culture held in common—a culture not unitary but composed of many differences. The base for understanding must be built and rebuilt over time.

. . . I am told that for a proper historian, the history always has a beginning and an end. But this bicentennial is not an end. Carlyle has observed that history is a book that all men write and read and try to understand, and in which they, too, are written.[88] So today at this place of learning we celebrate one volume of that book—the wisdom that it embodies and that we bring to it—before we return to the infinite task of completing the text.

Governing by Discussion

Government Basic Rights and the Citizenry[1]

A SPEECH TO THE AMERICAN JEWISH COMMITTEE

June 11, 1961

During his time as Attorney General, Levi often referred to the idea of a government by discussion, and this chapter includes examples of what he meant. This brief excerpt from a talk he gave much earlier suggests that— even before trying to stimulate a rich discussion, in post-Watergate Washington, of electronic surveillance, secrecy and the need for an energetic executive branch—he understood vividly what a challenge this was.

. . . [W]hile I suppose all of us like to talk, few of us like to listen, to have our thoughts jarred, or to reshape our ideas. My grandfather, who was a well-known rabbi, and who certainly liked to talk, came home one day and announced he was feeling very empty. "I have been exchanging thoughts," he explained, "with Rabbi X—." My grandfather, if not Rabbi X—, would forgive me this quotation. It aptly illustrates what goes on in most discussions, except that probably we don't feel empty; we feel full with the same old thoughts we always had. Most of us, perhaps all of us, to paraphrase Professor [Friedrich] Hayek, are at best only secondhand dealers in ideas.[2] The fact is we usually haven't had a new idea, even a new secondhand idea, in years. Our thoughts come wrapped up in clichés; our discussions usually take place with those who agree with us anyway, and if they don't, normally we have signed a truce so that they will keep their ideas and we will keep ours. Once you hear the first sentences and have the speaker pegged, you can normally fill in the rest for yourself. And if the speaker doesn't say what you expect, you probably won't hear him anyway. One of the weaknesses of our society is that we are all pegged, conservatives or liberals. How frequently, given a knowledge of our economic status, our ethnic and religious background and similar factors, our views on a host of social issues can be typed. . . . It should be the function of discussion—real discussion—to change this.

Real discussion, new inquiry and learning are not easy. We should not expect them to be. They are not easy when it comes to science, but somehow we think science is different—different possibly because the rewards of science seem more genuine to us. Moreover, we have accepted a great deal of dogma—conservatives and liberals alike—about the coming shape of events, and the movement of history. In this setting we treat discussions and inquiry as but another contest of wits, involving not discovery but only persuasion and propaganda. Yet the means to the ends which we all seek do not come tailor made. They have to be worked out. The first impulse wrapped in the best cliché may not forge the best tool. The problems which encumber our world are enormous. Each of us has his own check list. Free inquiry means that we should put ourselves to the test of finding out what is wrong with what we think—an unsettling, a disconcerting, at times a most unwelcome pursuit of knowledge. This kind of inquiry and discussion can forge better instruments for government, and better appraisals of the wisdom of legislation. The law reflects and will change and respond to community reactions in any event. It is from these community reactions that the persuasion of similar situations gains its strength. For the community's appraisal tells us what is indeed similar. And the distinction between wisdom and constitutionality only has meaning as the wisdom is examined and debated. The quality of the debate will determine the quality of our laws. Desegregation is one example where the failure long ago to seek common measures and understandings, through real discussion, has left the law naked, exposed and unprotected, and has resulted in a national tragedy. One of the disconcerting aspects of modern life is that in so many areas real discussion is not welcome. . . .

The Legal Framework for Electronic Surveillance

TESTIMONY BEFORE THE SENATE SELECT COMMITTEE TO
STUDY GOVERNMENTAL RELATIONS WITH RESPECT TO
INTELLIGENCE ACTIVITIES

November 6, 1975

*The Watergate scandals provoked a period of intense scrutiny of a wide
range of intelligence activities that had for decades been done in the name
of protecting national security. Electronic surveillance was one of the techniques that received the most skeptical attention by Congress and some
federal courts. Meantime, without a workable statute providing for judicial
warrants in these cases, Levi continued under a grant of authority from
President Ford to authorize for foreign intelligence and counterintelligence
purposes wiretaps and microphone surveillance without a warrant, the latter sometimes requiring breaking and entering to install the device. Against
this backdrop, and with the increasing risk that a federal appeals court or
even the Supreme Court might at some point rule this exercise of Presidential power unconstitutional and thus a potentially federal civil rights violation, Levi laid out in detail the dangerously unsettled legal situation and
how he was responding to it in practice. He delivered the entire text to the
Senate Select Committee orally. It is some measure of the tension of the
moment that when Britain's counterintelligence agency, MI-5, learned—
probably from its FBI counterparts—that Levi was going to mention Britain's legal approach to surveillances, a representative called me and strongly
objected, even though Levi's testimony referred to information from British official sources freely available to the public.*[3]

I am here today in response to a request from the Committee to discuss
the relationship between electronic surveillance and the Fourth Amendment of the Constitution. If I remember correctly, the original request
was that I place before the Committee the philosophical or jurisprudential framework relevant to this relationship which lawyers, those with executive responsibilities or discretion, and lawmakers, viewing this complex field, ought to keep in mind. If this sounds vague and general and
perhaps useless, I can only ask for indulgence. My first concern when I received the request was that any remarks I might be able to make would

be so general as not to be helpful to this Committee. But I want to be as helpful to the Committee as I can be.

The area with which the Committee is concerned is a most important one. In my view, the development of the law in this area has not been satisfactory, although there are reasons why the law has developed as it has. Improvement of the law, which in part means its clarification, will not be easy. Yet it is a most important venture. In a talk before the American Bar Association last August, I discussed some of the aspects of the legal framework. Speaking for the Department of Justice, I concluded this portion of the talk with the observation and commitment that "we have very much in mind the necessity to determine what procedures through legislation, court action or executive processes will best serve the national interest, including, of course, the protection of constitutional rights."[4]

I begin then with an apology for the general nature of my remarks. This will be due in part to the nature of the law itself in this area. But I should state at the outset there are other reasons as well. In any area, and possibly in this one more than most, legal principles gain meaning through an interaction with the facts. Thus, the factual situations to be imagined are of enormous significance.

As this Committee well knows, some of the factual situations to be imagined in this area are not only of a sensitive nature but also of a changing nature. Therefore, I am limited in what I can say about them, not only because they are sensitive, but also because a lawyer's imagination about future scientific developments carries its own warnings of ignorance. This is a point worth making when one tries to develop appropriate safeguards for the future.

There is an additional professional restriction upon me which I am sure the Committee will appreciate. The Department of Justice has under active criminal investigation various activities which may or may not have been illegal.[5] In addition, the Department through its own attorneys, or private attorneys specially hired, is representing present or former government employees in civil suits which have been brought against them for activities in the course of official conduct. These circumstances naturally impose some limitation upon what it is appropriate for me to say in this forum. I ought not give specific conclusory opinions as to matters under criminal investigation or in litigation. I can only hope that what I have to say may nevertheless be of some value to the Committee in its search for constructive solutions.

I do realize there has to be some factual base, however unfocused it may at times have to be, to give this discussion meaning. Therefore, as a beginning, I propose to recount something of the history of the Department's position and practice with respect to the use of electronic surveillance both for telephone wiretapping and for trespassory placement of microphones.

As I read the history, going back to 1931 and undoubtedly prior to that time, except for an interlude between 1928 and 1931 and for two months in 1940, the policy of the Department of Justice has been that electronic surveillance could be employed without a warrant in certain circumstances.

In 1928 the Supreme Court in *Olmstead v. United States*[6] held that wiretapping was not within the coverage of the Fourth Amendment. Attorney General [John G.] Sargent had issued an order earlier in the same year prohibiting what was then known as the Bureau of Investigations from engaging in any telephone wiretapping for any reason. Soon after the order was issued, the Prohibition Unit was transferred to the Department as a new Bureau. Because of the nature of its work and the fact that the Unit had previously engaged in telephone wiretapping, in January 1931 Attorney General William D. Mitchell directed that a study be made to determine whether telephone wiretapping should be permitted and, if so, under what circumstances. The Attorney General determined that in the meantime the Bureaus within the Department could engage in telephone wiretapping upon the personal approval of the bureau chief after consultation with the Assistant Attorney General in charge of the case. The policy during this period was to allow wiretapping only with respect to the telephones of syndicated bootleggers, where the agent had probable cause to believe the telephone was being used for liquor operations. The Bureaus were instructed not to tap telephones of public officials and other persons not directly engaged in the liquor business. In December 1931 Attorney General William Mitchell expanded the previous authority to include "exceptional cases where the crimes are substantial and serious, and the necessity is great and [the bureau chief and the Assistant Attorney General] are satisfied that the persons whose wires are to be tapped are of the criminal type."[7]

During the rest of the thirties it appears that the Department's policy concerning telephone wiretapping generally conformed to the guidelines adopted by Attorney General William Mitchell. Telephone wiretapping was limited to cases involving the safety of the victim (as in kidnappings), location and apprehension of "desperate" criminals and other cases considered to be of major law enforcement importance, such as espionage and sabotage.

In December 1937, however, in the first *Nardone* case[8] the United States Supreme Court reversed the Court of Appeals for the Second Circuit and applied Section 605 of the Federal Communications Act of 1934 to law enforcement officers, thus rejecting the Department's argument that it did not so apply. Although the Court read the Act to cover only wire interceptions where there had also been disclosure in court or to the public, the decision undoubtedly had its impact upon the Department's estimation of the value of telephone wiretapping as an investigative technique. In the second *Nardone* case[9] in December 1939, the Act was read to bar the use in court not only of the overheard evidence, but also of the fruits of that evidence. Possibly for this reason, and also because of public concern over telephone wiretapping, on March 15, 1940, Attorney General Robert Jackson imposed a total ban on its use by the Department. This ban lasted about two months.

On May 21, 1940, President Franklin Roosevelt issued a memorandum to the Attorney General stating his view that electronic surveillance would be proper under the Constitution where "grave matters involving defense of the nation" were involved. The President authorized and directed the Attorney General "to secure information by listening devices [directed at] the conversation or other communications of persons suspected of subversive activities against the Government of the United States, including suspected spies." The Attorney General was requested "to limit these investigations so conducted to a minimum and to limit them insofar as possible to aliens."[10] Although the President's memorandum did not use the term "trespassory microphone surveillance," the language was sufficiently broad to include that practice, and the Department construed it as an authorization to conduct trespassory microphone surveillances as well as telephone wiretapping in national security cases. The authority for the President's action was later confirmed by an opinion by the Assistant Solicitor General Charles Fahy, who advised the Attorney General that electronic surveillance could be conducted when matters affected the security of the nation.

On July 17, 1946, Attorney General Tom C. Clark sent President Truman a letter reminding him that President Roosevelt had authorized and directed Attorney General Jackson to approve "listening devices [directed at] the conversation of other communications of persons suspected of subversive activities against the Government of the United States, including suspected spies" and that the directive had been followed by Attorneys General Robert Jackson and Francis Biddle. Attorney General Clark recommended that the directive "be continued in force" in view of the "increase in subversive activities" and "a very substantial increase in crime." He stated that it was imperative to use such techniques "in cases vitally affecting the domestic security, or where human life is in jeopardy" and that Department files indicated that his two most recent predecessors as Attorney General would concur in this view. President Truman signed this concurrence on the Attorney General's letter.[11]

According to the Department's records, the annual total of telephone wiretaps and microphones installed by the [Federal] Bureau [of Investigation] between 1940 through 1951 was as follows:

Telephone Wiretaps	Microphones
1940—6	1940—6
1941—67	1941—25
1942—304	1942—88
1943—475	1943—193
1944—517	1944—198
1945—519	1945—186
1946—364	1946—84
1947—374	1947—81
1948—416	1948—67
1949—471	1949—75
1950—270	1950—61
1951—285	1951—75

It should be understood that these figures, as is the case for the figures I have given before, are cumulative for each year and also duplicative to some extent, since a telephone wiretap or microphone which was installed, then discontinued, but later reinstated would be counted as a new action upon reinstatement.

In 1952, there were 285 telephone wiretaps, 300 in 1953, and 322 in 1954. Between February 1952 and May 1954, the Attorney General's position was not to authorize trespassory microphone surveillance. This was the position taken by Attorney General [James H.] McGrath, who informed the FBI that he would not approve the installation of trespassory microphone surveillance because of his concern over a possible violation of the Fourth Amendment. FBI records indicate there were 63 microphones installed in 1952, there were 52 installed in 1953, and there were 99 installed in 1954. The policy against Attorney General approval, at least in general, of trespassory microphone surveillance was reversed by Attorney General Herbert Brownell on May 20, 1954, in a memorandum to Director Hoover instructing him that the Bureau was authorized to conduct trespassory microphone surveillances. The Attorney General stated the "considerations of internal security and the national safety are paramount and, therefore, may compel the unrestricted use of this technique in the national interest."

A memorandum from Director Hoover to the Deputy Attorney General on May 4, 1961, described the Bureau's practice since 1954 as follows:

> [I]n the internal security field, we are utilizing microphone surveillances on a restricted basis even though trespass is necessary to assist in uncovering the activities of Soviet intelligence agents and Communist Party leaders. In the interests of national safety, microphone surveillances are also utilized on a restricted basis, even though trespass is necessary, in uncovering major criminal activities. We are using such coverage in connection with our investigations of the clandestine activities of top hoodlums and organized crime. From an intelligence standpoint, this investigative technique has produced results unobtainable through other means. The information so obtained is treated in the same manner as information obtained from wiretaps, that is, not from the standpoint of evidentiary value but for intelligence purposes.

The number of telephone wiretaps and microphones from 1955 through 1964 was as follows:

Telephone wiretaps	Microphones
1955—214	1955—102
1956—164	1956—71
1957—173	1957—73
1958—166	1958—70
1959—120	1959—75
1960—115	1960—74
1961—140	1961—85
1962—198	1962—100
1963—244	1963—83
1964—260	1964—106

It appears that there was a change in the authorization procedure for microphone surveillance in 1965. A memorandum of March 30, 1965, from Director Hoover to the Attorney General states that "[i]n line with your suggestion this morning, I have already set up the procedure similar to requesting of authority for phone taps to be utilized in requesting authority for the placement of microphones."

President Johnson announced a policy for federal agencies in June 1965 which required that the interception of telephone conversation without the consent of one of the parties be limited to investigations relating to national security and that the consent of the Attorney General be obtained in each instance. The memorandum went on to state that use of mechanical or electronic devices to overhear conversations not communicated by wire is an even more difficult problem "which raises substantial and unresolved questions of Constitutional interpretation." The memorandum instructed each agency conducting such an investigation to consult with the Attorney General to ascertain whether the agency's practices were fully in accord with the law.[12] Subsequently, in September 1965, the Director of the FBI wrote the Attorney General and referred to the "present atmosphere, brought about by the unrestrained and injudicious use of special investigative techniques by other agencies and department, resulting in Congressional and public alarm and opposition to any activity which could in any way be termed an invasion of privacy." "As a consequence," the Director wrote, "we have discontinued completely the use of microphones." The Attorney General responded in part as follows:

> The use of wiretaps and microphones involving trespass present more difficult problems because of the inadmissibility of any evidence obtained in court cases and because of current judicial and public attitude regarding their use. It is my understanding that such devices will not be used without my authorization, although in emergency circumstances they may be used subject to my later ratification. At this time I believe it desirable that all such techniques be confined to the gathering of intelligence in national security matters, and I will continue to approve all such requests in the future as I have in the past. I see no need to curtail any such activities in the national security field.

The policy of the Department was stated publicly by the Solicitor General in a supplemental brief in the Supreme Court in *Black v. United States* in 1966. Speaking of the general delegation of authority by Attor-

neys General to the Director of the Bureau, the Solicitor General stated
in his brief:

> An exception to the general delegation of authority has been prescribed, since
> 1940, for the interception of wire communications, which (in addition to being
> limited to matters involving national security or danger to human life) has re-
> quired the specific authorization of the Attorney General in each instance. No
> similar procedure existed until 1965 with respect to the use of devices such as
> those involved in the instant case, although records of oral and written commu-
> nications within the Department of Justice reflect concern by Attorneys Gen-
> eral and the Director of the Federal Bureau of Investigation that the use of lis-
> tening devices by agents of the government should be confined to a strictly
> limited category of situations. Under Departmental practice in effect for a pe-
> riod of years prior to 1963, and continuing until 1965, the Director of the Fed-
> eral Bureau of Investigation was given authority to approve the installation
> of devices such as that in question for intelligence (and not evidentiary) pur-
> poses when required in the interests of internal security or national safety, in-
> cluding organized crime, kidnappings and matters wherein human life might be
> at stake. . . .
>
> Present Departmental practice, adopted in July 1965, for the entire federal
> establishment, prohibits the use of such listening devices (as well as the inter-
> ception of telephone and other wire communications) in all instances other
> than those involving the collection of intelligence affecting the national secu-
> rity. The specific authorization of the Attorney General must be obtained in
> each instance when this exception is invoked.[13]

The Solicitor General made a similar statement in another brief filed
that same term again emphasizing that the data would not be made available for prosecutorial purposes, and that the specific authorization of the
Attorney General must be obtained in each instance when the national
security is sought to be invoked.[14] The number of telephone wiretaps and
microphones installed since 1965 are as follows:

Telephone Wiretaps	Microphones
1965—233	1965—67
1966—174	1966—10
1967—113	1967—0
1968—82	1968—9

1969 — 123	1969 — 14
1970 — 102	1970 — 19
1971 — 101	1971 — 16
1972 — 108	1972 — 32
1973 — 123	1973 — 40
1974 — 190	1974 — 42

Comparable figures for the year 1975 up to October 29 are:

Telephone Wiretaps	*Microphones*
121	24

In 1968 Congress passed the Omnibus Crime Control and Safe Streets Act. Title III of the Act set up a detailed procedure for the interception of wire or oral communications. The procedure requires the issuance of a judicial warrant, prescribes the information to be set forth in the petition to the judge so that, among other things, he may find probable cause that a crime has been or is about to be committed. It requires notification to the parties subject to the intended surveillance within a period not more than ninety days after the application for an order of approval has been denied or after the termination of the period of the order or the period of the extension of the order. Upon a showing of good cause the judge may postpone the notification. The Act contains a saving clause to the effect that it does not limit the constitutional power of the President to take such measures as he deems necessary to protect the nation against actual or potential attack or other hostile acts of a foreign power, to obtain foreign intelligence information deemed essential to the security of the United States or to protect national security information against foreign intelligence activities. Then in a separate sentence the proviso goes on to say, "Nor shall anything contained in this chapter be deemed to limit the constitutional power of the President to take such measures as he deems necessary to protect the United States against the overthrow of the government by force or other unlawful means, or against any other clear and present danger to the structure or existence of the government."[15]

The Act specifies the conditions under which information obtained through a Presidentially authorized interception might be received into evidence. In speaking of this saving clause, Justice Powell in the *Keith* case in 1972 wrote: "Congress simply left presidential powers where it

found them."[16] In the *Keith* case the Supreme Court held that in the field
of internal security, if there was no foreign involvement, a judicial warrant was required by the Fourth Amendment. Fifteen months after the
Keith case Attorney General Richardson, in a letter to Senator Fulbright
which was publicly released by the Department, stated: "In general, before I approve any new application for surveillance without a warrant, I
must be convinced that it is necessary (1) to protect the nation against actual or potential attack or other hostile acts of a foreign power; (2) to obtain foreign intelligence information deemed essential to the security of
the United States; or (3) to protect national security information against
foreign intelligence activities."

I have read the debates and reports of the Senate Judiciary Committee
with respect to Title III and particularly the proviso. It may be relevant to
point out that Senator Philip Hart questioned and opposed the form of
the proviso reserving Presidential power. But I believe it is fair to say that
his concern was primarily, perhaps exclusively, with the language which
dealt with Presidential power to take such measures as the President
deemed necessary to protect the United States "against any other clear
and present danger to the structure or existence of the government."

I now come to the Department of Justice's present position on electronic surveillance conducted without a warrant. Under the standards and
procedures established by the President, the personal approval of the Attorney General is required before any non-consensual electronic surveillance may be instituted within the United States without a judicial warrant. All requests for surveillance must be made in writing by the Director
of the Federal Bureau of Investigation and must set forth the relevant circumstances that justify the proposed surveillance. Both the agency and
the Presidential appointee initiating the request must be identified. These
requests come to the Attorney General after they have gone through review procedures within the Federal Bureau of Investigation. At my request, they are then reviewed in the Criminal Division of the Department.
Before they come to the Attorney General, they are then examined by a
special review group which I have established within the Office of the
Attorney General. Each request, before authorization or denial, receives
my personal attention. Requests are only authorized when the requested
electronic surveillance is necessary to protect the nation against actual or
potential attack or other hostile acts of a foreign power; to obtain foreign
intelligence deemed essential to the security of the nation; to protect na-

tional security information against foreign intelligence activities; or to obtain information certified as necessary for the conduct of foreign affairs matters important to the national security of the United States. In addition the subject of the electronic surveillance must be consciously assisting a foreign power or foreign-based political group, and there must be assurance that the minimum physical intrusion necessary to obtain the information sought will be used. As these criteria will show and as I will indicate at greater length later in discussing current guidelines the Department of Justice follows, our concern is with respect to foreign powers or their agents. In a public statement last July 9th, speaking of the warrantless surveillances then authorized by the Department, I said, "[I]t can be said that there are not outstanding instances of warrantless wiretaps or electronic surveillance directed against American citizens and none will be authorized by me except in cases where the target of surveillance is an agent or collaborator of a foreign power." This statement accurately reflected the situation today as well.

Having described in this fashion something of the history and conduct of the Department of Justice with respect to telephone wiretaps and microphone installations, I should like to remind the Committee of a point with which I began, namely, that the factual situations to be imagined for a discussion such as this are not only of a sensitive but a changing nature. I do not have much to say about this except to recall some of the language used by General Allen[17] in his testimony before this Committee. The techniques of the NSA [National Security Agency], he said, are of the most sensitive and fragile character. He described as the responsibility of the NSA the interception of international communications signals sent through the air. He said there had been a watch list, which among many other names, contained the names of U.S. citizens. Senator Tower spoke of an awesome technology—a huge vacuum cleaner of communications—which had the potential for abuses. General Allen pointed out that "[t]he United States, as part of its effort to produce foreign intelligence, has intercepted foreign communications, analyzed, and in some cases decoded, these communications to produce such foreign intelligence since the Revolutionary War." He said the mission of the NSA is directed to foreign intelligence obtained from foreign electrical communications and also from other foreign signals such as radar. Signals are intercepted by many techniques and processed, sorted and analyzed by procedures which reject inappropriate or unnecessary signals. He mentioned that the interception of communications, however it may occur, is conducted in such a manner as to minimize the unwanted messages. Nevertheless, according to his statement, many unwanted communications are potentially selected for further processing. He testified that subsequent processing, sorting and selection for analysis are conducted in accordance with strict procedures to insure immediate and, wherever possible, automatic rejection of inappropriate messages. The analysis and reporting is accomplished only for those messages which meet specific conditions and requirements for foreign intelligence. The use of lists of words, including individual names, subjects, locations, et cetera, has long been one of the methods used to sort out information of foreign intelligence value from that which is not of interest.

General Allen mentioned a very interesting statute, 18 USC 952, to which I should like to call your particular attention. The statute makes it a crime for anyone who by virtue of his employment by the United States obtains any official diplomatic code and willfully publishes or furnishes to another without authorization any such code or any other matter which was obtained while in the process of transmission between any foreign government and its diplomatic mission in the United States. I call this to your attention because a certain indirection is characteristic of the development of law, whether by statute or not, in this area.

The Committee will at once recognize that I have not attempted to summarize General Allen's testimony, but rather to recall it so that this extended dimension of the variety of fact situations which we have to think about as we explore the coverage and direction of the Fourth Amendment is at least suggested.

Having attempted to provide something of a factual base for our discussion, I turn now to the Fourth Amendment. Let me say at once, however, that while the Fourth Amendment can be a most important guide to values and procedures, it does not mandate automatic solutions.

The history of the Fourth Amendment is very much the history of the American Revolution and this nation's quest for independence. The Amendment is the legacy of our early years and reflects values most cherished by the Founders. In a direct sense it was a reaction to the general warrants and writs of assistance employed by the officers of the British Crown to rummage and ransack colonists' homes as a means to enforce anti-smuggling and customs laws. General search warrants had been used for centuries in England against those accused of seditious libel and other offenses. These warrants, sometimes judicial, sometimes not, often general as to persons to be arrested, places to be searched and things to be seized, were finally condemned by Lord Camden in 1765 in *Entick v. Carrington*,[18] a decision later celebrated by the Supreme Court as a "landmark of English liberty . . . one of the permanent monuments of the British Constitution."[19] The case involved a general warrant, issued by Lord Halifax as Secretary of State, authorizing messengers to search for John Entick and to seize his private papers and books. Entick had written publications criticizing the Crown and was a supporter of John Wilkes, the famous author and editor of the *North Briton* whose own publications had prompted wholesale arrests, searches and seizures. Entick sued for trespass and obtained a jury verdict in his favor. In upholding the verdict, Lord Camden observed that if the government's power to break into and search homes were accepted, "the secret cabinets and bureaus of every subject in this kingdom would be thrown open to the search and inspection of a messenger, whenever the secretary of state shall see fit to charge, or even to suspect, a person to be the author, printer, or publisher of a seditious libel."[20]

The practice of the general warrants, however, continued to be known in the colonies. The writ of assistance, an even more arbitrary and oppressive instrument than the general warrant, was also widely used by revenue officers to detect smuggled goods. Unlike a general warrant, the writ of assistance was virtually unlimited in duration and did not have to be returned to the court upon its execution. It broadly authorized indiscriminate searches and seizures against any person suspected by a customs officer of possessing prohibited or uncustomed goods. The writs, sometimes judicial, sometimes not, were usually issued by colonial judges and vested Crown officers with unreviewed and unbounded discretion to break into homes, rifle drawers and seize private papers. All officers and subjects of the Crown were further commanded to assist in the writ's execution. In 1761 James Otis eloquently denounced the writs as "the worst instrument of arbitrary power, the most destructive of English liberty, and the fundamental principles of law, that ever was found in an English law book," since they put "the liberty of every man in the hands of every petty officer."[21] Otis's fiery oration later prompted John Adams to reflect that "then and there was the first scene of the first act of opposition to the arbitrary claims of Great Britain. Then and there the child Independence was born."[22]

The words of the Fourth Amendment are mostly the product of James Madison. His original version appeared to be directed solely at the issuance of improper warrants.[23] Revisions accomplished under circumstances that are still unclear transformed the Amendment into two separate clauses. The change has influenced our understanding of the nature of the rights it protects. As embodied in our Constitution, the Amendment reads: "The right of the people to be secure in their persons, houses, papers, and effects, against unreasonable searches and seizures, shall not be violated, and no Warrants shall issue, but upon probable cause, supported by Oath or affirmation, and particularly describing the place to be searched, and the persons or things to be seized."

Our understanding of the purposes underlying the Fourth Amendment has been an evolving one. It has been shaped by subsequent historical events, by the changing conditions of our modern technological society and by the development of our own traditions, customs and values. From the beginning, of course, there has been agreement that the Amendment protects against practices such as those of the Crown officers under the notorious general warrants and writs of assistance. Above all, the Amendment safeguards the people from unlimited, undue infringement by the government on the security of persons and their property.

But our perceptions of the language and spirit of the Amendment have gone beyond the historical wrongs the Amendment was intended to prevent. The Supreme Court has served as the primary explicator of these evolving perceptions and has sought to articulate the values the Amendment incorporates. I believe it is useful in our present endeavor to identify some of these perceived values.

First, broadly considered, the Amendment speaks to the autonomy of the individual against society. It seeks to accord to each individual, albeit imperfectly, a measure of the confidentiality essential to the attainment of human dignity. It is a shield against indiscriminate exposure of an individual's private affairs to the world—an exposure which can destroy, since it places in jeopardy the spontaneity of thought and action on which so much depends. As Justice Brandeis observed in his dissent in the *Olmstead* case, in the Fourth Amendment the Founders "conferred, as against the Government, the right to be let alone—the most comprehensive of rights and the right most valued by civilized man."[24] Judge Jerome Frank made the same point in a dissent in a case in which a paid informer with a concealed microphone broadcast an intercepted conversation to a narcotics agent. Judge Frank wrote that "[a] sane, decent, civilized society must provide some such oasis, some shelter from public scrutiny, some insulated enclosure, some enclave, some inviolate place which is a man's castle."[25] The Amendment does not protect absolutely the privacy of an individual. The need for privacy, and the law's response to that need, go beyond the Amendment. But the recognition of the value of individual autonomy remains close to the Amendment's core.

A parallel value has been the Amendment's special concern with intrusions when the purpose is to obtain evidence to incriminate the victim of the search. As the Supreme Court observed in *Boyd*, which involved an attempt to compel the production of an individual's private papers, at some point the Fourth Amendment's prohibition against unreasonable searches and seizures and the Fifth Amendment's prohibition against compulsory self-incrimination "run almost into each other."[26] The intrusion on an individual's privacy has long been thought to be especially grave when the search is based on a desire to discover incriminating evidence.[27] The desire to incriminate may be seen as only an aggravating circumstance of the search, but it has at times proven to be a decisive factor in determining its legality. Indeed, in *Boyd* the Court declared broadly that "compelling the production of [a person's] private books and papers, to convict him of crime, or to forfeit his property, is contrary to the principles of a free government."[28] The incriminating evidence point goes to the integrity of the criminal justice system. It does not necessarily settle the issue whether the overhearing can properly take place. It goes to the use and purpose of the information overhead.

An additional concern of the Amendment has been the protection of freedom of thought, speech and religion. The general warrants were used in England as a powerful instrument to suppress what was regarded as seditious libel or non-conformity. Wilkes was imprisoned in the Tower and all his private papers seized under such a warrant for his criticism of the King. As Justice Frankfurter inquired, dissenting in a case that concerned the permissible scope of searches incident to arrest, "How can there be freedom of thought or speech or freedom of religion, if the police can, without warrant, search your house and mine from garret to cellar ... ?"[29] So Justice Powell stated in *Keith* that "Fourth Amendment protections become the more necessary when the targets of official surveillance may be those suspected of unorthodoxy in their political beliefs."[30]

Another concern embodied in the Amendment may be found in its second clause dealing with the warrant requirement, even though the Fourth Amendment does not always require a warrant. The fear is that the law enforcement officer, if unchecked, may misuse his powers to harass those who hold unpopular or simply different views and to intrude capriciously upon the privacy of individuals. It is the recognition of the possibility for abuse, inherent whenever executive discretion is uncontrolled, that gives rise to the requirement of a warrant. That requirement constitutes an assurance that the judgment of a neutral and detached magistrate will come to bear before the intrusion is made and that the decision whether the privacy of the individual must yield to a greater need of society will not be left to the executive alone.

A final value reflected in the Fourth Amendment is revealed in its opening words: "The right of the people." Who are "the people" to whom the Amendment refers? The Constitution begins with the phrase, "We the People of the United States." That phrase has the character of words of art, denoting the power from which the Constitution comes. It does suggest a special concern for the American citizen and for those who share the responsibilities of citizens. The Fourth Amendment guards the right of "the people" and it can be urged that it was not meant to apply to foreign nations, their agents and collaborators. Its application may at least take account of that difference.

The values outlined above have been embodied in the Amendment from the beginning. But the importance accorded a particular value has varied during the course of our history. Some have been thought more important or more threatened than others at times. When several of the values coalesce, the need for protection has been regarded as greatest. When only one is involved, that need has been regarded as lessened. Moreover, the scope of the Amendment itself has been altered over time, expanding or contracting in the face of changing circumstances and needs. As with the evolution of other constitutional provisions, this development has been cast in definitional terms. Words have been read by different justices and different courts to mean different things. The words of the Amendment have not changed; we, as a people, and the world which envelops us, have changed.

An important example is what the Amendment seeks to guard as "secure." The wording of the Fourth Amendment suggests a concern with tangible property. By its terms, the Amendment protects the right of the people to be secure in their "persons, houses, papers, and effects." The emphasis appears to be on the material possessions of a person, rather than on his privacy generally. The Court came to that conclusion in 1928 in the *Olmstead* case,[31] holding that the interception of telephone messages, if accomplished without a physical trespass, was outside the scope of the Fourth Amendment. Chief Justice Taft, writing for the Court, reasoned that wiretapping did not involve a search or seizure; the Amendment protected only tangible material "effects" and not intangibles such as oral conversations. A thread of the same idea can be found in *Entick*, where Lord Camden said: "The great end for which men entered into society was to secure their property." But, while the removal and carrying off of papers was a trespass of the most aggravated sort, inspection alone was not: "[T]he eye," Lord Camden said, "cannot by the law of England be guilty of a trespass."[32]

The movement of the law since *Olmstead* has been steadily from protection of property to protection of privacy. In the *Goldman* case[33] in 1942 the Court held that the use of a detectaphone placed against the wall of a room to overhear oral conversations in an adjoining office was not unlawful because no physical trespass was involved. The opinion's unstated assumption, however, appeared to be that a private oral conversation could be among the protected "effects" within the meaning of the Fourth Amendment. The *Silverman* case[34] later eroded *Olmstead* substantially by holding that the Amendment was violated by the interception of an oral conversation through the use of a spike mike driven into a party wall, penetrating the heating duct of the adjacent home. The Court stated that the question whether a trespass had occurred as a technical matter of property law was not controlling; the existence of an actual intrusion was sufficient.

The Court finally reached the opposite emphasis from its previous stress on property in 1967 in *Katz v. United States*.[35] The Court declared that the Fourth Amendment "protects people, not places," against unreasonable searches and seizures; that oral conversations, although intangible, were entitled to be secure against the uninvited ear of a government officer; and that the interception of a telephone conversation, even if accomplished without a trespass, violated the privacy on which petitioner justifiably relied while using a telephone booth. Justice Harlan, in a concurring opinion, explained that to have a constitutionally protected right of privacy under *Katz* it was necessary that a person, first, "have exhibited an actual (subjective) expectation of privacy and, second, that the expectation be one that society is prepared to recognize as 'reasonable.'"[36]

At first glance, *Katz* might be taken as a statement that the Fourth Amendment now protects all reasonable expectations of privacy—that the boundaries of the right of privacy are coterminous with those of the Fourth Amendment. But that assumption would be misleading. To begin with, the Amendment still protects some interests that have very little if anything to do with privacy. Thus, the police may not, without warrant, seize an automobile parked on the owner's driveway even though they have reason to believe that the automobile was used in committing a crime. The interest protected by the Fourth Amendment in such a case is probably better defined in terms of property than privacy. Moreover, the *Katz* opinion itself cautioned that "the Fourth Amendment cannot be translated into a general constitutional 'right to privacy.'"[37] Some privacy interests are protected by remaining constitutional guarantees. Others are protected by federal statute, by the states, or not at all.

The point is twofold. First, under the Court's decisions, the Fourth Amendment does not protect every expectation of privacy, no matter how reasonable or actual that expectation may be. It does not protect, for example, against false friends' betrayals to the police of even the most private confidences. Second, the "reasonable expectation of privacy" standard, often said to be the test of *Katz*, is itself a conclusion. It represents a judgment that certain behavior should as a matter of law be protected against unrestrained governmental intrusion. That judgment, to be sure, rests in part on an assessment of the reasonableness of the expectation, that is, on an objective, factual estimation of a risk of intrusion under given circumstances, joined with an actual expectation of privacy by the person involved in a particular case. But it is plainly more than that, since it is also intermingled with a judgment as to how important it is to society that an expectation should be confirmed—a judgment based on a perception of our customs, traditions and values as a free people.

The *Katz* decision itself illustrates the point. Was it really a "reasonable expectation" at the time of *Katz* for a person to believe that his telephone conversation in a public phone booth was private and not susceptible to interception by a microphone on the booth's outer wall? Almost forty years earlier in *Olmstead* the Court held that such nontrespassory interceptions were permissible. *Goldman* reaffirmed that holding. So how could Katz reasonably expect the contrary? The answer, I think, is that the Court's decision in *Katz* turned ultimately on an assessment of the effect of permitting such unrestrained intrusions on the individual in his private and social life. The judgment was that a license for unlimited governmental intrusions upon every telephone would pose too great a danger to the spontaneity of human thought and behavior. Justice Harlan put the point this way: "The analysis must, in my view, transcend the search for subjective expectations or legal attribution of assumptions of risk. Our expectations, and the risks we assume, are in large part reflections of laws that translate into rules the customs and values of the past and present."[38]

A weighing of values is an inescapable part in the interpretation and growth of the Fourth Amendment. Expectations, and their reasonableness, vary according to circumstances. So will the need for an intrusion and its likely effect. These elements will define the boundaries of the interests which the Amendment holds as "secure."

To identify the interests which are to be "secure," of course, only begins the inquiry. It is equally essential to identify the dangers from which those interests are to be secure. What constitutes an intrusion will depend on the scope of the protected interest. The early view that the Fourth Amendment protected only tangible property resulted in the rule that a physical trespass or taking was the measure of an intrusion. *Olmstead* rested on the fact that there had been no physical trespass into the defendant's home or office. It also held that the use of the sense of hearing to intercept a conversation did not constitute a search or seizure. *Katz*, by expanding the scope of the protected interests, necessarily altered our understanding of what constitutes an intrusion. Since intangibles such as oral conversations are not regarded as protected "effects," the overhearing of a conversation may constitute an intrusion apart from whether a physical trespass is involved.

The nature of the search and seizure can be very important. An entry into a house to search its interior may be viewed as more serious than the overhearing of a certain type of conversation. The risk of abuse may loom larger in one case than the other. The factors that have come to be viewed as most important, however, are the purpose and effect of the intrusion. The Supreme Court has tended to focus not so much on what was physically done, but on why it was done and what the consequence is likely to be. What is seized, why it is seized, and what is done with what is seized are critical questions.

I stated earlier that a central concern of the Fourth Amendment was with intrusions to obtain evidence to incriminate the victim of the search. This concern has been reflected in Supreme Court decisions which have traditionally treated intrusions to gather incriminatory evidence differently from intrusions for neutral or benign purposes. In *Frank v. Maryland*,[39] the appellant was fined for refusing to allow a housing inspector to enter his residence to determine whether it was maintained in compliance with the municipal housing code. Violation of the code would have led only to a direction to remove the violation. Only failure to comply with the direction would lead to a criminal sanction. The Court held that such administrative searches could be conducted without warrant.

Justice Frankfurter, writing for the Court, noted that the Fourth Amendment was a reaction to "ransacking by Crown officers of the homes of
citizens in search of evidence of crime or of illegally imported goods."[40]
He observed that both *Entick* and *Boyd* were concerned with attempts to
compel individuals to incriminate themselves in criminal cases and that
"it was on the issue of the right to be secure from searches for evidence to
be used in criminal prosecutions or for forfeitures that the great battle for
fundamental liberty was fought."[41] There was thus a great difference, the
Justice said, between searches to seize evidence for criminal prosecutions
and searches to detect the existence of municipal health code violations.
Searches in this latter[42] category, conducted "as an adjunct to a regulatory
scheme for the general welfare of the community and not as a means of
enforcing the criminal law, [have] antecedents deep in our history," and
should not be subjected to the warrant requirement.[43]

  Frank was later overruled in 1967 in *Camara v. Municipal Court*,[44] and
a companion case, *See v. City of Seattle*.[45] In *Camara*, appellant was, like
Frank, charged with a criminal violation as a result of his refusal to permit
a municipal inspector to enter his apartment to investigate possible violations of the city's housing code. The Supreme Court rejected the *Frank*
rationale that municipal fire, health and housing inspections could be conducted without a warrant because the object of the intrusion was not to
search for the fruits or instrumentalities of crime. Moreover, the Court
noted that most regulatory laws such as fire, health and housing codes
were enforced by criminal processes, that refusal to permit entry to an
inspector was often a criminal offense, and that the "self-protection" or
"non-incrimination" objective of the Fourth Amendment was therefore
indeed involved.

  But the doctrine of *Camara* proved to be limited. In 1971 in *Wyman v.
James*[46] the Court held that a "home visit" by a welfare caseworker, which
entailed termination of benefits if the welfare recipient refused entry, was
lawful despite the absence of a warrant. The Court relied on the importance of the public's interest in obtaining information about the recipient,
the reasonableness of the measures taken to ensure that the intrusion was
limited to the extent practicable, and most importantly, the fact that the
primary objective of the search was not to obtain evidence for a criminal
investigation or prosecution. *Camara* and *Frank* were distinguished as involving criminal proceedings.

  Perhaps what these cases mainly say is that the purpose of the intrusion, and the use to which what is seized is put, are more important from

a constitutional standpoint than the physical act of intrusion itself. Where the purpose or effect is non-criminal, the search and seizure is perceived as less troublesome and there is a readiness to find reasonableness even in the absence of a judicial warrant. By contrast, where the purpose of the intrusion is to gather incriminatory evidence, and hence hostile, or when the consequence of the intrusion is the sanction of the criminal law, greater protections may be given.

The Fourth Amendment then, as it has always been interpreted, does not give absolute protection against government intrusion. In the words of the Amendment, the right guaranteed is security against *unreasonable* searches and seizures. As Justice White said in the *Camara* case, "[T]here can be no ready test for determining reasonableness other than by balancing the need to search against the invasion which the search entails."[47] Whether there has been a constitutionally prohibited invasion at all has come to depend less on an absolute dividing line between protected and unprotected areas, and more on an estimation of the individual security interests affected by the government's actions. Those effects, in turn, may depend on the purpose for which the search is made, whether it is hostile, neutral or benign in relation to the person whose interests are invaded, and also on the manner of the search.

By the same token, the government's need to search, to invade individual privacy interests, is no longer measured exclusively—if indeed it ever was—by the traditional probable cause standard. The second clause of the Amendment states, in part, that "no warrants shall issue but upon probable cause." The concept of probable cause has often been read to bear upon and in many cases to control the question of the reasonableness of searches, whether with or without warrant. The traditional formulation of the standard, as "reasonable grounds for believing that the law was being violated on the premises searched" relates to the governmental interest in the prevention of criminal offenses, and to seizure of their instruments and fruits.[48] This formulation once took content from the long-standing "mere evidence rule"—that searches could not be undertaken "solely for the purpose of . . . [securing] evidence to be used . . . in a criminal or penal proceeding, but that they may be resorted to only when a primary right to search and seizure may be found in the interest which the public . . . may have in the property to be seized."[49] The government's interest in the intrusion, like the individual's interest in privacy, thus was defined in terms of property, and the right to search as well as to seize was limited to items—contraband and the fruits and instrumentalities of crime—in which the government's interest was thought superior to the individual's. This notion, long eroded in practice, was expressly abandoned by the Court in 1967 in *Warden v. Hayden.*[50] Thus, the detection of crime—the need to discover and use "mere evidence"—may presently justify intrusion.

Moreover, as I have indicated, the Court has held that, in certain situations, something less than probable cause—in the traditional sense—may be sufficient ground for intrusion, if the degree of intrusion is limited strictly to the purposes for which it is made. In *Terry v. Ohio*[51] the Court held that a policeman, in order to protect himself and others nearby, may conduct a limited "pat down" search for weapons when he has reasonable grounds for believing that criminal conduct is taking place and that the person searched is armed and dangerous. Last term, in *United States v. Brignoni-Ponce*,[52] the Court held that, if an officer has a "founded suspicion" that a car in a border area contains illegal aliens, the officer may stop the car and ask the occupants to explain suspicious circumstances. The Court concluded that the important governmental interest involved, and the absence of practical alternatives, justified the minimal intrusion of a brief stop. In both *Terry* and *Brignoni*, the Court emphasized that a more drastic intrusion—a thorough search of the suspect or automobile—would require the justification of traditional probable cause. This point is reflected in the Court's decisions in *Almeida-Sanchez*[53] and *Ortiz*,[54] in which the court held that, despite the interest in stemming illegal immigration, searches of automobiles either at fixed checkpoints or by roving patrols in places that are not the "functional equivalent" of borders could not be undertaken without probable cause.

Nonetheless, it is clear that the traditional probable cause standard is not the exclusive measure of the government's interest. The kind and degree of interest required depend on the severity of the intrusion the government seeks to make. The requirement of the probable cause standard itself may vary, as the Court made clear in *Camara*.[55] That case, as you recall, concerned the nature of the probable cause requirement in the context of searches to identify housing code violations. The Court was persuaded that the only workable method of enforcement was periodic inspection of all structures, and concluded that because the search was not "personal in nature," and the invasion of privacy involved was limited, probable cause could be based on "appraisal of the conditions in the area as a whole," rather than knowledge of the condition of particular buildings. "If a valid public interest justifies the intrusion contemplated," the

Court stated, "then there is probable cause to issue a suitable restricted search warrant."[56] In the *Keith* case, while holding that domestic national security surveillance—not involving the activities of foreign powers and their agents—was subject to the warrant requirement, the Court noted that the reasons for such domestic surveillance may differ from those justifying surveillance for ordinary crimes, and that domestic security surveillances often have to be long-range projects. For these reasons, a standard of probable cause to obtain a warrant different from the traditional standard would be justified: "Different standards may be compatible with the Fourth Amendment if they are reasonable both in relation to the legitimate need of Government for intelligence information and the protected rights of our citizens."[57]

In brief, although at one time the "reasonableness" of a search may have been defined according to the traditional probable cause standard, the situation has now been reversed. Probable cause has come to depend on reasonableness—on the legitimate need of the government and whether there is reason to believe that the precise intrusion sought, measured in terms of its effect on individual security, is necessary to satisfy it.

This point is critical in evaluating the reasonableness of searches or surveillances undertaken to protect national security. In some instances, the government's interest may be, in part, to protect the nation against specific actions of foreign powers or their agents—actions that are criminal offenses. In other instances, the interest may be to protect against the possibility of actions by foreign powers and their agents dangerous to national security—actions that may or may not be criminal. Or the interest may be solely to gather intelligence, in a variety of forms, in the hands of foreign agents and foreign powers—intelligence that may be essential to informed conduct of our nation's foreign affairs. This last interest indeed may often be far more critical for the protection of the nation than the detection of a particular criminal offense. The Fourth Amendment's standard of reasonableness as it has developed in the Court's decisions is sufficiently flexible to recognize this.

Just as the reasonableness standard of the Amendment's first clause has taken content from the probable cause standard, so it has also come to incorporate the particularity requirement of the warrant clause—that warrants particularly describe "the place to be searched, and the persons or things to be seized." As one circuit court has written, although pointing out the remedy might not be very extensive, "[L]imitations on the fruit to be gathered tend to limit the quest itself."[58] The government's inter-

est and purpose in undertaking the search defines its scope, and the societal importance of that purpose can be weighed against the effects of
the intrusion on the individual. By precise definition of the objects of the
search, the degree of intrusion can be minimized to that reasonably necessary to achieve the legitimate purpose. In this sense, the particularity
requirement of the warrant clause is analogous to the minimization requirement of Title III,[59] that interceptions "be executed in such a way as
to minimize the interception of communications not otherwise subject to
interceptions" under the Title.

But there is a distinct aspect to the particularity requirement—one
that is often overlooked. An officer who has obtained a warrant based
upon probable cause to search for particular items may in conducting the
search necessarily have to examine other items, some of which may constitute evidence of an entirely distinct crime. The normal rule under the
plain view doctrine is that the officer may seize the latter incriminating
items as well as those specifically identified in the warrant so long as the
scope of the authorized search is not exceeded. The minimization rule responds to the concern about overly broad searches, and it requires an effort to limit what can be seized. It also may be an attempt to limit how it
can be used. Indeed, this minimization concern may have been the original purpose of the "mere evidence" rule.

The concern about the use of what is seized may be most important
for future actions. Until recently—in fact, until the Court's 1971 decision
in *Bivens*[60]—the only sanction against an illegal search was that its fruits
were inadmissible at any criminal trial of the person whose interest was
invaded. So long as this was the only sanction, the courts, in judging reasonableness, did not really have to weigh any governmental interest other
than that of detecting crimes. In practical effect, a search could only be
"unreasonable" as a matter of law if an attempt was made to use its fruits
for prosecution of a criminal offense. So long as the government did not
attempt such use, the search could continue and the government's interest, other than enforcing criminal laws, could be satisfied.

It may be said that this confuses rights and remedies; searches could be
unreasonable even though no sanction followed. But I am not clear that
this is theoretically so, and realistically it was not so. As I have noted earlier, the reasonableness of a search has depended, in major part, on the
purpose for which it is undertaken and on whether that purpose, in relation to the person whom it affects, is hostile or benign. The search most
hostile to an individual is one in preparation for his criminal prosecution.

Exclusion of evidence from criminal trials may help assure that searches
undertaken for ostensibly benign motives are not used as blinds for attempts to find criminal evidence, while permitting searches that are genuinely benign to continue. But there is a more general point. The effect of
a government intrusion on individual security is a function, not only of
the intrusion's nature and circumstances, but also of disclosure and of the
use to which its product is put. Its effects are perhaps greatest when it is
employed or can be employed to impose criminal sanctions or to deter,
by disclosure, the exercise of individual freedoms. In short, the use of the
product seized bears upon the reasonableness of the search.

These observations have particular bearing on electronic surveillance. By the nature of the technology the "search" may necessarily be far
broader than its legitimate objects. For example, a surveillance justified
as the only means of obtaining valuable foreign intelligence may require
the temporary overhearing of conversations containing no foreign intelligence whatever in order eventually to locate its object. To the extent that
we can, by purely mechanical means, select out only that information that
fits the purpose of the search, the intrusion is radically reduced. Indeed,
in terms of effects on individual security, there would be no intrusion at
all. But other steps may be appropriate. In this respect, I think we should
recall the language and the practice for many years under former Section 605 of the Communications Act [of 1934]. The Act was violated, not
by surveillance alone, but only by surveillance *and* disclosure in court or
to the public. It may be that if a critical governmental purpose justifies a
surveillance, but because of technological limitations it is not possible to
limit surveillance strictly to those persons as to whom alone surveillance
is justified, one way of reducing the intrusion's effects is to limit strictly
the revelation or disclosure or the use of its product. Minimization procedures can be very important.

In discussing the standard of reasonableness, I have necessarily described the evolving standards for issuing warrants and the standards governing their scope. But I have not yet discussed the warrant requirement
itself—how it relates to the reasonableness standard and what purposes
it was intended to serve. The relationship of the warrant requirement to
the reasonableness standard was described by Justice Robert Jackson:
"Any assumption that evidence sufficient to support a magistrate's dis-
interested determination to issue a search warrant will justify the officers
in making a search without a warrant would reduce the Amendment to a
nullity and leave the people's homes secure only in the discretion of po-

lice officers. . . . When the right of privacy must reasonably yield to the right of search is, as a rule, to be decided by a judicial officer, not by a policeman or government enforcement agent."[61] This view has not always been accepted by a majority of the Court; the Court's view of the relationship between the general reasonableness standard and the warrant requirement has shifted often and dramatically. But the view expressed by Justice Jackson is now quite clearly the prevailing position. The Court said in *Katz* that "searches conducted outside the judicial process, without prior approval by judge or magistrate, are *per se* unreasonable under the Fourth Amendment—subject only to a few specifically established and well-delineated exceptions."[62] Such exceptions include those grounded in necessity—where exigencies of time and circumstance make resort to a magistrate practically impossible. These include, of course, the *Terry* stop and frisk and, to some degree, searches incident to arrest. But there are other exceptions, not always grounded in exigency—for example, some automobile searches—and at least some kinds of searches not conducted for purposes of enforcing criminal laws—such as the welfare visits of *Wyman v. James*. In short, the warrant requirement itself depends on the purpose and degree of intrusion. A footnote to the majority opinion in *Katz*, as well as Justice White's concurring opinion, left open the possibility that warrants may not be required for searches undertaken for national security purposes. And, of course, Justice Powell's opinion in *Keith*, while requiring warrants for domestic security surveillances, suggests that a different balance may be struck when the surveillance is undertaken against foreign powers and their agents to gather intelligence information or to protect against foreign threats.

The purpose of the warrant requirement is to guard against overzealousness of government officials, who may tend to over-estimate the basis and necessity of intrusion and to underestimate the impact of their efforts on individuals. "The historical judgment, which the Fourth Amendment accepts, is that unreviewed executive discretion may yield too readily to pressures to obtain incriminating evidence and overlook potential invasions of privacy and protected speech."[63] These purposes of the warrant requirement must be kept firmly in mind in analyzing the appropriateness of applying it to the foreign intelligence and security area.

There is a real possibility that application of the warrant requirement, at least in the form of the normal criminal search warrant, the form adopted in Title III, will endanger legitimate government interest. As I have indicated, Title III sets up a detailed procedure for interception of wire or oral communications. It requires the procurement of a judicial warrant and prescribes the information to be set forth in the petition to the judge so that, among other things, he may find probable cause that a crime has been or is about to be committed. It requires notification to the parties subject to the surveillance within a period after it has taken place. The statute is clearly unsuited to protection of the vital national interests in continuing detection of the activities of foreign powers and their agents. A notice requirement—aside from other possible repercussions—could destroy the usefulness of intelligence sources and methods. The most critical surveillance in this area may have nothing whatever to do with detection of crime.

Apart from the problems presented by particular provisions of Title III, the argument against application of the warrant requirement, even with an expanded probable cause standard, is that judges and magistrates may underestimate the importance of the government's need, or that the information necessary to make that determination cannot be disclosed to a judge or magistrate without risk of its accidental revelation—a revelation that could work great harm to the nation's security. What is often less likely to be noted is that a magistrate may be as prone to over-estimate as to underestimate the force of the government's need. Warrants necessarily are issued *ex parte*; often decision must come quickly on the basis of information that must remain confidential. Applications to any one judge or magistrate would be only sporadic; no opinion could be published; this would limit the growth of judicially developed, reasonably uniform standards based, in part, on the quality of the information sought and the knowledge of possible alternatives. Equally important, responsibility for the intrusion would have been diffused. It is possible that the actual number of searches or surveillances would increase if executive officials, rather than bearing responsibility themselves, can find shield behind a magistrate's judgment of reasonableness. On the other hand, whatever the practical effect of a warrant requirement may be, it would still serve the important purpose of assuring the public that searches are not conducted without the approval of a neutral magistrate who could prevent abuses of the technique.

In discussing the advisability of a warrant requirement, it may also be useful to distinguish among possible situations that arise in the national security area. Three situations—greatly simplified—come to mind. They differ from one another in the extent to which they are limited in time or in target. First, the search may be directed at a particular foreign agent to detect a specific anticipated activity—such as the purchase of a secret document. The activity which is to be detected ordinarily would constitute a crime. Second, the search may be more extended in time—even virtually continuous—but still would be directed at an identified foreign agent. The purpose of such a surveillance would be to monitor the agent's activities, determine the identities of persons whose access to classified information he might be exploiting and determine the identity of other foreign agents with whom he may be in contact. Such a surveillance might also gather foreign intelligence information about the agent's own country, information that would be of positive intelligence value to the United States. Third, there may be virtually continuous surveillance which by its nature does not have specifically pre-determined targets. Such a surveillance could be designed to gather foreign intelligence information essential to the security of the nation.

The more limited in time and target a surveillance is, the more nearly analogous it appears to be with a traditional criminal search which involves a particular target location or individual at a specific time. Thus, the first situation I just described would in that respect be most amenable to some sort of warrant requirement, the second less so. The efficacy of a warrant requirement in the third situation would be minimal. If the third type of surveillance I described were submitted to prior judicial approval, that judicial decision would take the form of an *ex parte* declaration that the program of surveillance designed by the government strikes a reasonable balance between the government's need for the information and the protection of individuals' rights. Nevertheless, it may be that different kinds of warrants could be developed to cover the third situation. In his opinion in *Almeida-Sanchez*,[64] Justice Powell suggested the possibility of area warrants—issued on the basis of the conditions in the area to be surveilled—to allow automobile searches in areas near America's borders. The law has not lost its inventiveness, and it might be possible to fashion new judicial approaches to the novel situations that come up in the area of foreign intelligence. I think it must be pointed out that for the development of such an extended, new kind of warrant, a statutory base might be required or at least appropriate. At the same time, in dealing with this area, it may be mistaken to focus on the warrant requirement alone to the exclusion of other, possibly more realistic, protections.

What, then, is the shape of the present law? To begin with, several statutes appear to recognize that the government does intercept certain messages for foreign intelligence purposes and that this activity must be, and can be, carried out. Section 952 of Title 18, which I mentioned earlier, is one example; Section 798 of the same title is another. In addition, Title III's proviso, which I have quoted earlier, explicitly disclaimed any intent to limit the authority of the executive to conduct electronic surveillance for national security and foreign intelligence purposes. In an apparent recognition that the power would be exercised, Title III specifies the conditions under which information obtained through Presidentially authorized surveillance may be received into evidence. It seems clear, therefore, that in 1968 Congress was not prepared to come to a judgment that the executive should discontinue its activities in this area, nor was it prepared to regulate how those activities were to be conducted. Yet it cannot be said that Congress has been entirely silent on this matter. Its express statutory references to the existence of the activity must be taken into account.

The case law, although unsatisfactory in some respects, has supported or left untouched the policy of the executive in the foreign intelligence area whenever the issue has been squarely confronted. The Supreme Court's decision in the *Keith* case in 1972 concerned the legality of warrantless surveillance directed against a domestic organization with no connection to a foreign power and the government's attempt to introduce the product of the surveillance as evidence in the criminal trial of a person charged with bombing a CIA office in Ann Arbor, Michigan. In part because of the danger that uncontrolled discretion might result in use of electronic surveillance to deter domestic organizations from exercising First Amendment rights, the Supreme Court held that in cases of internal security, when there is no foreign involvement, a judicial warrant is required. Speaking for the Court, Justice Powell emphasized that "this case involves only the domestic aspects of national security. We have expressed no opinion as to the issues which may be involved with respect to activities of foreign powers or their agents."[65] As I observed in my remarks at the ABA convention,[66] the Supreme Court surely realized, "in view of the importance the government has placed on the need for warrantless electronic surveillance that, after the holding in *Keith*, the government would proceed with the procedures it had developed to conduct those surveillances not prohibited—that is, in the foreign intelligence area or, as Justice Powell said, 'with respect to activities of foreign powers or their agents.'"

The two federal circuit court decisions after *Keith* that have expressly addressed the problem have both held that the Fourth Amendment does not require a warrant for electronic surveillance instituted to obtain foreign intelligence. In the first, *United States v. Brown*,[67] the defendant, an American citizen, was incidentally overheard as the result of a warrantless wiretap authorized by the Attorney General for foreign intelligence purposes. In upholding the legality of the surveillance, the Court of Appeals for the Fifth Circuit declared that on the basis of "the President's constitutional duty to act for the United States in the field of foreign affairs, and his inherent power to protect national security in the conduct of foreign affairs . . . the President may constitutionally authorize warrantless wiretaps for the purpose of gathering foreign intelligence." The court added that "[r]estrictions on the President's power which are appropriate in cases of domestic security become artificial in the context of the international sphere."[68]

In *United States v. Butenko*,[69] the Third Circuit reached the same conclusion—that the warrant requirement of the Fourth Amendment does not apply to electronic surveillance undertaken for foreign intelligence purposes. Although the surveillance in that case was directed at a foreign agent, the court held broadly that the warrantless surveillance would be lawful so long as the primary purpose was to obtain foreign intelligence information. The court stated that such surveillance would be reasonable without a warrant even though it might involve the overhearing of conversations of "alien officials and agents, and perhaps of American citizens." I should note that although the United States prevailed in the *Butenko* case, the Department acquiesced in the petitioner's application for certiorari in order to obtain the Supreme Court's ruling on the question. The Supreme Court denied review, however, and left the Third Circuit's decision undisturbed as the prevailing law.

Most recently, in *Zweibon v. Mitchell*,[70] decided in June of this year, the District of Columbia Circuit dealt with warrantless electronic surveillance directed against a domestic organization allegedly engaged in activities affecting this country's relations with a foreign power. Judge Skelly Wright's opinion for four of the nine judges makes many statements questioning any national security exception to the warrant requirement. The court's actual holding made clear in Judge Wright's opinion was far narrower and, in fact, is consistent with holdings in *Brown* and *Butenko*. The court held only that "a warrant must be obtained before a wiretap is installed on a domestic organization that is neither the agent of nor acting in collaboration with a foreign power."[71] This holding, I should add, was fully consistent with the Department of Justice's policy prior to the time of the *Zweibon* decision.

With these cases in mind, it is fair to say electronic surveillance conducted for foreign intelligence purposes, essential to the national security, is lawful under the Fourth Amendment, even in the absence of a warrant, at least where the subject of the surveillance is a foreign power or an agent or collaborator of a foreign power. Moreover, the opinions of two circuit courts stress the purpose for which the surveillance is undertaken, rather than the identity of the subject. This suggests that in their view such surveillance without a warrant is lawful so long as its purpose it to obtain foreign intelligence.

But the legality of the activity does not remove from the executive or from Congress the responsibility to take steps, within their power, to seek an accommodation between the vital public and private interests involved. In our effort to seek such an accommodation, the Department has adopted standards and procedures designed to ensure the reasonableness under the Fourth Amendment of electronic surveillance and to minimize to the extent practical the intrusion on individual interests. As I have stated, it is the Department's policy to authorize electronic surveillance for foreign intelligence purposes only when the subject is a foreign power on an agent of a foreign power. By the term "agent" I mean a conscious agent; the agency must be of a special kind and must relate to activities of great concern to the United States for foreign intelligence or counterintelligence reasons. In addition, at present, there is no warrantless electronic surveillance directed against any American citizen, and although it is conceivable that circumstances justifying such surveillance may arise in the future, I will not authorize the surveillance unless it is clear that the American citizen is an active, conscious agent or collaborator of a foreign power. In no event, of course, would I authorize any warrantless surveillance against domestic persons or organizations such as those involved in the *Keith* case. Surveillance without a warrant will not be conducted for purposes of security against domestic or internal threats. It is our policy, moreover, to use the Title III procedure whenever it is possible and appropriate to do so, although the statutory provisions regarding probable cause, notification and prosecutive purpose make it unworkable in all foreign intelligence and many counterintelligence cases.

The standards and procedures that the Department has established within the United States seek to ensure that every request for surveillance receives thorough and impartial consideration before a decision is made whether to institute it. The process is elaborate and time-consuming, but it is necessary if the public interest is to be served and individual rights safeguarded.

I have just been speaking about telephone wiretapping and microphone surveillances which are reviewed by the Attorney General. In the course of its investigation, the Committee has become familiar with the more technologically sophisticated and complex electronic surveillance activities of other agencies. These surveillance activities present somewhat different legal questions. The communications conceivably might take place entirely outside the United States. That fact alone, of course, would not automatically remove the agencies' activities from scrutiny under the Fourth Amendment since at times even communications abroad may involve a legitimate privacy interest of American citizens. Other communications conceivably might be exclusively between foreign powers and their agents and involve no American terminal. In such a case, even though American citizens may be discussed, this may raise less significant, or perhaps no significant, questions under the Fourth Amendment. But the primary concern, I suppose, is whether reasonable minimization procedures are employed with respect to use and dissemination.

With respect to all electronic surveillance, whether conducted within the United States or abroad, it is essential that efforts be made to minimize as much as possible the extent of the intrusion. Much in this regard can be done by modern technology. Standards and procedures can be developed and effectively deployed to limit the scope of the intrusion and the use to which its product is put. Various mechanisms can provide a needed assurance to the American people that the activity is undertaken for legitimate foreign intelligence purposes, and not for political or other improper purposes. The procedures used should not be ones which by indirection in fact target American citizens and resident aliens where these individuals would not themselves be appropriate targets. The proper minimization criteria can limit the activity to its justifiable and necessary scope.

Another factor must be recognized. It is the importance or potential importance of the information to be secured. The activity may be undertaken to obtain information deemed necessary to protect the nation against actual or potential attack or other hostile acts of a foreign power, to obtain foreign intelligence information deemed essential to the security of the United States, or to protect national security information against foreign intelligence activities.

Need is itself a matter of degree. It may be that the importance of some information is slight, but that might be impossible to gauge in advance; the significance of a single bit of information may become apparent only when joined to intelligence from other sources. In short, it is necessary to deal in probabilities. The importance of information gathered from foreign establishments and agents may be regarded generally as high—although even here there may be wide variations. At the same time, the effect on individual liberty and security—at least of American citizens—caused by methods directed exclusively to foreign agents, particularly with minimization procedures, would be very slight.

There may be regulatory and institutional devices other than the warrant requirement that would better assure that intrusions for national security and foreign intelligence purposes reasonably balance the important needs of government and of individual interests. In assessing possible approaches to this problem it may be useful to examine the practices of other Western democracies. For example, England, Canada and West Germany each share our concern about the confidentiality of communications within their borders. Yet each recognizes the right of the executive to intercept communications without a judicial warrant in cases involving suspected espionage, subversion and other national security intelligence matters.

In Canada and West Germany, which have statutes analogous to Title III, the executive in national security cases is exempt by statute from the requirement that judicial warrants be obtained to authorize surveillance of communications. In England, where judicial warrants are not required to authorize surveillance of communications in criminal investigations, the relevant statutes recognize an inherent authority in the executive to authorize such surveillance in national security cases.[72] In each country, this authority is deemed to cover interception of mail and telegrams, as well as telephone conversations.

In all three countries, requests for national security surveillance may be made by the nation's intelligence agencies. In each, a Cabinet member is authorized to grant the request. In England and West Germany, however, interception of communications is intended to be a last resort, used only when the information being sought is likely to be unobtainable by any other means. It is interesting to note, however, that both Canada and

West Germany do require the executive to report periodically to the legislature on its national security surveillance activities. In Canada, the Solicitor General files an annual report with the Parliament setting forth the number of national security surveillances initiated, their average length, a general description of the methods of interception or seizure used and an assessment of their utility.

It may be that we can draw on these practices of other Western democracies, with appropriate adjustments to fit our system of separation of powers. The procedures and standards that should govern the use of electronic methods of obtaining foreign intelligence and of guarding against foreign threats are matters of public policy and values. They are of critical concern to the executive branch and to Congress, as well as to the courts. The Fourth Amendment itself is a reflection of public policy and values—an evolving accommodation between governmental needs and the necessity of protecting individual security and rights. General public understanding of these problems is of paramount importance, to assure that neither the executive, nor the Congress, nor the courts risk discounting the vital interests on both sides.

The problems are not simple. Evolving solutions probably will and should come—as they have in the past—from a combination of legislation, court decisions, and executive actions. The law in this area, as Lord Devlin once described the law of search in England, "is haphazard and ill defined."[73] It recognizes the existence and the necessity of the executive's power. But the executive and the legislature are, as Lord Devlin also said, "expected to act reasonably." The future course of the law will depend on whether we can meet that obligation.

A Proposed National Security Surveillance Statute

TESTIMONY BEFORE THE SENATE SELECT
COMMITTEE ON INTELLIGENCE

July 1, 1976

The Ford administration supported the establishment of a foreign electronic surveillance court with power to issue court orders in national security cases of the sort that other federal courts issued under the domestic wiretap statute. The bill that passed after the Ford administration ended was

in some respects different from the one discussed here. Levi's discussion
of the proposed bill's explicit recognition of residual Presidential power to
act without a court order—and the reasons for it—bear on the controversy
over post-9/11 electronic surveillance by the National Security Agency.

I am pleased to be here today to testify in support of S. 3197, a bill
that would authorize applications for court orders approving the use of
electronic surveillance to obtain foreign intelligence information. I want
to express . . . the great significance which I believe the bill to have. As I
am sure you know, the bill's provisions have evolved, from the initiative
of the President, through bipartisan cooperation and through discussion
between the executive branch and members of Congress, in an effort to
identify and serve the public interest. Enactment of the bill will, I believe,
provide major assurance to the public that electronic surveillance will be
used in the United States for foreign intelligence purposes pursuant to
carefully drawn legislative standards and procedures. The bill ensures accountability for official action. It compels the executive to scrutinize such
action at regular intervals. And it requires independent review at a crucial
point by a detached and neutral magistrate.

In providing statutory standards and procedures to govern the use
of electronic surveillance for foreign intelligence purposes in this country and in establishing critical safeguards to protect individual rights, the
bill also ensures that the President will be able to obtain information essential to protection of the nation against foreign threats. While guarding against abuses in the future, it succeeds, I trust, in avoiding the kind
of reaction against abuses of the past that focuses solely on these abuses,
but is careless of other compelling interests. To go in that direction would
bring a new instability and peril. In the area of foreign intelligence, the
avoidance of such cycles of reaction is the special responsibility of this
Committee. I know you are deeply conscious of this responsibility; I know
you are aware that it demands the most dispassionate attention, the most
scrupulous care. . . .

S. 3197 provides for the designation by the Chief Justice of seven district court judges, to whom the Attorney General, if he is authorized by
the President to do so, may make application for an order approving electronic surveillance within the United States for foreign intelligence purposes. The judge may grant such an order only if he finds that there is
probable cause to believe that the target of the surveillance is a foreign
power or an agent of a foreign power, and if a Presidential appointee con-

firmed by the Senate has certified that the information sought is indeed foreign intelligence information that cannot feasibly be gained by less intrusive techniques. Such surveillances may not continue longer than 90 days without securing renewed approval from the court. There is an emergency provision in the bill which is available in situations in which there is no possibility of preparing the necessary papers for the court's review in time to obtain the information sought in the surveillance. In such circumstances the Attorney General may authorize the use of electronic surveillance for a period of no more than 24 hours. The Attorney General would be required to notify a judge at the time of the authorization that such a decision has been made and to submit an application to the judge within 24 hours. Finally, the Attorney General must report annually both to the Congress and the Administrative Office of the United States Courts statistics on electronic surveillance pursuant to the bill's procedures. . . .

The bill responds . . . , not to constitutional necessity, but to the need for the branches of government to work together to overcome the fragmentation of the present law among the areas of legislation, judicial decisions and administrative action, and to achieve the coherence, stability and clarity in the law and practice that alone can assure necessary protection of the nation's safety and of individual rights. After 36 years in which succeeding Presidents have thought some use of this technique was essential, I believe the time has come when Congress and the executive together can take much-needed steps to give clarity and coherence to a great part of the law in this area, the part of the law that concerns domestic electronic surveillance of foreign powers and their agents for foreign intelligence purposes. To bring greater coherence to this field, one must, of course, build on the thoughts and experiences of the past; to give reasonable recognition, as the judicial decisions in general have done, to the confidentiality, judgments and discretion that the President's constitutional responsibilities require; to give legislative form to the standards and procedures that experience suggests; and to provide added assurance by adapting a judicial warrant procedure to the unique characteristics of this area. . . .

The bill allows foreign intelligence surveillance only of persons who there is probable cause to believe are agents of a foreign power. Moreover, the agency must be of a particular kind, directly related to the kinds of foreign power activities in which the government has a legitimate foreign intelligence interest. Thus, persons—not citizens or resident aliens— are deemed agents only if they are officers or employees of a foreign power. The standard is much higher for a citizen or resident alien. For the purpose of this bill, a citizen or resident alien can be found to be an agent only if there is probable cause to believe that the person is acting "pursuant to the direction of a foreign power," and "is engaged in clandestine intelligence activities, sabotage, or terrorist activities, or who conspires with, or knowingly aids or abets such a person in engaging in such activities." . . .

I understand that there have been suggestions to the Committee that electronic surveillance of citizens and permanent resident aliens should not be allowed absent a determination that such persons are violating federal law. My own view is that the concept of "foreign agent" safely cannot be limited in this way. As I noted in a letter to Senator [Edward] Kennedy, most of the activities that would, under the bill, allow surveillance of citizens and resident aliens, constitute federal crimes; other foreign agent activities—for example, foreign espionage to acquire technical data about industrial processes or knowledge about foreign personnel and facilities in this country—do not constitute federal crimes. Yet information about the latter activities may be vital to the national interest, not because the activities are or should be criminal, but because they are undertaken clandestinely within the United States "pursuant to the direction of a foreign power," the standard employed in the bill.

The point is critical. I realize that it has been suggested that federal criminal statutes could be broadened sufficiently to reach all clandestine activities of foreign agents covered by the bill's standard. Of course doing so would in no way limit the bill's reach. More important, any such effort would be based on a fundamental misconception. The purpose of criminalization, and of prosecutions for crime, is to deter certain activities deemed contrary to the public interest. The purpose of foreign intelligence surveillances is, of course, to gain information about the activities of foreign agents, not so much because those activities are dangerous in themselves—although they almost always are—but because they provide knowledge about the hostile actions and intentions and capabilities of foreign powers, knowledge vital to the safety of the nation. Indeed, it may be the case, and has been the case on occasions in the past, that such knowledge, provided through monitoring foreign agent activities, is more vital to the nation's safety than preventing or deterring the activities through criminal prosecutions. In short, the question, for purposes of properly limiting foreign intelligence surveillances, is not whether activities of foreign agents are now, or should be made, criminal offenses, but rather whether the activities are such that knowledge of them, gained through carefully restricted and controlled means, is essential to protection from foreign threats. While the answers to these two questions have a high correlation, the correlation is by no means necessarily complete.

I know that a certain discomfort comes in departing from the criminal law model of allowing searches only to obtain evidence of a crime. But the probable cause and reasonableness standards of the Fourth Amendment are not measured exclusively by the interest in detecting and thus deterring violations of criminal law. Searches for purposes other than criminal law enforcement historically have been permissible, if reasonable in light of the circumstances and the governmental interest involved. Information concerning the activities of foreign agents engaged in intelligence, espionage or sabotage activities is a valid—indeed a vital—government interest. I believe that the interest should be the proper standard of permissible surveillances under this legislation.

In addition to requiring that there be probable cause to believe that the subject of the proposed surveillance is an agent of a foreign power, the bill also provides that the Assistant to the President for National Security Affairs or another appropriate executive official appointed by the President and confirmed by the Senate must certify to the court that the information sought and described in the application is foreign intelligence information. Such information is defined in the bill as "information deemed necessary to the ability of the United States to protect itself against actual or potential attack or other hostile acts of a foreign power or its agents"; "information with respect to foreign powers or territories, which because of its importance is deemed essential to (a) the security or national defense of the Nation or (b) the conduct of the foreign affairs of the United States"; or "information deemed necessary to the ability of the United States to protect the national security against foreign intelligence activities."

I understand it has been suggested to the Committee that the court, in passing on applications for electronic surveillances, should be required to determine whether the information sought is foreign intelligence information as defined in the bill, rather than accepting the certification to that effect by a high Presidential appointee with national security responsibilities. I think the definition of "foreign intelligence information" contained in the bill itself indicates why this proposal would be unwise. The determination of whether information is or is not foreign intelligence information necessarily will require the exercise of judgment as to the degree of importance and need—judgment that must be informed by the most precise knowledge of national defense and foreign relations problems, and accurate perception of legitimate national security needs. Unless judges are to be given a continuing responsibility of an executive type, with constant access to the range of information necessary, under the proposal, to deal intelligently with the questions they would face, I doubt that the courts generally would be willing to substitute their judgments for those which the executive already has made. Of course, if mistakes are made, the costs could be incalculable. It must be noted in this connection that, in major part, it was precisely the felt incapacity of the courts to make judgments of this sort, and recognition that responsibility for such judgments properly resides in the executive, that led the Fifth Circuit in *Brown*[74] and the Third Circuit in *Butenko*[75] to conclude that the Fourth Amendment imposes no warrant requirement in this area. Indeed, the proposal could work a result quite the reverse of what its proponents would want. There would be a certain ease in proposing surveillance if the responsibility for determining its need lay ultimately with the court.

The point cannot be stressed too strongly. As it now stands, the bill places the responsibility for determining need where it belongs—in those officials who have the knowledge, experience and responsibility to make the judgment, and who have been nominated by the President and confirmed by the Senate to aid in carrying out his constitutional duty to protect the nation against foreign threats. With such responsibility clearly placed, there comes, in the long term at least, accountability—to the President, of course, but ultimately to the Congress, and to the people. I believe that this protection provided by clearly focused responsibility, when coupled with the probable clause requirement of the bill, a requirement that demands a kind of judgment the courts can responsibly make, ensures reasonable and certain barriers to abuse.

Finally, I want to express my understanding of the bill's Section 2528, which deals with the reservation of *Presidential Power*.[76] The bill's definition of electronic surveillance limits its scope, to gain foreign intelligence information when the target is a foreign power or its agents, to interceptions within the United States. The bill does not purport to cover interceptions of all international communications where, for example, the interception would be accomplished outside of the United States, or, to take another example, a radio transmission does not have both the sender and all intended recipients within the United States. Interception of international communications, beyond those covered by the bill, involves special problems and circumstances that do not fit the analysis and system this bill would impose. This is not to say that the development of legislative safeguards in the international communications area is impossible. I know it will be extremely difficult and will involve different considerations. I believe it will be unfortunate, therefore, to delay the creation of safeguards in the area with which this bill deals until the attempt is made to cover what is essentially a different area with different problems. An additional reason for the reservation of Presidential power is that, even in the area covered by the bill, it is conceivable that there may be unprecedented, unforeseen circumstances of the utmost danger not contemplated in the legislation in which restrictions unintentionally would bring paralysis where all would regard action as imperative. The Presidential power provision, therefore, simply makes clear that the bill was not intended to affect Presidential powers in areas beyond its scope, including areas which, because of utmost danger, were not contemplated by Congress in its enactment. In the reservation of Presidential power, where the circumstances are beyond the scope or events contemplated in the bill, the bill in no way expands or contracts, confirms or denies, the President's constitutional powers. As the Supreme Court said of Section 2511(3) of Title III, "Congress simply left Presidential powers where it found them."[77]

In conclusion I want to emphasize the critical safeguards the bill would erect: clear accountability for official action, scrutiny of the action by executive officials at regular intervals and prior, independent judgment, as provided, by a detached, neutral magistrate. I believe that the bill's enactment would be a significant accomplishment in the service of the liberty and security of our people.

Government Confidentiality and Individual Privacy

ASSOCIATION OF THE BAR OF THE CITY OF NEW YORK

April 28, 1975

The issue of executive branch confidentiality stood at the heart of the Watergate drama. It was against the backdrop of the attempt to use "executive privilege" to protect against the subpoena of President Nixon's secret Oval Office tapes that Attorney General Levi delivered this talk. When Nixon resigned, Congressional attention turned to the investigation of the intelli-

gence agencies, which led to demands that the executive branch turn over to investigating committees large amounts of highly classified information. Inside the executive branch, Levi had successfully argued that the Justice Department, not the intelligence agencies, would decide what to divulge and what to refuse to divulge on the basis of a privilege of executive branch confidentiality. He was inclined to provide Congress a lot of what it asked for, which caused tension with some of the intelligence agencies and the Departments of State and Defense. But at the same time he felt it essential to reestablish the legitimacy of the idea of executive privilege, which was the purpose of this talk.

I would like to speak to you this evening about confidentiality and democratic government. The subject is an important one. It is complicated and has many facets. I do not suggest there are easy answers. I do suggest, however, that public understanding of the issues involved and the relationship among the issues is extremely important. The bar as a profession has an enormous responsibility to help clarify these issues. My belief is that understanding may be increased by putting together certain doctrines and values with which most of us would agree. The relationship among these doctrines and values may have been obscured in the recent past. If hard cases sometimes make bad law, emergency situations also have distorted our perspective. The public good requires that we try to correct that distortion.

In recent years, the very concept of confidentiality in government has been increasingly challenged as contrary to our democratic ideals, to the constitutional guarantees of freedom of expression and freedom of the press, and to our structure of government. Any limitation on the disclosure of information about the conduct of government, it is said, constitutes an abridgement of the people's right to know and cannot be justified. Indeed, it is asserted that governmental secrecy serves no purpose other than to shield improper or unlawful action from public scrutiny. This perception of the relationship between confidentiality and government has been shaped in large measure by the Watergate affair. The unfortunate legacy of that affair is a pervasive distrust of public officials and a popular willingness to infer impropriety. Skepticism and distrust have their value; they are not the only values to which our society must respond.

Our understanding of what is involved in the present controversy over government confidentiality is further inhibited by the very words sometimes used to describe the legal authority of the executive branch to with-hold information. I am referring, of course, to the term "executive priv-ilege." The term fails to express the nature of the interest at issue; its emotive value presently exceeds and consumes what cognitive value it might have possessed. The need for confidentiality is old, common to all governments, essential to ours since its formation. The phrase "executive privilege" is of recent origin. It apparently made its first appearance in the case law in a Court of Claims opinion by Mr. Justice Reed in 1958. It is only in the last few years that the phrase has preempted public discussion of government confidentiality, and the phrase has changed in meaning and connotation. Because it has been seen against the background of the separation of powers, and in this setting has often involved the directive of the President, the phrase has come to be viewed by the public as an ex-ercise of personal Presidential prerogative, protecting the President and his immediate advisers or subordinates in their role of advising or formu-lating advice for the President. Whether or not disclosure in response to Congressional demands should be withheld only by Presidential directive, sweeping as was the case with President Eisenhower's order, or specific as President Kennedy promised, the phrase "executive privilege" has ceased to be a useful description of what is involved in the need for confidential-ity. Our ability to analyze the legal and public interests involved has be-come a prisoner of our vocabulary. Much more is involved than the Pres-ident's personal prerogative standing against the people's right to know. The problem is the need for confidentiality and its limitations in the pub-lic interest for the protection of the people in our country.

Let me suggest starting points for an analysis of the place of govern-ment confidentiality in our society. Government confidentiality does not stand alone. It is closely related to the individual's need for privacy and the recognition we frequently give to the needs of organizations for a de-gree of secrecy about their affairs. It also exists alongside the American citizenry's need to know and government's own right to investigate and discover what it needs to know. These rights are not always consistent or fully compatible. They are circumscribed where they conflict. Yet some-times these diverse interests are interrelated. One reason for confiden-tiality, for example, is that some information secured by government, if widely disseminated, would violate the rights of individuals to privacy. Other reasons for confidentiality in government go to the effectiveness—and sometimes the very existence—of important governmental activity.

Finally we should recognize that if there is a need for confidentiality, it is not necessarily based upon the doctrine of separation of powers found in our Constitution.

That doctrine may condition or shape the exercise of confidentiality, but governments having no doctrine of separation of powers have an essential need for confidentiality, and the doctrine does not diminish the need.

At the most general level of analysis, the question of confidentiality in government cannot be divorced from the broader question of confidentiality in the society as a whole. The recognition of a need for it reflects a basic truth about human beings, whether in the conduct of their private lives or in their service with the government. Throughout its history our society has recognized that privacy is an essential condition for the attainment of human dignity—for the very development of the individuality we value—and for the preservation of the social, economic and political welfare of the individual. Indiscriminate exposure to the world injures irreparably the freedom and spontaneity of human thought and behavior and places both the person and property of the individual in jeopardy.

As a result, protections against unwarranted intrusion whether by the government or public have become an essential feature of our legal system. Testimonial privileges protect the confidentiality of the most intimate and sensitive human relationships—between husband and wife, lawyer and client, doctor and patient, priest and penitent. A number of the rights enumerated in the Constitution's first ten amendments are said to cast "penumbras" which overlap to produce the "right of privacy," a shadow that obscures from public view and intrusion certain aspects of human affairs. Several amendments—most obviously the First and Fourth—mark off measures of confidentiality. The First Amendment—guaranteeing freedom of expression—shields the confidentiality of a person's thoughts and beliefs. The Fourth Amendment protects the "right of the people to be secure in their persons, houses, papers, and effects against unreasonable searches and seizures." In spirit this is an expression of the confidentiality of a person and his property and a recognition that a fundamental element of individuality would be sacrificed if all aspects of one's life were exposed to public view. In *Katz v. United States*[78] the Court held that the Fourth Amendment guards not only the privacy of the person but also the confidentiality of his communications.

The need for confidentiality applies not only to individuals but also to groups, professions and other social organizations. The Supreme Court in *NAACP v. Alabama*[79] noted that public scrutiny of membership lists might well expose the members to "economic reprisal, loss of employment, threat of physical coercion, and other manifestations of public hostility" and thereby condition their freedom of association upon their payment of an intolerable price. The point of the case is plain enough. Public disclosure would have destroyed the NAACP. Confidentiality was indispensable to its very existence. The claim of the news media for a privilege to protect the confidentiality of their sources of information is based on a belief that public disclosure of news sources, coupled with the embarrassment and reprisals that might ensue, could well deter informers from confiding in reporters. It would diminish the free flow of information. Another manifestation of the need for confidentiality of groups may be found in the law's protection of trade secrets. Again, businesses require some privacy as a prerequisite to economic survival.

Confidentiality is a prerequisite to the enjoyment of many freedoms we value most. The effective pursuit of social, economic and political goals often demands privacy of thought, expression and action. The legal rights created in recognition of that need undoubtedly infringe on the more generalized right of the society as a whole to know. But the absence of these legal rights would deprive our society of the quality we prize most highly.

The rationale for confidentiality does not disappear when applied to government. Indeed the Supreme Court recently noted that confidentiality at the highest level of government involves all the values normally deferred to in protecting the privacy of individuals and, in addition, "the necessity for protection of the public interest in candid, objective, and even blunt or harsh opinions in Presidential decisionmaking."[80]

I doubt if we would wish the conferences of the United States Supreme Court to be conducted in public. We accept as fact that each Justice must be free to confer in confidence with his colleagues and with his law clerks if decisions are to be reached effectively and responsibly. And insofar as the product of the Supreme Court is primarily its words, the words it speaks publicly must be shaped and nurtured with care. We realize that some words are so important that their meaning should not be diluted by exposure of the often ambiguous process by which they were chosen.

For similar reasons, confidentiality is required in the decision-making processes within the executive branch. As the Court recently stated, "Human experience teaches that those who expect public dissemination of their remarks may well temper candor with a concern for appearances and for their own interests to the detriment of the decisionmaking process."[81]

Now I realize that linking law's protection of personal or organizational privacy with the government's need for confidentiality may seem disingenuous. It is of course true that a good deal of the law protecting individual and organizational privacy has been created to guard against the intrusion of government. But the origin of the threat to privacy should not obscure the value to be protected. It is the underlying wisdom about human nature found in the law of individual privacy that suggests the analogy. Much as we are used to regarding government as an automaton — a faceless, mechanical creature — government is composed of human beings acting in concert, and much of its effectiveness depends upon the candor, courage and compassion of those individual citizens who compose it. They are vulnerable to the same fears and doubts as individuals outside government. Undoubtedly we expect government officials to rise to the responsibilities they must meet. But this is just as true of the demands of private life.

Moreover, the law's protection of privacy does not only go to individuals but also to organizations, some of which rightly regard themselves as important adjuncts and correctives to the government. Just as the ability of these organizations to function effectively has come within the law's concern, so must the ability of government to function.

Yet of course there is another side — a limit to secrecy. As a society we are committed to the pursuit of truth and to the dissemination of information upon which judgments may be made. This commitment is embodied in the First Amendment to our Constitution. In a democracy, the guarantee of freedom of expression achieves special significance. The people are the rulers; they are in charge of their own destiny; government depends on the consent of the governed. If the people are the rulers, then the people must have the right to discuss freely the issues relevant to the conduct of their government. As Professor [Alexander] Meiklejohn noted, the First Amendment is thus an integral part of the plan for intelligent self-government.[82] But it is equally clear that it is not enough that the people be able to discuss these issues freely. They must also have access to the information required to resolve those issues correctly. Thus, basic to the theory of democracy is the right of the people to know about the operation of their government. Our theory of government seeks an informed electorate. As James Madison wrote: "A popular government without popular information, or the means of acquiring it, is but a prologue to a farce or a tragedy; or, perhaps both. Knowledge will forever govern ignorance: And a people who mean to be their own governors, must arm themselves with the power which knowledge gives."[83]

So it has been urged that the news media should enjoy under the First Amendment an extraordinary right of access to information held by the government. Indeed, it cannot be doubted that our press has assumed a special role as an indispensable communicator of information vital to an informed citizenry. Investigative reporting, however annoying, has often served the public well by discovering governmental abuse and corruption.

The concern over the need of the general public for access to information about government has not gone unanswered. The Freedom of Information Act has conferred a visitatorial right on each citizen to inquire into the myriad workings of government. It is not an exaggeration to observe that the broad provisions of the Act have engendered a general uncertainty as to whether disclosure of almost any government document might not be compelled. The administrative burdens of compliance with the Act are enormous. The demands for information have constantly increased. . . . At present, the information released by the federal government pursuant to the Act, especially when coupled with information released as a matter of course, make it difficult to maintain that the volume of facts and opinions disclosed to the public about the conduct of government is not truly of leviathan proportions. Yet claims persist that even the Act does not extend far enough and that official secrecy still holds too much sway.

As is so often the case in human affairs, we are met with a conflict of values. A right of complete confidentiality in government could not only produce a dangerous public ignorance but also destroy the basic representative function of government. But a duty of complete disclosure would render impossible the effective operation of government. Some confidentiality is a matter of practical necessity. Moreover, neither the concept of democracy nor the First Amendment confer on each citizen an unbridled power to demand access to all the information within the government's possession. The people's right to know cannot mean that every individual or interest group may compel disclosure of papers and effects of government officials whenever they bear on public business. Under our Constitution, the people are the sovereign but they do not govern by the random and self-selective interposition of private citizens. Rather ours is a representative democracy, as in reality all democracies are, and our government is an expression of the collective will of the people. The concept of democracy and the principles of majority rule require a special role of the government in determining the public interest. The government must be accountable, so it must be given the means, including some confidentiality, to discharge its responsibilities.

For similar reasons, the special role of the news media cannot be understood to include a trespassorial easement over all that lies within the governmental realm. The Supreme Court addressed the point when it said: "It has generally been held that the First Amendment does not guarantee the press a constitutional right of access to information not available to the public generally. . . . Despite the fact that news gathering may be hampered, the press is regularly excluded from grand jury proceedings, our own conferences, the meetings of other official bodies in executive session, and the meetings of private organizations."[84]Just last term the Court reaffirmed this principle.

Demands by Congress for information from the executive, while obviously raising problems of comity among the branches of government, do not change the need of all governments, however organized, for some confidentiality. Such demands, however, emphasize the point that the preservation of confidentiality where really necessary requires special modes of responsibility, as it indeed does in the executive branch. The risk that the confidentiality of information may be breached, even by inadvertence, is of course ever present. In this country, constitutional guarantees create special limitations on the ability of the executive to prevent unauthorized disclosure of information. The Speech and Debate Clause, for example, confers on members of Congress and their aides absolute immunity from civil or criminal liability, including questioning by a grand jury, for conduct related to their legislative functions. The *Gravel* case,[85] in particular raises the question whether laws legitimately restricting the dissemination of classified or national defense information can provide any assurance of confidentiality. *New York Times Co. v. United States*,[86] or the so-called *Pentagon Papers Case*, further demonstrates the inability of the government to prevent publication of classified documents. The apparent lesson to be drawn from such cases is that once information is improperly released, its publication to the world becomes a certainty.

If the dissemination to Congress of some information is to be limited, acquiescence in this responsibility and limitation becomes a duty which must be willingly recognized. The choice which must be made concerns

the extent of dissemination, the likely travels of disclosure and the consequences which may follow. Successful democracies achieve an accommodation among competing values.

No provision of the Constitution, of course, expressly accords to any
branch the right to require information from another. Article II does state
that the President "shall from time to time give to the Congress information of the State of the Union," but the decision as to what information to
provide is left to the discretion of the President.

So far I have referred only to the free and candid discussion of policy matters that is promoted by the governmental confidentiality. There
are, however, several additional contexts in which confidentiality is also
required and where the primary effect of disclosure would be to prevent legitimate and important government activity from occurring altogether. Aspects of law enforcement, including the detection of crime and
the preparation of criminal prosecutions, cannot be conducted wholly in
public. Of particular importance is the confidentiality of investigative files
and reports. The rationale for confidentiality in this regard was stated by
Attorney General Robert Jackson in 1941 in declining to release investigative reports of the Federal Bureau of Investigation demanded by a
Congressional committee. The Attorney General wrote: "[D]isclosure of
the reports would be of serious prejudice to the future usefulness of the
Federal Bureau of Investigation. . . . [M]uch of this information is given
in confidence and can only be obtained upon pledge not to disclose its
sources. A disclosure of the sources would embarrass informants—
sometimes in their employment, sometimes in their social relations, and
in extreme cases might even endanger their lives. We regard the keeping of faith with confidential informants as an indispensable condition of
future efficiency. Disclosure could infringe on the privacy of those mentioned in the reports and might constitute "the grossest kind of injustice
to innocent individuals." Mr. Jackson observed that "investigative reports
include leads and suspicions, and sometimes even the statements of ma-
licious and misinformed people," and that "a correction never catches up
with an accusation."[87]

Government must also have the ability to preserve the confidentiality of matters relating to the national defense. Espionage statutes and
national security classification procedures are examples of the acknowledged need to prevent unauthorized dissemination of sensitive information that could endanger the military preparedness of the nation. The
Supreme Court addressed the issue in *United States v. Reynolds*, where

disclosure of information possibly relating to military secrets was sought in the context of a civil suit. The Court stated: "It may be possible to satisfy the court, from all the circumstances of the case, that there is a reasonable danger that compulsion of the evidence will expose military matters which, in the interest of national security, should not be divulged. When this is the case, the occasion for the privilege is appropriate, and the court should not jeopardize the security which the privilege is meant to protect by insisting upon an examination of the evidence, even by the judge alone, in chambers."[88] The value of safeguarding the confidentiality of national security intelligence activities has recently been made even more apparent with the publication of Fred [F. W.] Winterbotham's book, *The Ultra Secret*.[89] Britain's success in learning the Germans' cipher in 1939 later proved to be an important factor in the Allies' victory in World War II. Could anyone claim that Britain should not have worked secretly in peacetime to prepare itself in case of war? Or that once prepared, it should have disclosed that it had broken the code? To have disclosed that information would have destroyed its usefulness.

Closely related to this is the need for confidentiality in the area of foreign affairs. History is filled with instances where effective diplomacy demanded secrecy. In the first of his Fourteen Points, President Wilson exuberantly proclaimed his support for "Open Covenants of Peace openly arrived at." As Lord Devlin has recently pointed out, "What Wilson meant to say was that international agreements should be published; he did not mean that they should be negotiated in public."[90] Under our Constitution, the President has special authority in foreign affairs. In numerous decisions, the Supreme Court has recognized the unique nature of the President's diplomatic role and its relationship to confidentiality. Thus, in *United States v. Curtiss-Wright*, the court stated that Congress must

> ... often accord to the President a degree of discretion and freedom from statutory restriction that would not be admissible were domestic affairs alone involved. Moreover, he, not Congress, has ... confidential sources of information. He has his agents in the form of diplomatic, consular, and other officials. Secrecy in respect of information gathered by them may be highly necessary, and the premature disclosure of it productive of harmful results. Indeed, so clearly is this true that the first President refused to accede to a request to lay before the House of Representatives instructions, correspondence and documents relating to the negotiation of the Jay Treaty—a refusal the wisdom of which ... has never since been doubted.[91]

The inappropriateness of the judicial branch requiring disclosure of foreign policy information was emphasized in *C & S Air Lines v. Waterman Steamship Corp.*, where the court said: "The President, both as Commander-in-Chief and as the Nation's organ for foreign affairs, has available intelligence services whose reports neither are nor ought to be published to the world. It would be intolerable that courts, without the relevant information, should review and perhaps nullify actions of the Executive taken on information properly held secret."[92] In *United States v. Nixon*, the Court strongly intimated that disclosure of information held by the executive would not be required even in the context of a criminal trial if "diplomatic or sensitive national security secrets" were involved,[93] and expressly noted that "[a]s to these areas of Art. II duties the courts have traditionally shown the utmost deference to Presidential responsibilities."[94]

In the context of law enforcement, national security and foreign policy the effect of disclosure would often be to frustrate completely the government's right to know. Government ignorance in these areas clearly and directly endangers what has been said to be the basic function of any government, the protection of the security of the individual and his property.

Even as to national security and foreign policy, of course, the tensions between confidentiality and disclosure continue to place stress on the fragile structure of our government. The desire of Congress to know more about the activities of government in these areas, for example, has recently produced a legislative proposal that would impose extraordinary burdens on the ability of the executive to conduct electronic surveillance even where foreign powers are involved. It would require the government not only to procure a court order as a precondition to electronic surveillance, but also to report to both the Administrative Office of the United States Courts and to the Committee on the Judiciary of both the Senate and the House of Representatives detailed information, including a transcript of the proceedings in which the order was requested, the names of all parties and places involved in the intercepted communications, the disposition of all records and logs of the interceptions and the identity of and action taken by all individuals who had access to the interceptions.

The wisdom of this scheme is dubious at best, since it would represent a severe incursion on the executive's ability both to guard against the intelligence activities of foreign powers and to obtain foreign intelligence information essential to the security of this nation....

It is by no means clear that [such] legislative measures are compelled by the Fourth Amendment. . . . [It is] helpful to recall the exact words of the Fourth Amendment: "The right of the people to be secure in their persons, houses, papers, and effects against unreasonable searches and seizures shall not be violated." It is the "people" whose security is to be protected, not that of foreign powers. The Fourth Amendment was intended to protect the privacy, not of other nations, but of the "We the People" of this nation. Nor is there a requirement of public disclosure inherent in the Fourth Amendment. It was not designed to compel exposure of the government, but to prevent the unreasonable exposure of the individual. I think all of us understand the impulse which leads to such proposals. It comes in part from a desire to protect citizens from harassment and from unfair prosecutions and personal abuses of this nature. But this is to misstate the purpose and need of such surveillance and therefore to misconceive the remedy for possible abuses.

As history has shown, implicit in the concept of government, including democratic government, is the need and hence right to maintain the confidentiality of information. Confidentiality cannot be without limit, of course, and must be balanced against the right of all citizens to be informed about the conduct of their government. An exercise of discretion is clearly required. In each instance the respective interests must be assessed so that ultimately the public interest may be served.

In most governments, the question of which governmental body shall have the authority to determine the proper scope of the confidentiality interest poses no problem. Under our Constitution, however, the answer is complicated by the tripartite nature of the federal government and the doctrine of separation of powers. But history, I believe, has charted the course. For the most part, we have entrusted to each branch of government the decision as to whether, and under what circumstances, information properly within its possession should be disclosed to the other branches and to the public. Competing claims among the branches for information have been resolved mainly by the forces of political persuasion and accommodation. We have placed our trust that each branch will exercise its right of confidentiality in a responsible fashion, with the people as the ultimate judge of their conduct.

The only exception to this rule was established by the Supreme Court last term in *United States v. Nixon.* The Court held in effect that need for demonstrably relevant and material evidence in the context of a criminal trial prevailed over the need of the executive for confidentiality in decision-making. The Court also held, however, that the executive's right of confidentiality was founded in the Constitution and in the doctrine of separation of powers. Thus, the Court stated: "The privilege is fundamental to the operation of government and inextricably rooted in the separation of powers under the Constitution. . . . Nowhere in the Constitution . . . is there any explicit reference to a privilege of confidentiality, yet to the extent this interest relates to the effective discharge of a President's powers, it is constitutionally based."[95] The Court was careful to emphasize that the information sought was not claimed to involve military, diplomatic or sensitive national security secrets, the disclosure of which the Court has repeatedly suggested could never be compelled and which as a matter of historical fact no court has ever compelled.

The practice as between the executive and the Congress has been of a similar order. Each branch has traditionally accorded to the other that proper degree of deference and respect commanded by the doctrine of separation of powers and by the concomitant need for confidentiality in government. Attorney General Jackson, in declining to disclose investigative files to the Congressional committee, observed that the precedents for such refusals extended to the very foundation of the nation and to the administration of President Washington. He concluded: "This discretion in the executive branch has been upheld and respected by the judiciary. The courts have repeatedly held that they will not and cannot require the executive to produce such papers when in the opinion of the executive their production is contrary to the public interest. The courts have also held that the question whether the production of the papers would be against the public interest is one for the executive and not for the courts to determine."[96]

Congress, of course, has an oversight function under our Constitution. But that function has never been thought to include an absolute right of access to confidential information within the possession of the other branches. Its limits are necessarily defined by the legitimate need of the judiciary and the executive for confidentiality.

Comparative law may offer an insight in this regard. In resolving legal issues, we have often looked to Great Britain and the Parliament as helpful models. Many of our most cherished notions concerning justice and government have been shaped and influenced by the English tradition. The issue that presently confronts us is no exception. An examination of the British system reveals that little or no confidential information is ever disclosed by the Cabinet to parliamentary committees in the House of Commons. This is so despite the fact that maintaining the confidentiality of such information would be far easier than in this country. Parliamentary committees, for example, have far fewer members and staff than their American counterparts, thus appreciably minimizing the dangers of unauthorized disclosure. Moreover, the sweeping criminal provisions of the British Official Secrets Act, coupled with the absence of a First Amendment, deter unauthorized disclosure to a far greater extent than would be possible under our system.

More generally, having surveyed the democracies of Western Europe, it may be said without equivocation that it is not the practice of governments to disclose sensitive, national security or foreign policy information to parliamentary committees. Furthermore, Congressional committees in this country, through the cooperation and acquiescence of the executive, receive far more such information than do legislative counterparts in any other country.

The more general question of disclosure by government to the public may also be illuminated by a comparison between the American system and the Swedish system. Under the Freedom of the Press Act, which is a part of its constitution, Sweden is committed to the "principle of publicity," which states that both Swedish citizens and aliens alike shall have free access to all official documents. The extent of disclosure of official documents in Sweden is exceeded by few, if any, other governments in Western Europe. Sweden's principle of publicity is, however, subject to numerous exceptions specified in its Secrecy Act. These exceptions not only parallel but in many instances exceed the exceptions in our own Freedom of Information Act. It is also worth noting that under the Swedish Act the unauthorized release of a document excepted from disclosure subjects a civil servant to criminal liability. By contrast, under the Freedom of Information Act, it is the arbitrary failure to release a document required to be disclosed that subjects a civil servant to disciplinary action.

Again, when compared with the democratic governments in Western Europe, it is fair to conclude that there is by far a greater degree of public disclosure of information by the United States Government than by any other government. As Professor Gerhard Casper has recently written, "From the vantage point of comparative politics, I think, there can be little doubt that governmental *Geheimniskarämerei* (petty secretiveness) looms less large in the United States than anywhere else."[97]

Measured against any government, past or present, ours is an open society. But as in any society, conflicts among values and ideals persist, demanding continual reassessment and reflection. The problem which

I have discussed this evening is assuredly one of the most important of these conflicts. It touches on our most deeply-felt democratic ideals and the very security of our nation. I am reminded of the title which E. M. Forster gave to a collection of his essays, *Two Cheers for Democracy*. The third cheer, he suggested must still be earned. I do not share that hesitancy. The structure established by our Constitution itself represents a compromise and a genius for government.

What I have said is not intended to minimize in any way the need for candor between the government and the people to whom it is responsible. Indeed this talk is an exercise in candor — an attempt to confront the issues directly because the issues are there. The issues will not go away. The American public is misused if it does not understand that important values are involved, that these values must be balanced, and that among these values are confidentiality, the right of the people to know and the right of the government to obtain important information. No trick phrases will solve our problem. Reactions built upon crises in the immediate past are suspect. Rather we must reach back into the sources of our government, and to our own history of endeavor and accommodation, where wisdom has often been exercised to make the difficult choices.

As these choices are made I trust it is the bar's responsibility to enlighten them with understanding, to help all see them in perspective because that is essential for the future of our country and for the protection and freedom of our citizens.

Some Aspects of Separation of Powers

FOURTH SULZBACHER MEMORIAL LECTURE,
COLUMBIA LAW SCHOOL, NEW YORK[98]

December 2, 1975

I have chosen for the Sulzbacher Lecture in the bicentennial year to speak on some aspects of the separation of powers. It is a topic that has been of major importance since the birth of our Republic. Its significance as a special feature of our system of government continues to be recognized. In an essay written not long ago and recently reprinted, Scott Buchanan, searching for the essential spirit of our primary document, wrote, "All constitutions break down the whole governmental institution in parts with specific limited powers, but the Constitution of the United States is well known for its unusually drastic separation of powers."[99]

As we all know, in recent years there has been great controversy about the respective powers, limitations and responsibilities of the executive, legislative and judicial branches. During that period the Presidency was described by some writers as having become imperial. It appeared we might be developing an imperial judiciary as well. The idea of an imperial Congress is not unknown. The many-sided debate has been heated. This has emphasized the element of institutional conflict in the American constitutional system.

It is a recurring debate in America. It has often been the legacy of war and national scandal. In recent years it has taken concrete form in controversies about the power of the executive to withhold the expenditure of funds appropriated by the legislature; the power of the legislature to limit the executive's authority to use military force to protect the nation against foreign threats; the power of the executive to withhold information from the legislature and the judiciary; and the power of the legislature to publish documents taken from the executive.

The constitutional doctrine of separation of powers was invoked. Some have thought that the system has gone out of balance, that the imbalance can best be overcome by a reassertion of power by the Congress, which as the most democratic branch of government (or the branch mentioned first in the Constitution) should have primacy. Congressional supremacy is said to be at the heart of the American tradition which, after all, began in rebellion against prerogative and government without representation. We have had recent experience with the abuse of executive power. We have also seen the rise of modern totalitarian states and been reminded of the danger of the concentration of power in a single individual. But history has been mixed. Often, and for considerable periods of time, the concern in the United States has been with the weakness of the executive, not its strength. If we have forgotten this, it is only because memory is very short. There have been historical moments, some not so long ago, in which the great concern was about abuse of power by legislatures and their committees. Some have warned that Congressional resurgence threatens to be too great in reaction to the perceived lessons of recent history.

It may be useful to approach an understanding of the doctrine of separation of powers by looking to the origin of that idea in the interaction of intellectual theory and practical problems during the American revolutionary era. This reference to history will not resolve all the ambiguities of the doctrine of separation of powers. Perhaps the ambiguities ought not be resolved. Nor will a knowledge of the original understanding solve all our contemporary controversies. It may be that the expansion of governmental activity into wide areas of the nation's life and the corresponding growth of the federal bureaucracy have caused an irreversible change in our constitutional system that requires new modes of understanding. One example of the change is the movement for Congressional review of administrative action which is the product of expansive grants of authority by Congress to the executive at a time when judicially defined limitations on delegation have fallen.

The proposal for Congressional review of administrative action results in a new and ironic reversal of roles—the executive making laws and the legislature wielding, in effect, the veto, and often a one-house veto at that. We should also keep in mind that the disease of bureaucracy is as catching for the legislature as for any other branch.

History does not suggest complete answers to the questions we now ask ourselves. But in times of uncertainty when there are urgent calls for change, history may provide an understanding of the values thought to be served and the practical and salutary consequences thought to result from the separation of powers principle. It can help us calculate the consequences of proposed realignment of government power and what may be lost in the process.

The political theory developing in America through the period in which the Constitution was written was influenced by many sources. Writers of the era drew heavily upon classical accounts of the growth and decline of governments: Gibbon's first volume of *The Decline and Fall of the Roman Empire* was published, after all, in 1776. They also felt the fresh breath of new ideas. They read Voltaire and Rousseau. Adam Smith's *Wealth of Nations* was published in 1776, emphasizing the economic vitality of separating functions. The predominant experience of the American makers of government, however, was with the development of the British Constitution and the relationship of the British Crown and Parliament.

The political theory of the revolution was founded on a conception of the English experience advanced primarily by the radical Whigs. The central metaphor was that a compact existed between the rulers and the ruled by which the governors were authorized to act only so long as they did so in the interest of the nation as a whole. Liberty was conceived in terms of the right of the people collectively to act as a check and counterpoise to the actions of their rulers. The English Revolution of 1688 was seen as the result of the King's violation of the compact. After 1688 the House of Commons, as the institutional expression of one part of the nation, could limit the prerogative of the House of Lords, and more importantly, the King.

Yet before the American Revolution, the functioning of the British system, if not its elemental form, was being questioned. There was a fear that the colonies under British rule—and, indeed, Britain itself—were suffering moral decay of the sort that beset the republics of antiquity before their fall. There was also a characteristically ambivalent Calvinist notion that the colonists were chosen for unique greatness but that they had to struggle to attain it. The King and his officers were thought to have abused their power. Parliament offered the colonies no protection. In the Declaration of Independence and its bill of particulars against George III the colonists repeated the theory of 1688. The compact had again been broken.

Yet despite the complaints against the King and the scourge of the idea of hereditary monarchy in the writings of men such as Tom Paine, the ideology of the American Revolution was surprisingly moderate. As Gordon Wood has written, the colonists "revolted not against the English constitution but on behalf of it."[100]

This helps explain the influence in 1776 of Montesquieu, whose description of the British arrangement of government institutions, though it may be of questionable accuracy, in its primary intention was correct. Montesquieu emphasized the idea of separation of powers. "When the legislative and executive powers are united in the same person," Montesquieu wrote in *The Spirit of the Laws*, "there can be no liberty."[101] The doctrine of separation of powers took as its basis a particular view of men and power. It assumed that power corrupts. Its proponents, as Justice Frankfurter later wrote, "had no illusion that our people enjoyed biological or psychological or sociological immunities from the hazards of concentrated power."[102] The doctrine was based upon the skeptical idea that only the division of power among three government institutions—executive, legislative and judicial—could counteract the inevitable tendency of concentrated authority to overreach and threaten liberty.

But in 1776 the complaint was with the Crown. In the colonies the King, the executive power, had acted unchecked, often with the Parliament's—but not the colonists'—consent. Though the doctrine of separation of powers played a great role in the debate in 1776, it was seen as a means of controlling executive power, and its skeptical understanding of man and government and power did not wholly square with the buoyant optimism of the times, just as not so long ago the separation of powers seemed a frustrating barrier to the possible accomplishments which might follow from an assumed abundance of resources and to that creativity which could solve every problem. After 1776, as the new American states began to replace their colonial charters with new constitutions, strong language favoring separation of powers was a regular feature. As Gordon Wood has written, however, there was "a great discrepancy between the affirmations of the need to separate the several governmental departments and the actual political practice the state governments followed. It seems, as historians have noted, that Americans in 1776 gave only a verbal recognition to the concept of separation of powers in their Revolutionary constitutions, since they were apparently not concerned with a real division of departmental functions."[103] In 1776 separation of powers was a slogan; it meant that power was to be separated from the executive and given to legislatures.

After the Revolution was won, the optimism faded. The experience of the new American states with life under the Articles of Confederation and under the legislatures set up and made all-powerful in 1776 convinced George Washington that "[w]e have, probably, had too good an opinion of human nature in forming our confederation."[104]

The legislatures had assumed great power, and their rule—for a variety of reasons—was unstable. The supremacy of legislatures came to be recognized as the supremacy of faction and the tyranny of shifting majorities. The legislatures confiscated property, erected paper money schemes, suspended the ordinary means of collecting debts. They changed the law with great frequency. One New Englander complained: "The revised laws have been altered—realtered—made better—made worse; and kept in such a fluctuating position, that persons in civil commission scarce know what is law."[105]

Jefferson, in his *Notes on the State of Virginia*, wrote this stinging attack upon the interregnum period legislatures: "All the powers of government, legislative, executive and judiciary, result to the legislative body. The concentrating these in the same hands, is precisely the definition of despotic government. It will be no alleviation, that these powers will be exercised by a plurality of hands, and not by a single one. One hundred and seventy-three despots would surely be as oppressive as one. . . . And little will it avail us that they are chosen by ourselves. An elective despotism was not the government we fought for."[106]

The work of the Constitutional Convention of 1787 was in this respect a reaction to the unchecked power of the legislatures. In the later rewriting of history, the abuses to be corrected were sometimes seen solely in the context of federalism. But much more was involved. The doctrine of separation of powers, which had become a slogan for legislative supremacy in 1776, in 1787 was reinvigorated as a criticism of legislative power and was central to the theory of the new government. As Gordon Wood has written, "Tyranny was now seen as the abuse of power by any branch of government, even, and for some especially, by the traditional representatives of the people."[107] Madison wrote: "The accumulation of all powers, legislative, executive, and judiciary, in the same hands . . . may justly be pronounced the very definition of tyranny."[108] The liberty that was now emphasized was, as Wood has described, "the protection of individual rights against all governmental encroachments, particularly by the legislature, the body which the Whigs had traditionally cherished as the people's exclusive repository of their public liberty."[109] The structure of government had to be such that no single institution could exert all power. Against the "enterprising ambition" of legislative power, wrote Madison in *Federalist* 48, "which is inspired, by a supposed influence of the people, with an intrepid confidence in its own strength," the people should "indulge all their jealousy and exhaust all their precautions."[110] Hamilton in *Federalist* 71 warned:

> The representatives of the people in a popular assembly seem sometimes to fancy that they are the people themselves, and betray strong symptoms of impatience and disgust at the least sign of opposition from any other quarter; as if the exercise of its rights by either the executive or the judiciary were a breach of their privilege and an outrage to their dignity. They often appear disposed to exert an imperious control over the other departments; and as they commonly have the people on their side, they always act with such momentum as to make it very difficult for the other members of the government to maintain the balance of the Constitution.[111]

Hamilton's words and the *Federalist Papers* as a whole express two related aspects of the new American conception of politics that emerged from the experiences of the interregnum period. First, that the people and not the institutions of government are sovereign. The Constitution after all begins with "We the People." Second, that no institution of government is, or should be taken to be, the embodiment of society expressing the general will of the people. In the process of this fundamental shift away from the Whig theory and its conception of the British Constitution, the doctrine of separation of powers took on a new meaning. Each branch of government served the sovereign people. No branch could correctly claim to be the sole representative of the people. Representation was to be of different kinds according to the functions to be performed. Each branch derived its powers from the people, and its powers were subject to the limitations imposed by the constitutional grant of authority. Government power was divided among the branches, and a system of interdependence was erected by which each branch had certain limited powers to control the excesses of other branches. In this way it was hoped that the public interest could be achieved, and at the same time, liberty protected from tyranny. As Buchanan has written, "'We the People' are the authority that propagates the Constitution, a master law which in turn establishes other authorities or offices which in turn propagate other laws. . . . [T]he Constitution distinguishes three great offices, powers or functions: the legislative, the executive, and the judiciary; and to them are assigned respectively three uses of practical reason: the making of laws, the executing or administration of laws, and the adjudication of laws. Furthermore, the Constitution not only divides these functions but also separates them by making the institutions equal and independent."[112] The doctrine of federalism was based on a similar conception. The national government was made supreme, but only in a limited compass defined by limited powers. Thus, the sovereign people and the states retained all powers not delegated to the national government.

The compact between the rulers and the ruled had changed its fundamental terms. Rather than a general agreement to be governed for such time as the rulers acted in the interest of society as a whole, the new compact was seen to be something closer to a limited agency arrangement in which each branch of government was authorized to act in unique ways in limited areas. One must be cautious, as Alexander Bickel has taught, about using such contractual metaphors lest they make the institutions seem too sharply defined in their powers.[113] The provisions in the Constitution were, rather, the expression of compromises that mirror the sort of adaptation and accommodation envisioned by the process the Constitution set into motion. But there is no doubt that the separation of powers was consciously intended as a confrontation with problems to be solved, and in its new form an invention for the future.

The Congress was delegated enumerated legislative powers and such other power as was "necessary and proper" to the effectuation of the enumerated powers. The executive was to be made more energetic than it had been in the interregnum state constitutions. Whether executive power was meant to be limited by enumeration quickly became a matter of controversy between Hamilton and Madison once the Constitution was ratified. Some years ago Professor [William] Crosskey argued that the enumerated powers of the Congress were not so much a limitation on legislative power as a way of clearly stating the power of Congress so that the executive could not so easily encroach upon it. But Crosskey's concern was an opposition to states' rights, not with limiting the executive. And his argument was that the enumeration did not limit national power.[114] There was no question, however, that the Constitution meant to expand the power of the executive. "Energy in the Executive," wrote Hamilton in *Federalist* 70,[115] "is a leading character in the definition of good government. It is essential to the protection of the community against foreign attacks: It is not less essential to the steady administration of the laws, to the protection of property against those irregular and high handed combinations which sometimes interrupt the ordinary course of justice to the security of liberty against the enterprises and assaults of ambition, of faction, and of anarchy."[116] Jay, in *Federalist* 64, wrote that the President must be unitary and protected in the conduct of foreign affairs in part because those who would supply useful intelligence "would rely on the secrecy of the President" but would not confide "in that of the Senate and still less in that of a large popular Assembly."[117]

At the same time the judiciary, which had been subject to significant encroachments by the revolutionary period legislatures, began to be seen as another important bulwark against tyranny. Though distrusted before the Revolution as an arbitrary mechanism of the Crown, the courts rose dramatically in importance after the experiences of the interregnum period.[118] But the power courts were to assume was not that "energetic" power Hamilton asserted for the executive. It was a more passive power, not only to articulate and apply the principles of law with justice in individual cases but also to repel attacks, by the legislature or executive, on basic rights. It was a vital, but limited power. The view of the courts contained, I believe, a good deal of the continuing English view, articulated in our time by Lord Devlin, that "it would not be good for judges to act executively; it is better to expect executives to act judicially."[119] James Wilson, who in the Constitutional Convention debates favored judicial power to nullify constitutional statutes also warned against conferring "upon the judicial department a power superior, in its general nature, to that of the legislature."[120]

The constitutional system contemplated the possibility of disagreement among the branches, but it defined the channels through which those conflicts were to be resolved. Indeed, Madison was obliged to defend the draft constitution against the argument that the three branches had not been made separate enough. Appealing to Montesquieu, Madison wrote, "His meaning . . . can amount to no more than this, that where the *whole* power of one department is exercised by the same hands which possess the *whole* power of another department, fundamental principles of a free constitution are subverted."[121] Acting within its sphere, within the constitutional limits of its power and within the bounds placed by the institutional responsibilities of the other branches, each branch was to be supreme, subject only—ultimately, indirectly and in various ways—to the decisions of the people. Each branch had a degree of independence so that its activities would not be entirely taken over by another, but they were tied together with a degree of independence as well so that, in Madison's words, "ambition [could] be made to counteract ambition."[122]

The system also contemplated responsibility and accommodation, for though the branches were separate, they were part of one government. As Justice Jackson wrote, "While the Constitution diffuses power the better to secure liberty, it also contemplates that practice will integrate the dispersed powers into a workable government. It enjoins upon its branches separateness but interdependence, autonomy but reciprocity."[123]

The exhilaration of the Revolution and the despair of the misgovernment that followed it, the optimistic political philosophies of Locke and Rousseau and the pessimistic views of Montesquieu and Hobbes, these came together in the creation of the American republic. Michael Kammen has written: "What would eventually emerge from these tensions between liberty and authority, between society and its instruments of government? For one thing, a political style, a way of doing and viewing public affairs in which several sorts of biformities would be prevalent: pragmatic idealism, conservative liberalism, orderly violence, and moderate rebellion."[124] I would add to that list of paradoxes one more—skeptical optimism. It was this vision of man and government that formed the basis for the separation of powers doctrine.

At various times in the 19th century and after, the idea of the potential excellence of human nature and the trustworthiness of unchecked popular will reasserted itself. As Martin Diamond wrote recently in *Public Interest*: "In the 19th century, there were many who mocked Montesquieu for his fear of political power and for his cautious institutional strategies. ... But let those now mock who read the 20th century as warranting credence in such a conception of human nature, as entitling men to adventures in unrestrained power."[125]

The 19th century was a time of great Romantic idealism. The industrial revolution deified Energy, and the Romantic writers expressed their adulation because to them men and nature shared in the abundant energy and grace of life. The 20th century has slowly brought changes in this view, though in some respects it lingers. In literature the glorification of human energy and spirit is tempered by metaphors of entropy and humbling intellectual paradoxes. If the emphasis is still upon the self, that self shares the potential cruelty of nature, its ineluctable process of running down, and its fundamental impenetrability to observation. The skeptical vision embodied in the separation of powers doctrine again has its intellectual resonance.

But in the 19th century, particularly following the Civil War, there was a reemergence of the Whig theory that the legislature is the best expression of the people's will. Congress gained ascendency. During that period Woodrow Wilson finished his essay, *Congressional Government*.[126] It is an important work to study today since it challenges the American system of separation of powers. To Wilson the British parliamentary form of government seemed superior. He favored that system because to Wilson legislative ascendency and executive decline under our form of government seemed inevitable. The parliamentary system made the legislature responsible and effective and in that context provided for executive leadership. "The noble charter of fundamental law given us by the convention of 1787," he wrote, "is still our Constitution, but it is now our form of government rather in name than in reality, the *form of government* being one of nicely adjusted, ideal balances, while the actual form of our present government is simply a scheme of congressional supremacy. ... All niceties of constitutional restriction, and even many broad principles of constitutional limitation have been overridden and a thoroughly organized system of congressional control set up which gives a very rude negative to some theories of balance and some schemes for distributed powers."[127] To Wilson in the 1880s, the presidency had been incurably weakened.

"That high office has fallen from its just estate of dignity," he wrote, "because its power has waned; and its power has waned because the power of Congress has become predominant."[128] Though some years later he saw a greater hope in the reassertion of an energetic executive, in the 1880s the only remedy for the failings of Congressional supremacy seemed a fundamental change in the system. Referring to Wilson's warnings about Congressional power in the American system, Walter Lippmann in an edition of the book published in the 1950s wrote: "[T]he morbid symptoms which he identified are still clearly recognizable when the disease recurs and there is a relapse into Congressional supremacy. This was a good book to have read at the end of the Truman and at the beginning of the Eisenhower Administrations."[129] It is also excellent reading today, not the least because of Wilson's observations that "[i]f there be one principle clearer than another, it is this: that in any business, whether of government or of mere merchandising, *somebody must be trusted*, in order that when things go wrong it may be quite plain who should be punished. . . . *Power and strict accountability of its use* are the essential constituents of good government."[130]

President Taft in a 1912 message to Congress recommended that members of the cabinet be given seats in each house of Congress. "There has been much lost in the machinery," Taft wrote, "due to the lack of cooperation and interchange of views face to face between the representatives of the executive and the members of the two legislative branches of the government. It was never intended that they should be separated in the sense of not being in effective touch and relationship to each other."[131] This idea was, of course, never accepted. Had it been, the process of interchange between executive and legislature would have been much different than the model of Congressional inquiry by testimony to committees as it works today. Taft envisioned a new system just as Wilson did in his appeal to the parliamentary system.

The Wilson text, which arose out of a concern for the weakness of executive power, is often turned to these days because of a yearning for the perceived legislative power of the British system. Wilson in 1885 wrote that legislative inquiry into the administration of government is even more important than lawmaking. The answer to executive weakness was to be a form of parliamentary executive government. Wilson's model of the process of legislative inquiry was the question period in Parliament. "No cross-examination is more searching than that to which a minister of the Crown is subjected by the all-curious Commons," Wilson wrote.[132]

This gives a clue to what sort of questioning he thought appropriate. The question period in Parliament is not what it is often thought to be. It is a strictly disciplined affair. Precedent has been established as to the inadmissibility of a wide variety of questions—including those seeking an expression of opinion, or information about an issue pending in court, or proceedings of the Cabinet or Cabinet committee, or information about past history for purpose of argument. In addition, the Speaker has always held that a Minister has no obligation to answer a question—though if he fails to answer, he must suffer the political consequences. A Minister may always decline to answer either because the matter under inquiry is not within his responsibility or, more importantly, because to give the information requested would be contrary to the public interest.[133] The reason for such wide discretion for the Ministers seems clear to British writers, though it might shock those who would substitute parliamentary for our own because of distrust of the wisdom of separation of powers. "Had the Speaker ruled otherwise," wrote two approving contemporary students of the question period, "he would have had to devise some form of disciplinary action suitable for extracting an answer out of a stubborn Minister."[134]

While it is true that the Ministers in Britain are directly accountable to the legislators—and this might make it seem a commodious system to those who prefer legislative supremacy—the British system also allows the Prime Minister to choose whatever moment he may for a national election of legislators. The relationship between executive and legislative is neither more relaxed nor more one-sided in Britain than it is in our system. The Cabinet is directly accountable to Parliament, but Parliament sits only at the indulgence of the Cabinet.

That is not our system, and I doubt whether anyone seriously thinks of altering our Constitution so drastically as to make it our system. But one cannot have that kind of parliamentary system without such drastic changes. The features of parliamentary government that may seem most appealing to the proponents of legislative supremacy upon closer examination turn out to be imaginary—and this may be its strength—because the British system, as it was in Montesquieu's description, is also in fact a system of separated powers.

Nevertheless, the thought in quite recent time has been that the Congressional government Wilson wrote about gave way to an equally problematical Presidential government. One of the reasons given for this change was that the complexity and immediacy of the problems of the modern world required a strong President, though Jefferson saw the same need at the time of the Louisiana Purchase. He called that transaction "an act beyond the Constitution," but said it had been done "in seizing the fugitive occurrence which so advances the good of [the] country."[135] It was a necessary act, as he saw it, not only beyond executive but also beyond legislative authority. Whether the reasons for Presidential power be new or old, there has been a feeling that both the executive and the judiciary have assumed functions that properly belong to the legislature.

The encroachment of one branch of our federal government upon the functions of another is not a new phenomenon. The tendency of a governmental department to augment its own powers may be thought to be an inherent tendency of government generally, although its consequences are all the more serious in a system whose very genius is a tripartite separation of governing powers. The instances of such infringement throughout our history are reflected in the case law. *In re Debs*,[136] in which the Supreme Court upheld an injunction issued without express statutory authority, might be viewed as a case in which both the Court and the executive usurped the legislative function of Congress. The *Steel Seizure* case,[137] in which President Truman without statutory authority commandeered the nation's steel mills, is perhaps the most famous example of the executive arrogating to itself the law-making power of Congress. *Ex parte Milligan*[138] represented the executive's attempt during the Civil War to exercise the judicial power to try criminal cases. The Supreme Court, too, has not been entirely immune to the temptation to stray into the province of the other branches.[139]

The necessity of protecting each branch against encroachment by the others has not gone unanswered. The Speech and Debate Clause of the Constitution has been given a broad construction to insulate the Congress against unwarranted interference in the performance of its duties. The *Gravel* case[140] held that the Clause confers absolute immunity on Congressmen and their aides for acts performed in furtherance of their legislative functions. The protected act in that case involved Senator Gravel's decision to read classified documents, known popularly as the Pentagon Papers, into the public record at a meeting of a Congressional subcommittee. The *Eastland* case,[141] decided last term, held that the Speech and Debate Clause prevented the issuance of an injunction against a Congressional committee, its members and staff, so long as the committee is acting broadly within its "legitimate legislative sphere." The committee in that case had issued a subpoena against a bank to obtain the records of a dis-

sident organization as part of its study of the administration and enforcement of the Internal Security Act of 1950. The *Eastland* case states a reaffirmation of the separation of powers. Indeed, it says, quoting from *United
States v. Johnson*, that the Speech and Debate Clause "serves the . . . function of reinforcing the separation of powers so deliberately established by
the founders."[142]

But the problems are not simple. Congress has on occasion intruded
upon the functions of the other branches. *United States v. Klein*[143] involved
an attempt by Congress to limit the effect of the President's pardon power
by depriving federal courts of jurisdiction to enforce certain indemnifica-
tion claims. The Supreme Court held that the statute violated separation
of powers since it invaded the judicial province by "prescrib[ing] rules of
decision" in pending cases and infringed upon the power of the executive
by "impairing the effect of a pardon."[144]

Congressional investigations have also tended to assume a purpose divorced from legitimate legislative functions. In 1881 in *Kilbourn v. Thompson*[145] the Court severely curbed Congress's contempt power and warned
that Congress had "no general power of making inquiry into the private
affairs of the citizen."[146] The period after World War II, as perhaps is the
case after most wars, saw an exercise of the legislature's investigatory
power far broader than in any previous period and, eventually, a recognition that that power could be abused to impose sanctions on individual
conduct and beliefs, without the vital protections to personal liberty and
privacy that law and the judicial process affords, and with an accompany-
ing disruption of governmental functions. In some instances, the Court
identified the abuse, and pronounced appropriate limits on the power. In
Watkins v. United States,[147] it reversed a conviction resulting from a witness's refusal to answer certain questions before a House committee. The
Court reasoned that the conviction was improper since the ambiguous
purpose of the committee's inquiry precluded any determination whether
the questions were pertinent to the committee's proper legislative tasks.
The Court cautioned that although the power to conduct investigations is
inherent in the legislative power, "there is no general authority to expose
the private affairs of individuals without justification in terms of the functions of Congress. . . . Nor is Congress a law enforcement or trial agency.
These are functions of the executive and judicial departments."[148] On occasion, Congress has also used its legislative power directly to invade the
powers of other branches. In the *Lovett* case,[149] the Court held that a statute forbidding payment of compensation to three named government

employees was unconstitutional, since it imposed punishment without a judicial trial and thus constituted a "Bill of Attainder." *United States v. Brown*[150] presented a statute making it a crime for a member of the Communist Party to be an official or employee of a labor union. The court held this a bill of attainder. The constitutional prohibition against such bills of attainder, the Court observed, was an integral part of the separation of powers. The prohibition "reflected the Framers' belief that the Legislative Branch is not so well suited as politically independent judges and juries to the task of ruling upon the blameworthiness of, and levying appropriate punishment upon, specific persons."[151]

The Supreme Court has also attempted to protect the executive against improper Congressional intrusion on its prerogatives. It is interesting to note that [Samuel Eliot] Morrison in commenting on Washington's first administration writes that "[h]eads of departments had to be appointed by the President, with the consent of the Senate, but Congress, in organizing executive departments, might have made their heads responsible to and removable by itself. Instead it made the secretaries of state and war responsible to the President alone, and subject to his direction within their legal competence."[152] *Myers v. United States*[153] upheld the power of the President to remove executive officers appointed with the advice and consent of the Senate. In declaring unconstitutional a statute seeking to make removal dependent upon the consent of the Senate, the Court stated that the executive power vested in the President under Article II must include the unlimited discretion to remove subordinates whose performance the President regards, for whatever reason, as unsatisfactory. The statute attempting to limit that discretion, the Court noted, violated the principle of separation of powers and would have given Congress unwarranted authority "to vary fundamentally the operation of the great independent branch of government and thus most seriously weaken it."[154] The Court also rejected as a "fundamental misconception: the idea that Congress is the only defender of the people in government."[155] "The President," the Court observed, "is a representative of the people just as the members of the Senate and of the House are, and it may be, at some times, on some subjects, that the President elected by all the people is rather more representative of them all than are the members of either body of the Legislature."[156]

These cases occurred because on occasion each branch has abused the power entrusted to it and in some instances invaded the powers that properly belong to the others. In some instances the Court has been able and willing to provide remedies. In other instances, as in *Debs*, the Court has failed to perceive the problem or has participated in creating it.

In periods of reaction to past events—and we are in such a period—it is more than ever necessary to take time to contemplate the fundamental guidance which a living constitution is intended to provide. The essence of the separation of powers concept formulated by the Founders from the political experience and thought of the revolutionary era is that each branch, in different ways, within the sphere of its defined powers and subject to the distinct institutional responsibilities of the others, is essential to the liberty and security of the people. Each branch, in its own way, is the people's agent, its fiduciary for certain purposes. Two points, I think, follow from this conception and, in the course of our history, have been perceived as following from it. First, the question of whether power has been rightly exercised, or exercised within the limits the Constitution defines, is not always a problem of separation of powers. Some powers have been confided to no branch. Abuse of power may mean that the limits should be enforced on all branches of government, not that the power is better conferred on and exercised by a branch other than that which has abused it. A corollary of this is that a weakness in one branch of the government is not always best corrected by a weakening of another branch.

Second, perhaps what is most remarkable about the various cases that to some extent define the allocation of power among the branches is that their number is relatively few. That fact is a testament to the respect that each branch generally has maintained for the powers and responsibilities of the others, and to an understanding that each branch, within its sphere, represents and serves the people's interest. As Scott Buchanan has written, in our constitutional system, each branch ultimately relies for its authority on its power to persuade the people. In this sense, each branch is democratic, as each is specially representative, whatever its manner of selection. Fiduciaries do not meet their obligations by arrogating to themselves the distinct duties of their master's other agents. Inevitably in a system of divided powers there are points where responsibility conflicts, where legitimate interests and demands appear on either side. In such instances, accommodation and compromise reflecting the exigencies of the matter at hand have been not only possible but a felt necessity. The essence of compromise is that there is no surrender of principle or power on either side, but there is a respect for the responsibility of others and recognition of the need for flexibility and reconciliation of competing interests.

This general respect and the felt need for accommodation has been part of the role of the courts. Recognizing the limits of their own proper functions and institutional competence, the courts had long employed a series of devices that had, as their ultimate purpose, avoiding interference with the powers and functions of other branches. These restrictions, founded in the case or controversy requirement of Article III or frankly in prudential considerations that must govern the exercise of judicial power, defined and narrowed the occasions in which judicial resolution may be sought. But they recognized, too, that certain questions may be better left without resolution in law, and allowed to work themselves out in the political process and in the *ad hoc* process of accommodation.

To some extent, and perhaps to a more substantial extent than had been thought, these barriers to judicial resolution remain. In *United States v. Richardson*,[157] the Supreme Court held that the plaintiff, as a taxpayer, lacked standing to obtain an injunction requiring, under the Constitution's Statement and Account Clause, a published accounting of Central Intelligence Agency expenditures. Justice Powell, in his concurring opinion, wrote that "[r]elaxation of standing requirements is directly related to the expansion of judicial power. . . . [A]llowing unrestricted taxpayer or citizen standing would significantly alter the allocation of power at the national level."[158]

There is a discomfort in uncertainty. There is, on the part of some, a longing for simple, straight answers about the allocation of powers among the branches and the responsibilities of each to the other. There is a corresponding tendency to assume that the courts can provide the answers by deduction from constitutional principles and properly act as umpire between the other branches. In some instances, as in the *Steel Seizure* case, this may be the inevitable consequence of the courts' performance of their duties properly where private interests are immediately affected. But there are other instances in which the dispute may be purely one between the institutional interests of the Congress and the executive. The intervention of the courts in such matters may be furthered if courts recognize standing in members of Congress to challenge the legality of executive actions. Some courts have done so, apparently on the ground that the executive's action diminishes Congressional power and thus the power of each member.[159]

Resolution of such disputes provides a kind of certainty. But this is an area of great difficulty, requiring caution. There is no doubt that judicial intervention is sometimes essential. The danger is that in attempting to provide final answers not only will the courts inevitably alter the balance between Congress and the executive in the context of a particular situation, but the very nature of this kind of determination, when the interactions of a government of checks and balances are involved, may then require continuing judicial supervision. This would constitute a removal to the courts of judgments of responsibility and discretion, contrary to the fundamental conception of different functions to be differently performed by the divisions of government. It would significantly alter the balance between the courts and the other branches. The consequence may well be a weakening rather than a strengthening of accountability. We are sometimes said to be a litigious people, but the Constitution, while it establishes a rule of law, was not intended to create a government by litigation. A government by representation through different branches, and with interaction and discussion, would be much nearer the mark.

The current controversies concerning the demands of one branch of the government for information in the hands of another reflect some of the complexities. Congress has in some instances through its own legislation placed statutory restrictions on the disclosure of information in the executive's possession.[160] Some of these statutes, no doubt, would never have been enacted without such restrictions. When the executive acts under such statutes, his action has nothing to do with executive privilege. It has to do with the good faith interpretation of a statute. Some of these statutes by their own terms represent a government's pledge of confidentiality to its citizens.[161] Congress which passed the statute took part in making that pledge. The construction of these statutes, if the appropriate forum can be found, can be regarded as a standard judicial task, identical to the kinds of decisions which courts make frequently. The issue raises separation of powers problems only to the extent that it concerns the ability of the legislature, having enacted a statute, to later place its own interpretation by committee action, without later enactment, on the meaning to be given to the words used. There have, of course, been many disputes between Congress and the courts on similar issues. To be sure, some interpretations of such statutes recently advanced do concern most directly the power of the Congress to the point of asserting that Congress may not constitutionally grant a confidentiality against itself.[162] Such a principle bears no resemblance to the system the Constitution established. The primary argument has been that such statutes, unless they mention Congress specifically, do not mean what they appear to say.[163] In the long run a dispute of this latter nature might best be resolved by Congress establish-

)

ing a commission to review such statutes, of which there are many, involving citizens' claims to privacy, and then through revision and reenactment making explicit the limitation on the apparent confidentiality conferred.

In other quite different instances, the demand of a legislative committee for documents or testimony can raise the issue of executive privilege as part of the doctrine of separation of powers. Even in such instances, however, it is important to stress that the requirement for some confidentiality is not unique to any one branch of the government. It is a need that Congress and the judiciary as well as the executive have asserted and attempted to meet. It is a need which all advanced countries have recognized, whether or not they have a doctrine of separation of powers. Nor is it, of course, solely a governmental necessity. As the Supreme Court acknowledged in *NAACP v. Alabama*,[164] the invasion of privacy by investigation and publication can pose grave harm, and, indeed, can at times be employed to deter the exercise of fundamental rights.

One primary area of responsibility has been the confidentiality of the decision-making process. The Constitution provides a structure where some decisions are normally made in public; the Founders were quite explicit that others should not be. There is a theory in science that one can never know with certainty what one is observing since the process necessary for observation can change what is observed. Scientists among you will know, far better than I, whether the analogy is apt. But the principle is suggestive. As the Supreme Court recently said: "Human experience teaches that those who expect public dissemination of their remarks may well temper candor with a concern for appearances and for their own interests to the detriment of the decisionmaking process."[165] The need for confidentiality to protect the safety of citizens and individual rights goes beyond the decision-making process to the protection of some information essential to the security of the nation and the conduct of foreign affairs. Of course there are competing considerations. An informed public is essential in a democratic republic, and Congress requires information for informed legislation. The courts, on occasion, must have access to information in the possession of the executive if it is essential to informed adjudication. There is a conflict of values, a necessary ordering of means and ends, with the public good as the common objective. Concern for the functioning of each branch must be accompanied by recognition of, and accommodation to, the responsibilities of others. Historically, in this area as in others, compromise has been our course.

This has been so of demands for information in the hands of the executive in the context of judicial proceedings. From the *Burr* case[166] early in our history to very recent years, means have been found for leaving the decision on disclosure to the executive in ways found and enforced by the courts to be consistent with fairness to litigants. The only exception to that rule was established by the Supreme Court in 1974 in *United States v. Nixon*.[167] The case was singular in the circumstances that foreclosed the normal means of accommodation to protect both the public and private interests involved. But although requiring disclosure in the unique circumstances of the case, the Court expressly recognized that the executive's right of confidentiality is a necessary adjunct to the executive's constitutional power. While this right obviously should be used with care and discretion, and with an understanding of the comity which must exist among the branches of government, it is perhaps well to remind those who in the past have been concerned about an imperial presidency that a too limited version of the scope of the right can drive deliberations into a more centralized and dependent focus—a result directly contrary to what they would wish.

But in recent years there have been calls for final resolution, perhaps generated by abuses on both sides, for clear definition by the courts of Congress's right to demand disclosure and of the executive power to refuse. To a limited degree these calls have been satisfied, although in a way that can have been satisfactory neither to the advocates of Congressional power nor to the advocates of the executive. In *United States v. Nixon*, private interests were, as the Court recognized, immediately affected. Moreover, in a conflict involving, in one of its dimensions, the integrity of the judicial process, it was necessary for the Court to come to a judgment of relative interests. But in *Senate Select Committee v. Nixon*,[168] in which jurisdiction was based on a statute specially enacted for purposes of the case,[169] the Court of Appeals for the District of Columbia Circuit held that because the Senate committee's need for information did not, in the circumstances, outweigh the executive's need for confidentiality, the executive did not have a legal obligation to comply with the committee's subpoena. The values and needs asserted on both sides were matters not perhaps susceptible to judicial calibration. The Court's statements about the Congress's need for information provide little comfort to those who insist on unrestricted Congressional access.

Cases may come in which judicial resolution is necessary. They are most likely to come if the Congress, as some of its committees have recently threatened to do, asserts its authority by attempting to hold in contempt executive officers who act under a Presidential assertion of privilege or who are conforming to the mandate of a statute, which has nothing to do with executive privilege, and when the Attorney General, as he is required to do by statute, has given his opinion. Under present circumstances if Congress were to take such a course, it would be either to ask for the official's indictment—a road with incredible problems, outside the spirit of the Constitution, and carrying a mandatory minimum term of imprisonment of one month—or take the more traditional course, little used in this century and never against an incumbent cabinet officer, of attempting itself to impose coercive or punitive restraints, in which case, I suppose, an application for habeas corpus would be the appropriate remedy. Either course would be, at the least, unedifying, although the more so when punishment rather than clarification is sought—an attempt by one branch to assert its authority by imposing personal sanctions on those who seek to perform their duty as officials of another branch equal to the Congress in responsibility to serve the people. This is not the statesmanship which created our Republic, nor is it justified by past abuses. Such an argument would have made our present Constitution an impossibility. It does not rectify abuses; it supplants them with new ones.

Such resolution has been little used in the past, not only because considerations of respect and comity have overcome the pressures of the moment, but because, I think, there has been an implicit, perhaps intuitive appreciation that judicial resolution, whatever it ultimately might be, and which at times is necessary, would have severe costs.

The separation of powers doctrine, as Scott Buchanan wisely emphasized, is a political doctrine. It is based, he wrote, on the idea that government institutions given separate functions, organizations and powers will operate with different modes of reasoning. Each mode is important to the processes of law formation and to the generation of popular consent to the law.[170]

The doctrine of separation of powers was also designed to control the power of government by tension among the branches, with each, at the margin, limiting the other. But there is a misperception about that tension. For example, Arthur Schlesinger once described the doctrine as creating "permanent guerrilla warfare" between the executive and legislative branches.[171] To be sure, the authors of the Constitution had a realistic view of man and government and power. They assumed that from time to time men in power might grow too bold and engage in overreaching that threatens liberty and the balance of the system. They designed the system in such a way that the overreaching—the threatened tyranny—might be checked. But they did not envision a government in which each branch seeks out confrontation; they hoped the system of checks and balances would achieve a harmony of purpose differently fulfilled.

The branches of government were not designed to be at war with one another. The relationship was not to be an adversary one, though to think of it that way has become fashionable. Adversaries make out their claims with a bias, and one would not want to suggest that the Supreme Court, for example, ought to view each case before it as a chance to increase or protect its institutional power. Justice Stone and others have written of the importance of the Court's sense of self-restraint. That insight applies as well to the executive and legislature. If history were to teach, that might be its lesson rather than new cycles of aggression.

Institutional self-restraint does not mean that we must have a government of hesitancy. It does mean that the duty to act is coupled with a duty to act with care and comity and with a sense of the higher values we all cherish. This is the wisdom of the separation of powers, for as Buchanan wrote, "Under our constitution the law divides itself so that reason can rule."[172]

The Founders of the Republic, as the *Federalist Papers* state, thought they had found "means, and powerful means, by which the excellences of republican government may be retained and its imperfections lessened or avoided."[173] Among those means was "the regular distribution of power into distinct departments."[174] For a country which has come through a storm, aided so greatly by the wisdom of the basic document thus fashioned, some reflection and an ability to take the longer view is now called for. We owe that much to the Founders; we owe that much to ourselves.

The Ideal of Political and Economic Democracy

THE EIGHTY-FIFTH ANNIVERSARY OF THE SHERMAN ACT

June 19, 1975

Attorney General Levi served in the Antitrust Division of the Department of Justice during the administration of Franklin Delano Roosevelt. After returning to the University of Chicago Law School, he was instrumental in the development of the law and economics movement, teaming up

*with economist Aaron Director of the law faculty to use economic analy-
sis to teach antitrust law. As this talk shows, despite his belief in the important contribution economics makes to the development of the law, he did
not believe that economic theory was the only thing antitrust policy should
consider.*

I need hardly say it is an enormous pleasure for me to take part in this
85th anniversary celebration of the Sherman Act. It is a homecoming, a
reunion and a pledge to help maintain the values which each of us sees
in our way in that historic charter of freedom. As alumni, conscious as we
are that many of us had our experiences with the Antitrust Division at
different times, we are prepared to welcome outsiders to our group. And
we know that outsiders are here. I would like to say this conforms with
the modern temper, witness the Freedom of Information Act. But the fact
is that those of us who were involved with the antitrust laws realize that
these laws have always moved with bursts of publicity and occasionally
with high drama. The antitrust laws are the public's business, and so we
welcome the outsiders. But we hope they have the faith, shared by plaintiff's and defense counsel alike. In some sense I choose to believe this is a
gathering of true believers. It is because we are true believers that in the
past at least there have been so many sects among us, so many contrary
positions strongly held.

The most important thing, of course, is that the antitrust laws have survived. I believe they have survived in strength. They have been of ines-
timable value to our country. They are an expression of the importance
of a recognition that liberty is to be found not only in the First Amendment but in the ability to make choices free of overwhelming government
directions and intervention. The antitrust laws, in their basic theory, are
built upon a view of enterprise and of choice, which property and access
to the market give, and I would claim them among the most important
civil liberties. This is an older view, often in disrepute. Although often violated, this view has been sufficiently strongly held to give our country unusual diversity and creativity. This view and its manifestations in the Sherman Act have shaped and protected our democracy.

The survival of the Sherman Act has not always been a sure thing.
Throughout its existence the Act has been under periodic attack. There
have been frequent revivals. Revivals fit our faith. Some of us came to
the Antitrust Division only a few years after the demise of the Sherman
Act was firmly predicted. The revival of the forties was chiefly the vision

of Thurman Arnold. I don't think it is unfair to put it that way, although Thurman was surrounded by persons of exceptional ability. Some of them are here. They will forgive me for this statement, because I think they will agree with it. But the opportunity for Thurman's entrance was given by Robert Jackson, who began the revival in 1937 with more than a note of skepticism—a thought that this was the last try, a lurking belief, which many thinking people shared, that a different form of government control might be necessary.

"The policy to restrain concentration of wealth through combination or conspiracies to restrict competition," Assistant Attorney General Robert Jackson wrote, "[has][175] not achieved its purpose." "Concentration of ownership and control of wealth were never greater than today," he said. Looking over the forty-seven-year history of the Sherman Act, he observed that the "almost unanimous verdict . . . would be that the enforcement has been more spectacular than successful, that legal prosecutions have not suppressed monopoly . . . [,] a half century of litigation has not made the law either understandable or respected." The antitrust laws were "full of loopholes," failed to "break up price controlling organizations, or to check the continuing concentration of wealth and of industrial control." He noted the antitrust laws represented "an effort to avoid detailed government regulation of business by keeping competition in control of prices."[176] It was hoped to save government from the conflicts and accumulations of grievances which continuous price control would produce, but perhaps if the antitrust laws failed in this one last effort, government regulation of a different type would be necessary. The regulation he had in mind was regulation by governmental commission. Perhaps in some instances it might have gone further to government ownership.

The Jackson doubts were natural. His last chance remarks were written in the aftermath of the National Recovery Administration—an attempt to replace the Sherman Act with the collusion of industrial self-government. The first director of the NRA, after he departed from his post, wrote a book explaining what he had been up to. Here are his 1935 remarks:

> You can't have recovery without amending the Antitrust Acts because you must prevent a repetition of 1922–29. You can't do that without control and can't have that control under Antitrust legislation. Those Acts have failed in every crisis. They had to be forgotten during the war to enable the country to defend itself. When they came back to memory in 1919, they set the stage for what happened up to 1929. They contributed to the boom and they were help-

less in the crash. Without amendment, following the principles of NIRA, they will go on (as they did) to create the very conditions of monopoly and erasure of the individualism which they were conceived to prevent and in the future, as in the past, they will have to be abandoned in any crisis, economic or military. Unless so amended, they have no place in the mechanized, highly organized, and integrated civilization in which we live. There is no more vital and fundamental issue before the country than whether we are going to control modern scientific and industrial development to our use or suffer it to our destruction.

The only forces that can control it are industrial self-government under Federal supervision.[177]

In the background of these remarks by Hugh Johnson were the frequent complaints from some economists and businessmen that the American antitrust laws had made it impossible for American firms to compete with giant foreign companies or cartels in world markets. Those complaints appeared before World War I, were repeated in the period between the two world wars and, not surprisingly, seem to be reappearing today in a somewhat different version. The Johnson remarks also carried forward an extreme version of some aspects of the trade association movement of the twenties, and of course he was stating much of the language of the technocrats.

The Jackson skeptical last chance did turn into one of[178] the most creative periods of the Sherman Act, rivaling in doctrinal development the Taft period, exceeding all prior times in the reach of the Act, providing the platform for what has come since. Many, perhaps most, of you here today made and shared in the subsequent experience. And some of you indeed are providing the current leadership or response to the leadership of the present Antitrust Division. This experience is the more surprising and the more important because in the forest of regulatory commissions created since Jackson's last chance, the Antitrust Division is almost an oasis. So there is a bond among us; we share something quite unique.

In response to this bond and the affection that goes with it, I thought it might be appropriate to use this occasion to attempt to state some of the things I believe I have learned about antitrust enforcement. I would rather have a discussion on these points, because I am rather sure we do not all agree. We probably never did agree in all respects, anyway, and subsequent experiences have caused us to change our minds, or at least given us time to rethink the bases for our opinions. Yet I thought it might be a worthwhile exercise for me to attempt to set down some conclusions. I hasten to add I don't think my views will surprise anyone, nor do I think they should be given any particular weight. Indeed perhaps they should be discounted because of the government position I presently hold.

I believe my knowledge of the general direction of the present Antitrust Division is fairly complete. I admire Tom Kauper and his deputies and staff. I did have a conversation with Tom Kauper about what I thought I might say on this occasion. I was afraid someone might think I was setting forth a program for the Antitrust Division, and of course if I did that, I would really want it to come from him although through my mouth. But Tom Kauper is away and I have had to write this speech myself. My humility on this matter is not put on. I don't feel humble. I have just been well trained.

I cannot get out of my mind two incidents among many which occurred when I was in the Antitrust Division. One was in the very early days when Thurman Arnold took me up with him in the private elevator to show the Attorney General, who was Robert Jackson—two floors above—a document which Thurman thought was quite exciting and "hot." The document seemed in any event to implicate a large company in a cartel arrangement. Before anyone asks me under the Freedom of Information Act to supply a copy of that document, let me say at once I have forgotten what the document was. But I do recall that Thurman flashed the page in front of Jackson without further explanation, and I didn't see how anyone could possibly understand from that glimpse what the significance of the disclosure would be. After getting some appropriate expression from Jackson to the effect that it seemed to be quite a document, Thurman whisked out of the room—I trailing after him—and down the elevator we went. "Why didn't you tell the Attorney General what the case was about?" I asked as we descended. "You should never tell the Attorney General anything," Thurman said. That was my first lesson on Attorney Generalship.

I remember as a second occasion Francis Biddle saying quite seriously and plaintively that he always opened the morning paper with apprehension because it would probably report something the Antitrust Division was doing which he didn't know about. And he had reason to be apprehensive. So the second lesson.

I would not have thought I needed a third lesson, but as a useful reminder not to take too seriously the twelve-hour-a-day minimum I put in on my present job, I was given a lesson by the *Washington Star* the other day. The *Star* asked a friend of mine, not in the Antitrust Division, to be sure—but nevertheless I think it has some relevance—whether the turmoil in the Justice Department, the rapid turnover of Attorneys General, hadn't left the Department suffering badly. With the graciousness which all of us cherish as part of Washington life, my friend responded brightly that he thought things had settled down, but anyway the Justice Department consisted of dedicated professionals, so it didn't make too much difference what the political leadership at the top looked like.

So now that I have been given the freedom which comes from being ineffectual, let me seriously try to state what my views or observations are.

As a starter, I think that experience shows one should not expect the defense trial bar to attempt to campaign seriously for a quiet Antitrust Division. I certainly don't mean that the defense antitrust bar wants the Division to win all its cases, or even to bring them all. But quietude does not seem to be the aim, and perhaps that is a good thing.

I have another observation which perhaps derives from too little experience. When I was in the Antitrust Division and for some time thereafter, I remained amazed not only at what people put into writing but the collusive arrangements they sometimes sought to achieve. It is of course true that documents written in the heat of a transaction or at the end of a tiring day often appear in a false light when they appear years later. My thought was, however, that due to the great increase in antitrust prosecutions and the plethora of lawyers surrounding most large companies, there never would be again the kind of conspiratorial price fixing cases which appeared in the early antitrust cases. Indeed I was rather sorry for my successors, which include many in this audience, because I thought they never would have the thrill of that kind of macabre discovery. Indeed when I was teaching the antitrust laws, I used to tell my classes that such simple but overtly[179] conspiratorial cases were a thing of the past. It was on such a day in February 1961, when I was giving forth with this profound wisdom, that a student showed me a newspaper item describing an indictment, fines and prison terms and an arrangement among major electrical firms couched in terms of phases of the moon, meetings described as choir practices and a variety of other codes used for price fixing. My conclusion undoubtedly over-reaches this jolting experience, but it tends to confirm a view that Adam Smith was probably right, and vigilance both within and outside such companies will always be needed. If this is true, it says something important about the everlasting necessity for vigorous antitrust enforcement against price fixing or collusive production-controlling or division-of-territory arrangements. In our excitement about problems of concentration, I think we often tend to forget this. Indeed as some of the experts have pointed out, the nub of the problem of concentration is likely to be the greater ease with which collusive arrangements may be arrived at....

The antitrust laws have great symbolic value. This is true with the enforcement of most laws, and is one reason, although of course there are other reasons as well, that laws ought not to be enforced in secrecy. But there is a special reason why this is true of antitrust. Antitrust is supported as a viable alternative to more severe, more interfering, more bureaucratic forms of government regulation. It is in that sense that antitrust is regarded as nonregulatory. But this viability must be believed. It must be demonstrated. It must be shown that cases can and will be brought. I do not think this aspect of antitrust enforcement is in any sense illicit. And if this is so, it does suggest, although there are other reasons for this suggestion as well, that antitrust enforcement ought to be programmatic. I mean two things by this. First, I do not think a successful antitrust program can be launched merely by waiting for complaints to arrive. Collusive arrangements do often break down; there is bickering and some disclosure. But successful enforcement in this and other fields of non-violent crime must be based on a much more affirmative scrutiny of what is going on. Second, I think the effectiveness of antitrust action, as well as the ability to uncover other violations, is greatly enhanced if one proceeds industry by industry. I don't think this is the only way to proceed. Violations, as we know, sometimes follow the pattern of the assumed loopholes of new devices. I would want to be reassured, for example, that the Supreme Court's *Kewanee Oil Co.*[180] case, which gave patent-like monopoly to non-patented secrets, was not to be used as the basis for cartel-like exchange agreements. As we know, this was the history of many cartel arrangements in the past. In any event I think an enforcement program requires an articulate explanation of its focus, both to help the enforcement program itself and to give reassurance to the public of the viability of the law....

A central question concerning antitrust enforcement is whether it must be based solely on correct economic theory. I find the answer to this rather simple. The answer is "no." I do think it is proper to criticize antitrust cases and doctrines when they justify results on economic grounds which do not stand up. But antitrust laws in a proper sense have always had political overtones. The over-riding purpose of the law, particularly the law against monopolies, was to give assurance that private firms would not be exercising what was taken as the equivalent of governmental power. When Senator Hoar[181] explained his bill, which became the Sherman Act, he emphasized the menace which monopolies, as they were perceived, would have on republican institutions. When Robert Jackson gave his last chance speech, he spoke of the ideal of political and economic democracy. I am prepared to accept therefore, as one indeed must, the judgment of the courts or Congress as to banned conduct even though from an economic standpoint in many cases the ban may make very little sense, or be fairly trivial in its economic impact. This is not an appeal in favor or in defense of nonsense. I think it is a realistic interpretation of the way the law has developed, and is more consistent with its common law background and process. I would not myself otherwise know how to explain the outcome of the *DuPont–General Motors* case,[182] although I believe the result was to be expected. This is to say there are some limits as to what size can do—because that is in fact what the law is, quite apart from what it says it is, and there are also some practices which may be banned, such as tie-in arrangements attached to patents, even though economic theory may or may not, depending on the facts, find an actual enlargement of the patent monopoly.

I realize this statement, since it seems to leave the often illusory security of economic doctrine, might suggest I advocate no sensible limits to the extension of the antitrust laws in many directions and that I do not see the necessity for the development of consistent judicial or legislative activities for antitrust. But I have not said either of these things, and I should at once affirm that an antitrust doctrine which can be shown to be seriously harmful in its economic impact is of course subject to the greatest questioning. My guess is that the antitrust laws have suffered more from the development of assumed economic doctrine to justify continually the further extension and reach of the laws. The basic problem of the antitrust laws is not only that they have to be vigorously enforced, but also that they have to be saved from their friends.

The basic guidelines for present problems I think have to be faced up to are these: (1) Collusive behavior to restrict production must be vigorously pursued. I believe this should be done on[183] an articulated industry-to-industry basis. (2) In the field of concentration or structure of industry, short of the problem of monopolization or monopolizing to foreclose entry, there still must be some concern for that kind of felt or believed domination, or for that lack of inventiveness or creativity in industry which gives rise to an overwhelming doubt as to whether the antitrust laws can perform their function. This may be a restatement of traditional doctrines which emphasize the way monopoly power was acquired or the way it has been maintained. But I go back to the symbolic nature or the antitrust laws, and their paramount purpose to be seen as a viable alternative to more[184] stringent and managerial forms of government regulation. I cannot emphasize too strongly that I am not advocating the bringing of cases where violation is doubtful; on the contrary, I am saying that in fixing the priority for cases one must consider not only the effect within an industry but also the more general impact in law enforcement.[185] In this sense — and perhaps this is paradoxical, but I believe it is true — catching monopoly in what is called its incipiency by preventing acquisitions when the market control is very small, under Section 7[186] as it has been interpreted, may be a great disservice to the administration of the antitrust laws, which, from time to time, need splendid demonstrations of the power to deal with the real thing. To talk this way opens one to a double charge I realize. I am sure the notion, which I think a necessary one, of symbolic concentration cases is very troublesome. Conversely, the way I have stated the matter may be regarded as being too unsympathetic to the assumed need to stop the trend of concentration or to increase the number of industries now dominated, as the saying always goes, by four or five firms. As to the assumed concentration increase over the years, I think there is very little to support this picture, although it may be true. To adopt a change in the law which creates a rebuttable presumption that monopoly power exists if it is shown that four or fewer firms account for 50% or more of the aggregate market share, or which automatically goes after any firm having a market share of at least 70% seems to be destined to create a different form of government control over industry. But as to this, perhaps one might consider a suggestion. The issues can be enormously complicated in concentration cases; at least not many can be prepared and tried at once. It might be a valuable step to have legislation through which the President every five years would appoint a short-term independent commission, composed of attorneys, economists and other experts from outside government, which would report on the concentration and structure of American industry from the standpoint of apparent anticompetitive or monopoly behavior. Such a commission if formed should not have a prosecutorial purpose and should not have the power of compulsory process. But its report would focus attention on apparent problem areas. A good report would enlighten public discussion. It also would enlighten the direction of the enforcement of the antitrust laws. Needless to say, this suggestion has not been cleared with anyone. . . .

If the antitrust laws have played their role, as more or less they have, of insuring creativity and diversity, of upholding the ideals of freedom of entry into the marketplace and into the channels of manufacture and trade, and have contributed to the reality of our democracy, I hope the Antitrust Division itself will not fall victim to over-regulation. It might be poetic justice if it did. For the antitrust laws at birth and thereafter were never quite as pure on the side of competition as we have tried to make them. They were, after all, in origin at least in some respects part of the Populist tradition, with a strong dose of unfair competition theory and desire to regulate mixed in. Moreover, the Antitrust Division in some ways was the original consumer's advocate, as it still is. But as Thurman Arnold wrote in another connection: the answer to the poetic justice argument is that I don't like poetic justice.

I guess no one does. But I hope the Sherman Act and the Antitrust Division will be here with you, loud and clear, at least at every five-year interval.

Guidelines for the FBI

TESTIMONY BEFORE THE SENATE SELECT COMMITTEE ON
INTELLIGENCE ACTIVITIES

December 11, 1975

The review of practices and establishment of standards and procedures for the intelligence activities of the Federal Bureau of Investigation were a high priority for Attorney General Levi from the moment he took office. He issued guidelines in a number of areas, none more controversial—then or later—than those governing investigation into what had often been known as subversive organizations. Under these guidelines ongoing investigations were for the first time reviewed by a special unit within the Department of Justice.[187] For the first time, the guidelines established a written standard of proof that domestic security investigations had to meet in order to continue. Failure to meet this standard led to Levi's decision to discontinue a decades-long investigation of the Socialist Workers' Party. During the first nine months after the guidelines went into effect, the number of active domestic security investigations declined from about five thousand to fewer than three hundred.[188]

The Committee has asked me to talk with you today about the future of the Federal Bureau of Investigation. I thought it might be helpful if I outline quite briefly some of the points I would like to make, some of the problems I think ought to be considered and some of the steps we have taken.

The first point is that the statutory base for the operations of the Bureau cannot be said to be fully satisfactory. . . . A number of questions are often asked about this statutory base. It has the virtue of simplicity, but the executive orders which deal with government employee investigations are complicated and confusing, and Presidential memoranda or, perhaps, oral instructions from a President may be difficult to collate. I think it is important, in any case, to separate out the kinds of questions which are asked about the Bureau's authority base. Some questions are constitutional in nature, relating to the inherent power of the President; others go to the interpretation of the statutes and the relationship between the statutes and Presidential directives; others go to the failure of the statutes to define sufficiently the areas of the Bureau's jurisdiction or to spell out sufficiently—and this is partly constitutional—the means and methods which the Bureau is permitted to use in carrying out its assigned tasks.

The second point, related to the first, is a continuing discussion of the role of the Bureau in intelligence investigations or domestic security investigations. The argument is sometimes made that the Bureau's proper role, at least in purely domestic matters, should be limited to investigations of committed crimes. The basic statute for the Bureau is broader than this, as have been executive orders and Presidential mandates to the Bureau. The basic statute is broader since it refers to investigations regarding official matters under the control of the Department of Justice and the Department of State as may be directed by the Attorney General. A disparity is sometimes seen among the different roles of the Bureau in crime detection, in on-going domestic security matters and in foreign intelligence or foreign counterintelligence matters. In recent days a statement by the then Attorney General Harlan Fiske Stone, who reorganized

the Bureau and chose J. Edgar Hoover as its director, has been quoted as
a relevant warning.

Stone warned,

> There is always the possibility that a secret police may become a menace to
> free government and free institutions because it carries with it the possibility
> of abuses of power which are not always quickly apprehended or understood.
> . . . [I]t is important that its activities be strictly limited to the performance of
> those functions for which it was created and that its agents themselves be not
> above the law or beyond its reach. . . . The Bureau of Investigation is not con-
> cerned with political or other opinions of individuals. It is concerned only with
> their conduct and then only with such conduct as is forbidden by the laws of
> the United States. When a police system passes beyond these limits, it is dan-
> gerous to the proper administration of justice and to human liberty, which it
> should be our first concern to cherish.[189]

I should like to suggest that Stone's warning always must be considered relevant to the proper conduct of the Bureau's duties, but it does
not necessarily follow that domestic security investigations are, therefore,
outside the Bureau's proper functions. The detection of crime in some areas requires preparation and at least some knowledge of what is likely to
be going on. What is at issue, I think, is the proper scope, the means and
methods used, the attention paid to conduct and not views and the close-
ness of the relationship of the conduct and that which is forbidden by the
laws of the United States.

Third, I realize that some proposals . . . might separate out in some
fashion domestic and foreign intelligence functions from the FBI or from
one another within the FBI. This is, of course, an issue to be looked at. I
assume it is recognized that there may be some relationship between that
intelligence which is domestic and that intelligence which is involved in
foreign counterintelligence work. One may lead to the other. And there
may be a relationship between foreign counterintelligence and foreign intelligence. If the work were separated out into different agencies, I do not
know if the decision about when an investigation should pass from one
agency to another always could be made easily. Moreover, even so, information presumably would pass from one agency to the other. I know
that one consideration has been that it might be decided that information
collected by some permitted means in intelligence investigations under

some circumstances should not be used in criminal prosecutions. But if there is an exchange of information, this must always be a consideration, whether there are separate agencies or not, and the basic question then is of use and not organization. The more active concern, I believe, is that there is a risk that conduct proper for one area may be improper for another, and that the combination can work a contamination. My view on this is that in any case we must decide what conduct is appropriate and is inappropriate for each of the areas, and we must take steps to make sure that proper conduct is lived up to. My hope is that the fact that the FBI has criminal investigative responsibilities, which must be conducted within the confines of constitutional protections strictly enforced by the courts, gives the organization an awareness of the interests of individual liberties that might be missing in an agency devoted solely to intelligence work. I know the argument can be run the other way. I believe the dangers are greater if there is separation.

Fourth, there is a question as to the proper role of the FBI in crime prevention and whether or not it should be considered authorized to take steps under some circumstances to reduce the likelihood that crimes will be committed or that serious injury to persons or property will occur. Preventive action has raised serious questions and these must be dealt with. I suppose an initial question is whether it should be allowed at all. Yet I believe under special circumstances and with proper controls most would believe this to be a proper function.[190]

Fifth, the problem of proper controls, supervision and accountability is all-embracing. By statute the Federal Bureau of Investigation is in the Department of Justice, and also by statute the Attorney General is head of the Department of Justice. The history is mixed, of course, and we all have a tendency to over-simplify, but it is a fair statement that there have been times in the past when the supervision by Attorneys General, granted that the Bureau must have considerable autonomy, has been sporadic, practically nonexistent or ineffective. I hope that is not the case now. The responsibility is a heavy one. But in any event the problem of proper controls, supervision and accountability goes beyond the Director of the Bureau and the Attorney General. I have already mentioned that in my view the statutory base for the operations of the Bureau cannot be said to be fully satisfactory. I think that better controls and performance can be achieved through statutory means, executive orders, guidelines and reporting to appropriate Congressional committees.

Sixth, before I come to a resumé of some of the steps which have been taken, let me say I know we all realize that in the past there have been grave abuses. I am uncomfortable with a kind of writing of history, however, which sees it only in terms of the abuses and not in terms of past and present strength. It is very difficult to be fair to the past in which many institutions of government carried a share of responsibility. But more than unfairness is involved. If we are not careful, we will turn to solutions of the moment which a better reading of history might indicate are not the best solutions. I know we must seize the moment, if I may use such a phrase in this setting. I know also that this Committee realizes that a very important agency with dedicated, highly professional, greatly disciplined government servants is involved. The importance is to the security and domestic tranquility of the United States. Stone's warning was given in an act of creation. He was proud of his creation. In spite of the abuses, there is a proper place for pride. I take it our mutual work should be to nurture that pride and the conditions which justify it.

I turn now to a review of some of the steps which have been taken or are in process. We have tried most diligently, under safeguards to protect the privacy of individuals and with an awareness of the unfairness of instant history, to give a great deal of information to Congressional committees. Attorney General [William] Saxbe made public and Deputy Attorney General [Laurence] Silberman and [FBI] Director [Clarence] Kelley testified about the so-called COINTELPRO.[191] When the FBI discovered evidence of several more COINTELPRO projects after I became Attorney General, these were revealed. One of my first acts as Attorney General, my third week in office, was to testify before a Congressional committee about possible incidents of political misuse of the FBI by the White House in the past and about the nature of FBI file-keeping systems, particularly the files kept by Director Hoover in his office suite. Director Kelley has spoken publicly and before Congressional committees about the incidents in the past in which FBI agents engaged in break-ins to gather or photograph physical evidence in intelligence investigations. On a number of occasions, most recently in testimony before this Committee, I have described the history of the use of electronic surveillance by the FBI. We have welcomed such opportunities.

On February 26, 1975, I instructed Director Kelley to report to me any requests made of the Bureau, or practices within the Bureau, which he deems improper or which present the appearance of impropriety. On February 28, 1975, Director Kelley ordered FBI personnel to report such requests or practices to him. In July 1975, I reaffirmed my February directive and also asked for a report of all sensitive investigative practices. The Director promptly complied. Director Kelley has regularly provided information on conduct by Bureau agents and programs underway within the Bureau that could raise questions. These matters have been reviewed and discussed within the Department so that a consistent and appropriate policy can be achieved. This is a continuing process. I do not assert that we are aware of everything about the Bureau. Nor do I suggest that we ought to know everything. Appropriate communication, consultation and supervision at this level have to be selective. I make this point, which I think may sound disconcerting, not in any way to minimize the responsibility of the Bureau to keep the Department informed nor to minimize the Department's duty to find out. Rather I want to be realistic about a learning and organization problem which requires realism if it is to be understood and perfected.

With respect to possible legislation, the Department has in preparation various drafts of possible bills which may be of assistance in the area of what is now warrantless electronic surveillance.[192] Although obtaining a judicial warrant does not automatically eradicate the possibility of abuse, it is perceived to be an important safeguard of individual privacy interests, and we are exploring, as we said we would do, various possibilities and alternatives. Finally, a committee within the Department of Justice—chaired by Mary Lawton, Deputy Assistant Attorney General in the Office of Legal Counsel, and composed of representatives of my office, the Criminal and Civil Rights Divisions, the Office of Policy and Planning and the FBI—has been working for eight months reviewing FBI procedures in many areas and drafting guidelines to govern those procedures in the future. The committee has produced draft guidelines covering White House inquiries, Congressional and judicial staff appointment investigations, unsolicited mail and domestic security investigations. It is currently at work on guidelines covering counterespionage investigations and will later consider the use of informants, the employee loyalty program, organized crime investigations, criminal investigations and all other aspects of FBI practice.[193] The committee's work has been extensive and time-consuming. It has involved not only questions of proper safeguards but also of efficiency in the proper functioning of the Bureau. It has been an effort to translate into words the complicated and important mechanisms for controlling the FBI. I hope the committee's efforts at articulation will be of use to this Committee and others as it considers drafting legislation.

You have received copies of the latest drafts of the guidelines that have been substantially completed by the committee. These guidelines do not yet represent Department policy. There is disagreement within the Department on some aspects of these guidelines. I have disagreed with the committee recommendations from time to time, and the FBI has raised substantial questions about other recommendations—particularly with respect to the treatment of unsolicited mail. Some of the proposals in the guidelines could be promulgated as departmental regulations. Congress may feel some ought to be enacted into statutory law. Other provisions would require implementation by executive order.

I would be glad to discuss these draft guidelines with you in detail in response to your questions, but a brief discussion of the guidelines on domestic security may be useful at the outset.

The guidelines begin by attempting to impose some order and definiteness to the domestic security field. To begin with, these guidelines do not deal with FBI efforts to counteract the work of foreign intelligence services operating within the United States. Standards for determining when there is foreign involvement sufficient to place a subject in the category of foreign counterintelligence investigation are now being debated within the guidelines committee. The domestic security guidelines also are not meant to cover security or background investigations of federal appointees or investigations of ordinary crimes. Under the draft guidelines, domestic security investigations are only to be authorized when there is a likelihood that the activities of individuals or groups involve or will involve the use of force or violence in violation of federal law. Domestic security investigations are to be limited to activities of individuals or groups intended to accomplish one of five purposes: overthrowing the government of the United States or a state; interfering with the activities within the United States of foreign governments or their representatives; influencing government policies by interfering by force or violence with government functions or interstate commerce; depriving individuals of their civil rights; and creating domestic violence or rioting when such violence or rioting would necessitate as a countermeasure the use of federal armed forces. There is also a provision for limited investigation when there is a clear and immediate threat of domestic violence which is likely to result in a request by a state for federal armed assistance.

Currently there is no procedure requiring the review outside the FBI of all domestic intelligence investigations conducted by the FBI, though the FBI has a long-standing policy of reporting its investigative findings to the Criminal Division. Under the draft guidelines there would be a comprehensive program of reporting to the Attorney General or his designee of all preliminary and full domestic intelligence investigations. The Attorney General would be required under the draft guidelines to put a stop to any full investigation whose justification did not meet an established standard. The standard would be that there must be specific and articulable facts giving reason to believe that the individual or group under investigation is engaged in the activities I have just listed.

Another feature of the draft guidelines is to place strict controls upon the use of any technique by the FBI which goes beyond the gathering of information. COINTELPRO was the name given to the use of some such techniques. As I have said before, some of the activities in COINTELPRO were outrageous and the others were foolish. Nonetheless, there may be circumstances involving an immediate risk to human life or to extraordinarily important government functions that could only be countered by some sort of preventive action. The guidelines require that any such preventive action proposal be submitted to the Attorney General. He could authorize the preventive action only when there is probable cause to believe that violence is imminent and when such measures are necessary to minimize the danger to life or property. The preventive action would in all cases have to be nonviolent. The Attorney General would be required to report to Congress periodically and no less often than once a year on the use of preventive action by the FBI.[194]

I make no claim that during this rather difficult but interesting and—I must trust—promising period we have achieved all that might have been possible. In many ways the work has been disappointingly slow. But I do think we have made advances in nurturing and helping to improve a structure which will be supportive of the best efforts of the men and women in the Department of Justice and in the Federal Bureau of Investigation. No procedures are fail-safe against abuse. The best protection remains the quality and professionalism of the members of the Bureau and of the Department.

Appendix

FBI Guidelines on Domestic Security Investigations[1]

I. BASES OF INVESTIGATION

A. Domestic security investigations are conducted, when authorized under Section II(C), II(F), or II(I), to ascertain information on the activities of individuals, or the activities of groups, which involve or will involve the use of force or violence and which involve or will involve the violation of federal law, for the purpose of:

(1) overthrowing the government of the United States or the government of a State;

(2) substantially interfering, in the United States, with the activities of a foreign government or its authorized representatives;

(3) substantially impairing for the purpose of influencing U.S. government policies or decisions:

(a) the functioning of the government of the United States;

(b) the functioning of the government of a State; or

(c) interstate commerce.

(4) depriving persons of their civil rights under the Constitution, laws, or treaties of the United States.

II. INITIATION AND SCOPE OF INVESTIGATIONS

A. Domestic security investigations are conducted at three levels—preliminary investigations, limited investigations, and full investigations—differing in scope and in investigative techniques which may be used.

B. All investigations undertaken through these guidelines shall be designed and conducted so as not to limit the full exercise of rights protected by the Constitution and laws of the United States.

Preliminary Investigations

C. Preliminary investigations may be undertaken on the basis of allegations or other information that an individual or a group may be engaged in activities which involve or will involve the use of force or violence and which involve or will involve the violation of federal law for one or more of the purposes enumerated in IA(1)–IA(4). These investigations shall be confined to determining whether there is a factual basis for opening a full investigation.

D. Information gathered by the FBI during preliminary investigations shall be pertinent to verifying or refuting the allegations or information concerning activities described in paragraph IA.

E. FBI field offices may, on their own initiative, undertake preliminary investigations limited to:

    1. examination of FBI indices and files;[2]

    2. examination of public records and other public sources of information;

    3. examination of federal, state, and local records;

    4. inquiry of existing sources of information and use of previously established informants; and

    5. physical surveillance and interviews of[3] persons not mentioned in E(1)–E(4) for the limited purpose of identifying the subject of an investigation.

Limited Investigations

F. A limited investigation must be authorized in writing by a Special Agent in Charge or FBI Headquarters when the techniques listed in paragraph E are inadequate to determine if there is a factual basis for a full investigation. In addition to the techniques set forth in E(1)–E(4) the following techniques also may be used in a limited investigation:

    1. physical surveillance for purposes other than identifying the subject of the investigation;

    2. interviews of persons not mentioned in E(1)–E(4) for purposes other than identifying the subject of the investigation, but only when authorized by the Special Agent in Charge after full consideration of such factors as the seriousness of the allegation, the need for the

interview, and the consequences of using the technique. When there is a question whether an interview should be undertaken, the Special Agent in Charge shall seek approval of FBI Headquarters.

G. Techniques such as recruitment or placement of informants in groups, "mail covers,"[4] or electronic surveillance may not be used as part of a preliminary or a limited investigation.

H. All preliminary and limited investigations shall be closed within 90 days of the date upon which the preliminary investigation was initiated. However, FBI Headquarters may authorize in writing extension of a preliminary or limited investigation for periods of not more than 90 days when facts or information obtained in the original period justify such an extension. The authorization shall include a statement of the circumstances justifying the extension.

Full Investigations[5]

I. Full investigations must be authorized by FBI Headquarters. They may only be authorized on the basis of specific and articulable facts giving reason to believe that an individual or group is or may be engaged in activities which involve the use of force or violence and which involve or will involve the violation of federal law for one or more of the purposes enumerated in IA(1)–I(A)4. The following factors must be considered in determining whether a full investigation should be undertaken:

(1) the magnitude of the threatened harm;

(2) the likelihood it will occur;

(3) the immediacy of the threat; and

(4) the danger to privacy and free expression posed by a full investigation.

Investigative Techniques

J. Whenever use of the following investigative techniques is[6] permitted by these guidelines, they shall be implemented as limited herein:

(1) Use of informants to gather information, when approved by FBI Headquarters, and subject to review at intervals not longer than 180 days; provided,

(a) When persons have been arrested or charged with a crime, and criminal proceedings are still pending, informants shall not be used to gather information concerning that crime from other person(s) charged; and

(b) informants shall not be used to obtain privileged information; and where such information is obtained by an informant on his own initiative no record or use shall be made of the information.

(2) "mail covers," pursuant to postal regulations, when approved by the Attorney General or his designee, initially or upon request for extension; and

(3) electronic surveillance in accordance with the requirement of Title III of the Omnibus Crime Control and Safe Streets Act of 1968.

Provided that whenever it becomes known that person(s) under surveillance are engaged in privileged conversation (e.g., with attorney), interception equipment shall be immediately shut off and the Justice Department advised as soon as practicable. Where such a conversation is recorded it shall not be transcribed, and a Department attorney shall determine if such conversation is privileged.

NOTE: These techniques have been the subject of strong concern. The committee[7] is not yet satisfied that all sensitive areas have been covered (e.g., inquiries made under "pretext;"[8] "trash covers,"[9] photographic or other surveillance techniques.)[10]

III. TERMINATING INVESTIGATIONS

A. Preliminary, limited, and full investigations may be terminated at any time by the Attorney General, his designee, or FBI Headquarters.

B. FBI Headquarters shall periodically review the results of full investigations, and at such time as it appears that the standard under II(I) can no longer be satisfied and all logical leads have been exhausted or are not likely to be productive, FBI Headquarters shall terminate the full investigation.

C. The Department of Justice shall review the results of full domestic intelligence investigations at least annually, and shall determine in writing whether continued investigation is warranted. Full investigations shall not continue beyond one year without the written approval of the Department. However, in the absence of such notification the investigation may continue for an additional 30-day[11] period pending response by the Department.

IV. REPORTING, DISSEMINATION, AND RETENTON

A. Reporting

1. Preliminary investigations which involve a 90-day extension under IIH and limited investigations under IIF, shall be reported periodically to the Department of Justice. Reports of preliminary and

limited investigations and limited investigations shall include the identity of the subject of the investigation, the identity of the person interviewed or the person or place surveilled, and shall indicate which investigations involved at 90-day extension. FBI Headquarters shall maintain, and provide to the Department of Justice upon request, statistics on the number of preliminary investigations instituted by each field office, the number of limited investigations under IIF, the number of preliminary investigations that involved 90-day extensions under IIH, and the number of preliminary or limited investigations that resulted in the opening of a full investigation.

2. Upon opening a full domestic security investigation the FBI shall, within one week, advise the Attorney General or his designee thereof, setting forth the basis for undertaking the investigation.

3. The FBI shall report the progress of full domestic security investigations to the Department of Justice not later than 90 days after the initiation thereof, and the results at the end of each year the investigation continues.

4. Where the identity of the source of information is not disclosed in a domestic security report, an assessment of the reliability of the source shall be provided.

B. Dissemination

1. Other Federal Authorities

The FBI may disseminate facts or information obtained during a domestic security investigation to other federal authorities when such information:

(a) falls within their investigative jurisdiction;

(b) may assist in preventing the use of force or violence; or

(c) may be required by statute, interagency agreement approved by the Attorney General, or Presidential directive. All such agreements and directives shall be published in the *Federal Register*.

2. State and Local Authorities

The FBI may disseminate facts or information relative to activities described in paragraph IA to state and local law enforcement authorities when such information:

(a) falls within their investigative jurisdiction;

(b) may assist in preventing the use of force or violence; or

(c) may protect the integrity of a law enforcement agency.

3. When information relating to crimes not covered by paragraph

IA is obtained during a domestic security investigation, the FBI may refer the information to the appropriate lawful authorities if it is within the jurisdiction of state and local agencies.

4. Nothing in these guidelines shall limit the authority of the FBI to inform any individual(s) whose safety or property is directly threatened by planned force or violence, so that they may take appropriate protective safeguards.

5. The FBI shall maintain records, as required by law, of all disseminations made outside the Department of Justice, of information obtained during domestic security investigations.

C. Retention[12]

1. The FBI shall, in accordance with a Records Retention Plan approved by the National Archives and Records Service, within _____ years after closing domestic security[13] investigations, destroy all information obtained during the investigation as well as all index references thereto, or transfer all information and index references to the National Archives and Records Service.

NOTE: We[14] are not yet certain whether empirical data exists to help define a period of retention for information gathered in preliminary or full investigations. Whatever period is determined should take into account the retention period for other categories of information (e.g., general criminal, organized crime, and background checks); since we have not yet considered these areas we cannot fix a period for retention at this time.

NOTE: It may also be possible to establish a sealing procedure to preserve investigative records for an interim period prior to destruction. After being sealed, access would be permitted only under controlled conditions.

2. Information relating to activities not covered by paragraph IA obtained during domestic security investigations, which may be maintained by the FBI under other parts of these guidelines, shall be retained in accordance with such other provisions.

3. The provisions of paragraphs one (1), and two (2) above apply to all domestic security investigations completed after the promulgation of these guidelines, and apply to investigations completed prior to promulgation of these guidelines when use of these files serves to

identify them as subject to destruction or transfer to the National Archives and Records Service.

4. When an individual's request pursuant to law for access to FBI records identifies the records as being subject to destruction or transfer under paragraph one (1), the individual shall be furnished all information to which he is entitled prior to destruction or transfer.

Notes

Foreword

1. "An Approach to Law." All of the quotes contained in the foreword come from this volume. Each citation provides the title of the speech from which the quoted material was drawn.
2. "The Damaging Cycle."
3. "An Approach to Law."
4. "A Burden of Mistrust."
5. *Id.*
6. "Guidelines for the FBI."
7. *Id.*
8. "A Great Trust Waiting to be Reawakened."
9. "Security, Power and Equality."
10. "Some Aspects of Separation of Powers."
11. "Security, Power and Equality."
12. "The Tone of Our Asking."
13. "In the Service of the Republic."
14. "An Approach to Law."
15. "The Rule of Law."
16. "In the Service of the Republic."
17. "The Damaging Cycle."
18. "Security, Power and Equality."
19. *Id.*
20. "The Tone of Our Asking."
21. "The Infinite Task."
22. "In the Service of the Republic."
23. "Government Basic Rights and the Citizenry."
24. "The Infinite Task."

25. "Some Aspects of Separation of Powers."

26. "The Tone of Our Asking."

Editor's Introduction

1. Facsimiles of the original press releases of this and all other talks and testimony Levi gave as Attorney General are available at http://pi.lib.uchicago.edu/1001/law/pub/ehlevi.

2. Edward Levi, Speech to Los Angeles County Bar Association (Nov. 18, 1976), in Press Release, Department of Justice (Nov. 18, 1976), at 2–3.

3. Robert Bork, "Presentation of Citation of Merit to Edward Levi," *Yale L. Rep.*, Winter 1977–78, at 7.

4. See "A Lawyer among Humanists," a talk at a dinner honoring Freund, in this volume.

5. He decided against prosecution because the statute of limitations had run out on all but a few lower-level people. It would be wrong, he concluded, to indict an era at the very end of it by prosecuting a few individuals who simply thought they were doing work legitimated over decades. But at the same time, Levi issued a report making clear that the domestic mail opening without a warrant was illegal and that any further violation would be subject to prosecution.

6. Ron Carr, "Mr. Levi at Justice," 52 *Univ. of Chicago L. Rev.* 300, 314–15 (1985).

7. Because of Levi's leadership in the development of the law and economics movement and his time working on antitrust matters in the Justice Department during the Second World War and later on Capitol Hill, I have also included in this collection his talk upon the anniversary of the Sherman Act ("The Ideal of Political and Economic Democracy"). That speech questions the idea that economic theory is the only guide to the interpretation and enforcement of antitrust laws. Given his role as a pioneer in the use of economic reasoning in the law, the talk is an example of the paradox of leading change that Levi once described to me this way: "You push and push and push to get the thing moving, then you have to run around to the front and push the opposite direction to keep it from going over a cliff."

8. Levi told me of his literary aspirations some years after we left the Department of Justice.

9. Levi told me this story when Douglas retired in November 1975.

10. The Atomic Energy Act of 1946, ch. 724, 60 Stat. 755 (1946).

11. Gerald Ford, *A Time to Heal: The Autobiography of Gerald Ford* 235–36 (Harper & Row/Readers Digest Association 1979).

12. *Id.* at 236.

13. "Security, Power and Equality," in this volume.

NOTES TO PAGES xxiv–xxx

14. His conviction for conspiracy to obstruct justice was overturned on procedural grounds.

15. United States v. U.S. Dist. Court, 407 U.S. 297, 303 (1972).

16. For example, in "Guidelines for the FBI," in this volume.

17. *9/11 Commission Report*, p. 75, available at www.9-11commission.gov/report/911Report.pdf.

18. I attended the meeting as Levi's representative and felt confident I was speaking for him when I responded that keeping secrets from the President is a good way of getting in serious trouble.

19. "Government Confidentiality and Individual Privacy" in this volume.

20. "Some Aspects of Separation of Powers" in this volume.

21. The Director's office later moved across the street to the Bureau's new headquarters, the J. Edgar Hoover Building.

22. For a discussion of the provisions of the domestic security guidelines, see "Guidelines for the FBI" in this volume. The guidelines themselves are in the appendix. The foreign intelligence and counterintelligence guidelines were classified.

23. Available at vault.fbi.gov/FBI Domestic Investigations and Operations Guide (DIOG)/fbi-domestic-investigations-and-operations-guide-diog-2011-version/fbi-domestic-investigations-and-operations-guide-diog-october-15-2011/view.

24. *Id.* § 3.1.

25. For a more thorough discussion of the kind of activities the Bureau engaged in, see Geoffrey R. Stone, *Perilous Times: Free Speech in Wartime from the Sedition Act of 1798 to the War on Terrorism* 487–90 (W. W. Norton & Company 2004).

26. See "Guidelines for the FBI," in this volume.

27. See "The Legal Framework for Electronic Surveillance," in this volume.

28. *Id.*

29. "A Proposed National Security Surveillance Statute," in this volume.

30. The Foreign Intelligence Surveillance Act, 92 Stat. 1783 (1978); amended at 50 U.S.C. ch 36 (2011).

31. In 1978 three former FBI officials—L. Patrick Gray, former acting Director; Mark Felt, former Deputy Director; and Ed Miller, former chief of intelligence—were indicted in connection with these break-ins. Charges against Gray were dropped in 1980. President Ronald Reagan pardoned Felt and Miller. Tim Weiner, *Enemies: A History of the FBI* (Random House 2012), includes an account of these matters.

32. Levi recounted to me what happened at the White House meeting when he returned from it. Not long afterwards, Ford replaced Kissinger with Brent Scowcroft as National Security Advisor, obviating the problem of Kissinger's refusal to make the certification.

33. Edward Levi, "The Sovereignty of the Courts," 50 *Univ. of Chicago L. Rev.* 679 (1991).

34. University of Chicago News Office obituary, March 7, 2000, available at www-news.uchicago.edu/releases/00/000307.levi.shtml.

35. Gerald Ford, "A President's Tribute to Edward H. Levi," *Chicago Daily Law Bulletin*, Apr. 7, 2000, at 2.

A Note on the Text

1. They are available in bound volumes in the University of Chicago law library, which has also made the full original texts of all Levi's talks as Attorney General available at http://pi.lib.uchicago.edu/1001/law/pub/ehlevi.

Acknowledgments

1. Ron Carr's essay, "Mr. Levi at Justice," 52 *Univ. of Chicago L. Rev.* 300 (1985), reflects importantly on many of the themes—and talks—treated in this volume.

Chapter One

1. The inauguration was of Leon Botstein as president of Bard College.

2. See Alexander Bickel, *The Morality of Consent* (Yale University Press 1975).

3. 2 Alexis de Tocqueville, *Democracy in America* 10 (Francis Bowen ed., Henry Reeve trans., Century 1898).

4. In 1950 Levi was chief counsel of the Subcommittee on Monopoly Power of the House Judiciary Committee.

5. John Henry Newman, *The Idea of a University* (University of Notre Dame Press 1990).

6. Guidelines on organized crime investigations and other matters were planned but not completed when Levi left the Department of Justice at the time of President Jimmy Carter's inauguration.

7. The word "include" was missing in the original typescript.

8. The Levi guidelines on domestic security investigations are in the appendix of this volume. A full discussion of these is in Levi's testimony to the Senate Select Committee on Intelligence, "Guidelines for the FBI," in this volume. I have shortened the discussion of the guidelines in this talk to avoid repetition. Guidelines on White House personnel security and background investigations, use of informants and reporting on civil disorders and demonstrations can be found in the appendices of John T. Elliff, *The Reform of FBI Intelligence Operations* (Princeton University Press 1979).

9. Levi treated the subject of national security electronic surveillance fully in testimony before the Senate Select Committee on Intelligence, "The Legal Frame-

work for Electronic Surveillance," in this volume. I have abbreviated Levi's discussion in this speech in order to avoid repetition.

10. DeFunis v. Odegaard, 416 U.S. 312 (1974).

11. Levi persuaded President Ford to support a gun control bill. No Republican sponsors could be found. Sen. Edward Kennedy of Massachusetts introduced it. It never passed.

12. S.1 was a bill to reorganize and revise the Federal Criminal Code. It never passed.

13. Lord Patrick Devlin, *The Criminal Prosecution in England* 65 (Oxford University Press 1960).

14. Branzburg v. Hayes, 408 U.S. 665 (1972).

15. *Id.* at 745–46 (Stewart, J., dissenting, joined by Brennan and Marshall, JJ.).

16. 28 *C.F.R* § 50.10(f)(5)(1976).

17. The guidelines were issued in 1970 and revised in 1973.

18. The original typescript reads "close to the reach of policy of constitutional protection."

19. Abbate v. United States, 359 U.S. 187 (1959).

20. United States v. Lanza, 260 U.S. 377 (1922).

21. *Abbate*, 359 U.S. at 203.

22. *Id.* at 203.

23. Bartkus v. Illinois, 359 U.S. 121 (1959).

24. *Id.* at 150.

25. Press Release, Department of Justice (Nov. 6, 1959).

26. The current policy refers to "substantial federal interest." U.S. Dep't of Justice, "Dual and Successive Prosecution Policy ('Petite Policy')," *United States Attorneys' Manual*, tit. 9 § 2031. http://www.justice.gov/usao/eousa/foia_reading_room/usam/title9/2mcrm.htm#9-2031.

27. Quoted in United States v. Mechanic, 454 F.2d 849, 855, n. 5 (8th Cir. 1971).

28. Watts v. United States, 422 U.S. 1032, 1038 (1975).

29. Levi dealt extensively with the legal issues involved in warrantless electronic surveillance in his testimony, "The Legal Framework for Electronic Surveillance," before the Senate Select Committee to Study Governmental Operations with Respect to Intelligence Activities. It can be found in this volume.

30. A more extensive discussion of this proposed bill can be found in Levi's testimony to the Senate Select Committee on Intelligence, "A Proposed National Security Surveillance Statute," in this volume.

31. A similar bill was finally enacted during the Carter administration. 50 *U.S.C* § 1801–1812 (2006).

32. Wicker and the team of Evans and Novak were syndicated newspaper columnists.

33. Levi had served during the Roosevelt administration as, among other posi-

tions, first assistant to Thurman Arnold in the Antitrust Division and as special assistant to Attorney General Francis Biddle.

34. Transcript available in box 303, folder 7, Edward H. Levi Papers, Special Collections Research Center, University of Chicago D'Angelo Law Library.

Chapter Two

1. Transcript available in box 303, folder 7, Edward H. Levi Papers, Special Collections Research Center, University of Chicago D'Angelo Law Library.

2. Lawrence A. Kimpton led the University of Chicago from 1951 to 1960.

3. Burton-Judson is a residence hall.

4. Brown v. Bd of Educ. of Topeka, 347 U.S. 483, 494 and note 11 (1954).

5. Muller v. Oregon, 208 U.S. 412 (1908).

6. This punctuation is Levi's.

7. Oliver Wendell Holmes, "The Path of the Law," 10 *Harvard L. Rev.* 457, 469 (1897).

8. Edmund Burke, *Speech on Conciliation with the Colonies*, in 1 *The Founders' Constitution* 3, 5, (Philip Kurland and Ralph Lerner eds., Univ. of Chicago Press 1987).

9. *A Federalist* from *Boston Gazette and Country Journal, Nov. 26, 1787*, in 4 *The Complete Anti-Federalist Papers* 117, 118, (Herbert Storing ed., Univ. of Chicago Press 1981).

10. John Austin, *The Province of Jurisprudence Determined* 118 (John Murray 1832).

11. Samuel Johnson, definition of "Critick," in *Dictionary of the English Language* (Longman, Hurst, Reese, and Orme 1805).

12. Johnson, definition of "Adversary," in *id.*

13. George Washington, *Letter to John Jay, Aug. 1, 1786*, in *George Washington: Writings* 605, 606, (John Rhodehamel ed., Library of America 1997).

14. *Id.* at 605.

15. Benjamin Franklin, *Motion for Prayers in the Convention, June 28, 1787*, in *Benjamin Franklin: Writings* 1138, (J. A. Leo Lemay ed., Library of America 1987). [Emphasis in original.]

16. Charles and Mary Beard, *The Rise of American Civilization* 317 (Macmillan 1957).

17. James Madison, *Letter to Thomas Jefferson, March 18, 1786*, in 1 *Letters and Other Writings of James Madison* 227 (R. Worthington 1884).

18. See J. B. McMaster, *The Struggle for Commercial Independence (1783–1812)*, in 7 *The Cambridge Modern History* 305 (A. W. Ward, G. W. Prothero and Stanley Leathes eds., Macmillan 1903).

19. Thomas Jefferson, *Revolt of the Nobles: To John Adams, Aug. 30, 1787*, in

Thomas Jefferson: Writings 906, 908 (Merrill D. Peterson ed., Library of America 1984).

20. Washington, *The Diary of George Washington* 128 (Benson Lossing ed., Kessenger Publishing 2006).

21. Joel Barlow, from an oration delivered in Hartford, CT, on July 4, 1787, quoted in Richard Buel, Jr., *Joel Barlow: American Citizen in a Revolutionary World* 95 (Johns Hopkins University Press 2011).

22. John Stuart Mill, *The Basic Writings of John Stuart Mill* 35 (Modern Library 2002).

23. The capital "E" in "Economist" is preserved from original typescript.

24. Walter Bagehot, *Physics and Politics* 219 (D. Appleton 1873).

25. John Jay, *Letter from John Jay to Thomas Jefferson of June 27, 1786*, in Galliard Hunt, James Madison, and James Scott Brown, *The Debates in the Federal Convention of 1787 Which Framed the Constitution of the United States of America* 586, 587 (Oxford University Press 1920).

26. Washington, *The Diary of George Washington* 17 (Benson J. Lossing ed., Kessenger Publishing 2006).

27. Madison, *The Federalist No. 14*, in 1 *The Debate on the Constitution* 431, 433 (Bernard Bailyn ed., Library of America 1993).

28. Barrett Wendell, *The American Intellect*, in 7 *Cambridge Modern History* 723, 734–35 (A. W. Ward, G. W. Prothero and Stanley Leathes eds., Macmillan 1903).

29. The word is "have" in the original typescript.

30. François Rabelais, *Gargantua and Pantagruel* 199 (Thomas Urquhart and Antony Motteux trans., Laurence and Bullen 1892).

31. Paul Freund, "The Challenge of the Law," 40 *Tul. L. Rev.* 475, 477 (1966).

32. In the text of the Department of Justice press release, these last three sentences are included within the quote, but they are not in the Freund article. Since they are written in a style characteristic of Levi, the quotation marks were probably misplaced in the typing of the release.

33. Archibald MacLeish, "Apologia," 85 *Harv. L. Rev.* 1505, 1508 (1972).

34. The idea appears with slightly different wording in the book Warren developed from his Jefferson Lecture: Robert Penn Warren, *Democracy and Poetry* 45 (Harvard University Press 1975).

35. Prohibitions del Roy, (1607) 77 Eng. Rep. 1342 (K.B.), 1343; 12 Co. Rep. 64, 65.

36. The typescript lacks the word "its."

37. *Id.* Levi also drew on Catherine Drinker Bowen, *The Lion and the Throne: The Life and Times of Sir Edward Coke* 303–6 (Little, Brown 1956), apparently accepting her conclusion in the face of ambiguous evidence that Coke actually did fall prostrate before the King. As Bowen put it, "It was that or a cell in the Tower."

38. "Legislator" in the original.

39. The original typescript text of the Department of Justice press release reads "before it."

40. 2 David Ramsay, *History of the American Revolution* 405 (James J. Wilson 1811).

41. James Wilson, *Of the Study of Law in the United States*, in 1 *The Works of James Wilson* 7 (James DeWitt Andrews ed., Callaghan and Company 1895).

42. Gordon Wood, *The Creation of the American Republic, 1776–1787* 10 (W. W. Norton 1972).

43. The original typescript read "branches of governments."

44. Alexander Hamilton, *The Federalist No. 9*, in 1 *The Debate on the Constitution* 339, 340 (Bernard Bailyn ed., Library of America 1993).

45. Jack Greenberg, *Litigation for Social Change: Methods, Limits, and Role in Democracy*, in 30 *Benjamin N. Cardozo Lectures* 320, 321 (Ass'n of Bar of City of N.Y. 1974).

46. I do not know what translation Levi used for this quotation. In 1 Alexis de Tocqueville, *Democracy in America* 279 (Harvey C. Mansfield and Delba Winthrop trans. and eds., Univ. of Chicago Press 2000), the passage is rendered this way: "[E]verything is certain and fixed in the moral world, although the political world seems to be abandoned to the discussion and attempts of men."

47. Madison quoted in 2 *Debate on the Constitution* 121, 123 (Bernard Bailyn ed., Library of America 1993). [Emphasis in original.]

48. *Id.* at 163, 164.

49. Lawrence Friedman, *The Legal System: A Social Science Perspective* 23 (Russell Sage Foundation 1975).

50. John Winthrop, thesis written on board the *Arbella* (1630), available at religiousfreedom.lib.virginia.edu/sacred/charity.html.

51. Ezra Stiles, "The United States Elevated to Glory and Honor, 1783," Electronic Texts in American Studies, Libraries at University of Nebraska–Lincoln, http://digitalcommons.unl.edu/etas/41/.

52. Herman Melville, *White-Jacket*, in *Redburn, White-Jacket and Moby Dick* 341, 506 (G. Thomas Tanselle ed., Library of America 1983).

53. I do not know what text of Rabbi Einhorn's talk Levi used in preparing this speech. But the quotes parallel passages in a published version: Rev. Dr. David Einhorn, *Centennial Sermon delivered on the 1st of July, 1876, in the Temple Bethel, Newport, R.I.*, p. 4, in Sermons, 1855–1876, box 1, folder 6, MS-155, David Einhorn Papers, American Jewish Archives, Cincinnati, Ohio.

54. Jefferson, *A Profession of Political Faith: A Letter to Elbridge Gerry, Jan. 26, 1799*, in *Thomas Jefferson: Writings* 1055, 1061 (Merrill D. Peterson ed., Library of America 1984).

55. Madison, *Memorial and Remonstrance against Religious Assessments*, in *James Madison: Writings* 29, 30 (Jack N. Rakove ed., Library of America 1999).

56. Washington, *To the Hebrew Congregation in Newport Rhode Island, Aug. 18, 1790*, in *George Washington: Writings* 766, 767 (John Rhodehamel ed., Library of America 1997).

57. H. M. Brackenridge, *Recollections of Persons and Places in the West* 294 (J. P. Lippencott 1868).

58. Einhorn, *Centennial Sermon delivered on the 1st of July* at 5–6.

59. Henry Wadsworth Longfellow, *The Jewish Cemetery at Newport*, in *Henry Wadsworth Longfellow: Poems and Other Writings* 335, 336–37 (J. D. McClatchy ed., Library of America 2000). Levi omitted the first word of the stanza, "for."

60. Pericles quoted in 1 *Thucydides* 118 (Benjamin Jowett, trans., Clarendon 2d ed. 1881).

61. *Id.* at 120.

62. The original typescript released by the Department of Justice contains a double negative, "The vision does not deny that there might not be burdens."

63. Plato, *The Apology*, in *Plato's Apology of Socrates and Crito with a Part of His Phaedo* 49 (Benjamin Jowett trans., Century 1903).

64. 2 Alexis de Tocqueville, *Democracy in America* 275 (Francis Bowen ed., Henry Reeve trans., Century 1898).

65. Jay, *Letter of John Jay to George Washington*, in James Madison, Gaillard Hunt, and James Brown Scott, *The Debates in the Federal Convention of 1787 Which Framed the Constitution of the United States of America* 587 (Oxford University Press 1920).

66. Washington, *Letter to John Jay, Aug. 1, 1786*, in *George Washington: Writings* 605–7 (John Rhodehamel ed., Library of America 1997).

67. Bagehot, *Physics and Politics* 219 (D. Appleton and Co. 1873).

68. John Adams, *A Dissertation on the Canon and the Feudal Law No. 1*, in *John Adams: Revolutionary Writings 1755–1775* 114 (Gordon Wood ed., Library of America 2011).

69. *Id.* at 691 (note 118.2).

70. Barrett Wendell, *The American Intellect*, in 7 *Cambridge Modern History* 75 (A. W. Ward, G. W. Prothero and Stanley Leathes eds., Macmillan 1903).

71. Franklin, *Remarks Concerning the Savages of North America*, in *Benjamin Franklin: Writings* 970 (J. A. Leo Lemay ed., Library of America 1987).

72. 1 Richard Crossman, *Diaries of a Cabinet Minister* (Holt, Rinehart and Winston, 1978) (first published in Great Britain in 1975).

73. Reinhold Neibuhr, *Moral Man and Immoral Society* (Charles Scribner's Sons 1932).

74. Matthew Arnold, 2 *The Complete Prose Works of Matthew Arnold: Democratic Education* 17 (R. H. Super ed., University of Michigan Press 1962).

75. Sir Eric Ashby, *Masters and Scholars: Reflections on the Rights and Responsibilities of Students* 79 (Oxford University Press 1970).

NOTES TO PAGES 78–87

76. André Malraux, *Anti-Memoirs* 245 (Terence Kilmartin trans., Holt, Rinehart and Winston, 1968). (Malraux purports to be quoting an ambassador in New Delhi.)

77. Franklin, *Speech in the Convention at the Conclusion of its Deliberations*, in *Benjamin Franklin: Writings* 1139, 1141 (J. A. Leo Lemay ed., Library of America 1987).

78. Madison, *The Federalist No. 14*, in *James Madison: Writings* 168, 172 (Jack N. Rakove ed., Library of America 1999).

79. Abrams v. United States, 250 U.S. 616, 630 (1919) (Holmes, J., dissenting).

80. *Id.* at 630.

81. Jay, *The Federalist No. 2*, in *The Federalist* 54, 55 (John C. Hamilton ed., J. B. Lippincott 1864).

82. Hamilton, *The Federalist No. 9*, in *Alexander Hamilton: Writings 196,* 197 (Joanne B. Freeman ed., Library of America 2001).

83. Hamilton, *The Federalist No. 71*, in *Alexander Hamilton: Writings* 383, 385 (Joanne B. Freeman ed., Library of America 2001).

84. Hamilton, *The Federalist No. 70*, in *Alexander Hamilton: Writings* 374, 375 (Joanne B. Freeman ed., Library of America 2001).

85. James Joyce, *Portrait of the Artist as a Young Man* 189 (Viking Press 1974). [Italics in original.]

86. Jay, *The Federalist No. 2*, in *The Federalist* 55 (John C. Hamilton ed., J. B. Lippincott 1864).

87. Washington, *Farewell Address*, in *George Washington: Writings* 962, 965 (John Rhodehamel ed., Library of America 1997).

88. This follows the wording used by Jorge Luis Borges in *Other Inquisitions 1937–1952* 46, (Ruth L. C. Simms trans., Clarion Books, Simon and Schuster 1968).

Chapter Three

1. Transcript available in box 296, folder 6, Edward H. Levi Papers, Special Collections Research Center, University of Chicago D'Angelo Law Library.

2. F. A. Hayek, *Intellectuals and Socialism*, in *The Intellectuals: A Controversial Portrait* 371 (George B. de Huszar ed., The Free Press 1960).

3. Some of the notes in this speech were included, in one form or another, in the Department of Justice typescript press release, and some of these I have edited for accuracy or completeness. Other notes I have supplied.

4. "A Burden of Mistrust."

5. Among other matters, the Department of Justice investigated the opening of mail by agents of the Central Intelligence Agency and warrantless break-ins by the Federal Bureau of Investigation not authorized by the President or Attorney General in domestic security cases.

6. Olmstead v. United States, 277 U.S. 438 (1928).

7. When Levi refers to internal Department of Justice documents I have generally not added citations. Most of the original texts are not readily accessible.

8. Nardone v. United States, 302 U.S. 379 (1937).

9. Nardone v. United States, 308 U.S. 338 (1939).

10. *Memorandum for the Att'y Gen. from President Franklin D. Roosevelt* (May 21, 1940), reprinted in United States v. White, 401 U.S. 745, 766–767 (1971) (app. to Douglas, J., dissenting).

11. *Letter from Tom C. Clark to President Harry Truman* (July 17, 1946), reprinted in 117 Cong. Rec. 14056 (1971).

12. *Memorandum for the Heads of Exec. Dep'ts and Agencies from President Lyndon B. Johnson* (June 30, 1965), reprinted in United States v. White, 401 U.S. 745, 767–68 (1971) (app. to Douglas, J., dissenting).

13. Supp. Brief of Respondent, Black v. United States, 385 U.S. 26 (1966) (No. 1029).

14. Supp. Brief of Respondent, Schipani v. United States, 385 U.S. 372 (1966) (No. 504).

15. Public Law 90-351, § 2511(3) (June 19, 1968).

16. United States v. U.S. Dist. Court, 407 U.S. 297, 303 (1972) [hereinafter referred to in the text and notes as the "*Keith* case"].

17. Air Force General Lew Allen, then director of the National Security Agency.

18. Entick v. Carrington, 19 *Howell, St. Tr.* 1029 (1765).

19. Boyd v. United States, 116 U.S. 616, 627 (1886).

20. *Entick*, 19 *Howell, St. Tr.* 1029, 1063 (1765).

21. William Tudor, *Life of James Otis* 63, 66 (Wells and Lilly 1823).

22. Charles Francis Adams, 10 *The Works of John Adams* 248 (Little, Brown 1856).

23. James Madison's proposal read as follows: "The rights of the people to be secured in their persons, their houses, their papers, and their other property, from all unreasonable searches and seizures, shall not be violated by warrants issued without probable cause, supported by oath or affirmation, or not particularly describing the places to be searched, or the persons or things to be seized." 1 *Annals of Cong.* 452 (1789).

24. Olmstead v. United States, 277 U.S. 438, 478 (1928).

25. United States v. On Lee, 193 F.2d 306, 315–16 (2d Cir. 1951).

26. United States v. Boyd, 116 U.S. 616, 630 (1886).

27. The concern with self-incrimination is reflected in the test of standing to invoke the exclusionary rule. As the Court stated in United States v. Calandra, 414 U.S. 338, 348 (1974): "Thus, standing to invoke the exclusionary Rule [under the Fourth Amendment] has been confined to situations where the Government seeks to use such evidence to incriminate the victim of the unlawful search. . . .

This standing rule is premised on a recognition that the need for deterrence, and hence the rationale for excluding the evidence are strongest where the Government's unlawful conduct would result in imposition of a criminal sanction on the victim of the search."

28. *Boyd*, 116 U.S., at 631–32.

29. Harris v. United States, 331 U.S. 145, 163 (1947).

30. *Keith* case, at 314.

31. Olmstead v. United States, 277 U.S. 438 (1928).

32. *Entick*, 19 *Howell, St. Tr.* 1029, 1066 (1765).

33. Goldman v. United States, 316 U.S. 129 (1942).

34. Silverman v. United States, 365 U.S. 505 (1961).

35. Katz v. United States, 389 U.S. 347 (1967).

36. *Id.* at 361.

37. *Id.* at 350.

38. United States v. White, 401 U.S. 745, 786 (1971) (Harlan, J., dissenting).

39. Frank v. Maryland, 359 U.S. 360 (1959).

40. *Id.* at 363.

41. *Id.* at 365.

42. The typescript reads "later."

43. *Id.* at 367.

44. Camara v. Mun. Ct. of S.F., 387 U.S. 523 (1967).

45. See v. Seattle, 387 U.S. 541 (1967).

46. Wyman v. James, 400 U.S. 309 (1971).

47. *Camara*, 387 U.S. at 536–37.

48. Brinegar v. United States, 338 U.S. 160, 175 (1949).

49. Gouled v. United States, 255 U.S. 298, 309 (1921).

50. Warden V. Hayden, 387 U.S. 294 (1967).

51. Terry v. Ohio, 392 U.S. 1 (1968).

52. United States v. Brignoni-Ponce, 422 U.S. 873 (1975).

53. Almeida-Sanchez v. United States, 413 U.S. 266 (1973).

54. United States v. Ortiz, 422 U.S. 891 (1975).

55. Camara v. Mun. Ct. of S.F., 387 U.S. 523 (1967).

56. *Id.* at 539.

57. *Keith* case at 322.

58. United States v. Poller, 43 F.2d 911, 914 (2d Cir. 1930).

59. 18 U.S.C. § 2518(5) (1970).

60. Bivens v. Six Unknown Named Agents of the Fed. Narc. Bureau, 403 U.S. 388 (1971).

61. Johnson v. United States, 333 U.S. 10, 13–14 (1948).

62. Katz v. United Sates, 389 U.S. 347 (1967).

63. *Keith* case at 317.

64. Almeida-Sanchez v. United States, 413 U.S. 266, 275 (1973).

65. *Keith* case at 322.

66. "A Burden of Mistrust," in this volume. The portion dealing with electronic surveillance is for the most part not included, since its points are repeated and greatly elaborated in this testimony.

67. United States v. Brown, 484 F.2d 418 (5th Cir. 1973), *cert. denied*, 415 U.S. 960 (1974).

68. *Id.* at 426.

69. United States v. Butenko, 494 F.2d 593 (3d Cir. 1974) (*en banc*), *cert. denied sub nom.* Ivanov v. United States, 419 U.S. 881 (1974).

70. Zweibon v. Mitchell, 516 F.2d 594 (D.C. Cir. 1975) (*en banc*).

71. *Id.* at 614.

72. Committee of Privy Councillors Appointed to Inquire into the Interception of Communications, Report, 1957, at 5 (U.K.), which states, "The origin of the power to intercept communications can only be surmised, but the power has been exercised from very early times; and has been recognized as a lawful power by a succession of statutes covering the last 200 years or more."

73. Lord Patrick Devlin, *The Criminal Prosecution in England* 53 (Oxford University Press 1960).

74. United States v. Brown, 484 F.2d 418 (5th Cir. 1973), *cert. denied* 415 U.S. 960 (1974).

75. United States v. Butenko, 494 F.2d 593 (3d Cir. 1974) (*en banc*), *cert. denied sub nom.* Ivanov v. United States, 419 U.S. 881 (1974).

76. Capitals and italics in original Department of Justice press release text.

77. *Keith* case at 303.

78. Katz v. United States, 389 U.S. 347 (1967).

79. NAACP v. Alabama ex rel. Patterson, 357 U.S. 449 (1958).

80. United States v. Nixon, 418 U.S. 683, 708 (1974) [hereinafter cited as *Nixon*].

81. *Id.* at 705.

82. Alexander Meiklejohn, *Political Freedom* (Greenwood Press 1979).

83. Madison, *Letter to William T. Barry Aug. 4, 1822*, in *James Madison: Writings* 790 (Jack N. Rakove ed., Library of America 1999).

84. Branzburg v. Hayes, 408 U.S. 665, 684–685 (1972).

85. Gravel v. United States, 408 U.S. 606 (1972).

86. New York Times Co. v. United States, 403 U.S. 713 (1971).

87. Robert Jackson, *Position of the Exec. Dep't Regarding Investigative Reports*, in 40 *Op. Att'y Gen.* 45, 47 (1941).

88. United States v. Reynolds, 345 U.S. 1, 10 (1953).

89. Fred [F. W.] Winterbotham, *The Ultra Secret* (Harper and Row 1974).

90. Lord Devlin, *Too Proud to Fight* (Oxford University Press 1974).

91. United States v. Curtiss-Wright Export Corp., 299 U.S. 304, 320 (1936).

92. C & S Air Lines v. Waterman Steamship Corp., 333 U.S. 103, 111 (1948).

93. *Nixon* at 706.

94. *Id.* at 710.

95. *Nixon* at 708, 711.

96. Jackson, *Position of the Exec. Dep't Regarding Investigative Reports*, in 40 *Op. Att'y Gen.* 45, 49 (1941).

97. Gerhard Casper, *American Geheimniskrämerei*, in 3 *Reviews in American History* 154, 158 (1975) (reviewing Raoul Berger, *Executive Privilege: A Constitutional Myth* [Harvard University Press 1974]).

98. A revised version of this talk was published in 76 *Col. L. Rev.* 371 (1976). Notes were added later by the Department of Justice and the law review editors. I have used the original Department of Justice typescript press release for the main text, with minor spelling, punctuation and other typographical errors corrected.

99. Scott Buchanan, *So Reason Can Rule: The Constitution Revisited*, in *1975 Annual Volume of Great Books of the Western World Library* 145, 441 (Encyclopaedia Britannica 1975) [hereinafter cited as Buchanan].

100. Gordon Wood, *The Creation of the American Republic, 1776–1787* 10 (W. W. Norton 1969) [hereinafter cited as Wood].

101. Charles de Secondat, Baron de Montesquieu, *The Spirit of the Laws*, 38 *Great Books of the Western World* 70 (Robert Maynard Hutchins ed., Encyclopaedia Brittanica 1952).

102. Youngstown Sheet & Tube Co. v. Sawyer, 343 U.S. 579, 593 (1952) (Frankfurter, J., concurring).

103. Wood at 153–54.

104. George Washington, *Letter to John Jay, Aug. 1, 1786*, in *George Washington: Writings* 605, 606 (John Rhodehamel ed., Library of America 1997).

105. Anonymous New Englander quoted in Wood at 405.

106. Thomas Jefferson quoted in Madison, *The Federalist No. 48*, in *Federalist Papers*, 43 *Great Books of the Western World* 158 (Robert Maynard Hutchins ed., Encyclopaedia Britannica 1952) [hereinafter cited as *The Federalist*].

107. Wood at 608.

108. Madison, *The Federalist No. 47*, in *The Federalist* at 153..

109. Wood at 609.

110. Madison, *The Federalist No. 48*, in *The Federalist* at 157.

111. Alexander Hamilton, *The Federalist No. 71*, in *The Federalist* at 215.

112. Buchanan at 442.

113. See Alexander Bickel, *The Morality of Consent* (Yale University Press 1975).

114. See William W. Crosskey, *Politics and the Constitution in the History of the United States* (Univ. of Chicago Press 1981).

115. Hamilton, *The Federalist No. 70*, in *The Federalist* at 210.

116. Punctuation follows 2 *The Debate on the Constitution* 346 (Bernard Bailyn, ed., Library of America 1993).

117. John Jay, *The Federalist No. 64*, in *The Federalist* at 196.

118. Wood at 453.

119. Lord Devlin, *The Criminal Prosecution in England* 65 (Oxford University Press 1960).

120. James Wilson quoted in Wood at 305.

121. Madison, *The Federalist No. 47*, in *The Federalist* at 154.

122. Madison, *The Federalist No. 51*, in *The Federalist* at 163.

123. Youngstown Sheet & Tube Co. v. Sawyer, 343 U.S. 579, 635 (1952) (Jackson, J., concurring).

124. Michael Kammen, *People of Paradox: An Inquiry Concerning the Origins of American Civilization* 165 (Alfred A. Knopf 1972).

125. Martin Diamond, *Liberty, Democracy and the Founders*, 41 *Public Interest* 54 (1975).

126. Woodrow Wilson, *Congressional Government: A Study in American Politics* (Meridian Books 1956) [hereinafter cited as Wilson].

127. *Id.* at 28, 31.

128. *Id.* at 48.

129. Walter Lippmann, *Introduction*, in Wilson at 8.

130. Wilson at 186–87.

131. 49 Cong. Rec. 895, 62d Cong., 3d Sess. (1912).

132. Wilson at 196.

133. Thomas Erskine May, *Treatise on the Law, Privileges, Proceedings and Usage of Parliament* 357 *et seq.* (16th Ed., Butterworth 1957).

134. Daniel Norman Chester and Nona Bowring, *Questions in Parliament* 300 (Clarendon Press 1962).

135. Jefferson, *Letter to John Breckinridge*, in 4 *Annals of America* 172 (Encyclopaedia Britannica 1968).

136. In re Debs, 158 U.S. 564 (1895).

137. Youngstown Sheet & Tube Co. v. Sawyer, 343 U.S. 579 (1952).

138. Ex parte Milligan, 71 U.S. 2 (1866).

139. See Edward Levi, *The Collective Morality of Maturing Society*, 30 *Wash. & Lee L. Rev.* 399 (1973).

140. Gravel v United States, 408 U.S. 606 (1972).

141. Eastland v. U. S. Serv. Men's Fund, 421 U.S. 491 (1975).

142. *Id.* at 502 (quoting United States v. Johnson, 383 U.S. 169, 178 [1966]).

143. United States v. Klein, 80 U.S. 128 (1872).

144. *Id.* at 146, 147.

145. Kilbourn v. Thompson, 103 U.S. 168 (1880).

146. *Id.* at 190.

147. Watkins v. United States, 354 U.S. 178 (1957).

148. *Id.* at 187.

149. United States v. Lovett, 328 U.S. 303 (1946).

150. United States v. Brown, 381 U.S. 437 (1965).

151. *Id.* at 445.

152. Samuel Morrison, *The Oxford History of the American People* 319 (Oxford University Press 1965).

153. Myers v. United States, 272 U.S. 52 (1926).

154. *Id.* at 127.

155. *Id.* at 123.

156. *Id.* at 123.

157. United States v. Richardson, 418 U.S. 166 (1974).

158. *Id.* at 188.

159. E.g., Kennedy v. Sampson, 511 F. 2d 430, 433–36 (D.C. Cir. 1974).

160. E.g., 26 U.S.C. § 6103 (1970) (tax returns); 42 U.S.C. § 1306(a)–(d) (1970) (social security returns).

161. E.g., 42 U.S.C. § 260(d) (1970) (medical records of narcotics addicts who have voluntarily undertaken treatment).

162. *Contempt Proceedings against Secretary of Commerce Rogers C. B. Morton before the Subcommittee on Oversights and Investigations of the House Committee on Interstate and Foreign Commerce,* 94th Cong. 56 (1975) (testimony of Raoul Berger).

163. *Id.* at 107–8 (testimony of Philip Kurland).

164. NAACP v. Alabama ex rel. Patterson, 357 U.S. 449 (1958).

165. *Nixon* at 705.

166. U. S. v. Burr, 25 Fed. Cas. 30 (C.C.D. Va. 1807) (No. 14,692d); U. S. v. Burr, 25 Fed. Cas. 187 (C.C.D. Va. 1807) (No. 14,694).

167. *Nixon,* 418 U.S. 683 (1974).

168. Senate Select Comm. on Presidential Campaign Activities v. Nixon, 498 F.2d 725 (D.C. Cir. 1974) (*en banc*).

169. Act of Dec. 18, 1973, Pub. L. No. 93-190, 87 Stat. 736 (1973).

170. Buchanan at 460.

171. Arthur Schlesinger, *First Lecture,* in Arthur Schlesinger and Alfred De Grazia, *Congress and the Presidency: Their Roles in Modern Times* 3 (American Enterprise Institute for Public Policy Research 1967).

172. Buchanan at 460.

173. Hamilton, *The Federalist No. 9,* in *The Federalist* at 47.

174. *Id.*

175. The Department of Justice press release text of this speech has the word "had." The text of the Jackson article on the Robert Jackson website has it as "have."

176. Quotes are from Jackson, *The Struggle against Monopoly,* 1937 *Georgia Bar Association Report* 203, available at http://www.roberthjackson.org/the-man/ speeches-articles/speeches/speeches-by-robert-h-jackson/the-struggle-against -monopoly/.

177. Hugh S. Johnson, *The Blue Eagle from Egg to Earth* 188 (Doubleday, Doran 1935).

178. The Department of Justice press release text does not include the words "one of" but has "periods" plural.

179. This appears as "overly" in the original Justice Department typescript press release.

180. Kewanee Oil Co. v. Bicron Corp., 416 U.S. 470 (1974).

181. Sen. George Frisbie Hoar of Massachusetts.

182. United States v. E. I. DuPont de Nemours & Co., 353 U.S. 586 (1957).

183. Department of Justice press release of the text has this as "in."

184. In the Department of Justice typescript press release, this passage reads "more stringent forms of government managerial forms of regulation," which I have tried to ungarble.

185. The Department of Justice typescript press release reads "consider not only the effect within an industry but on the more general impact."

186. Clayton Act, § 7, 15 U.S.C. § 18 (1970).

187. This unit was led by Jeffrey Harris.

188. John T. Elliff, *The Reform of FBI Intelligence Operations* 77 (Princeton University Press 1979).

189. Harlan Fiske Stone quoted in *Sen. George Norris Letter to Att'y Gen. Robert Jackson* (April 24, 1940), in 86 Cong. Rec. 5642 (1940).

190. In the end Levi chose not to include provisions for preventive action in the domestic security guidelines. (A text of the guidelines is in the appendix of this volume; it includes the preventive action section.)

191. COINTELPRO was an FBI program aimed at the disruption of various activities and groups the Bureau claimed constituted a domestic security threat.

192. See "The Legal Framework for Electronic Surveillance," in this volume, for a thorough discussion of electronic surveillance and "A Proposed National Security Surveillance Statute" for a discussion of the draft legislation.

193. Guidelines were not completed in all these areas before the end of the Ford administration in January 1977.

194. These preventive action provisions were not included in the final domestic security guidelines.

Appendix

1. Hearings on FBI Statutory Charter, Committee on the Judiciary, United States Senate, 95th Congress, Second Session, April 20 and 25, 1978. This is the only text of the guidelines that I know of published in an official, publicly available source. It appears in typescript, facsimile form. This text was published after Levi left office, but I do not believe it was the last draft prepared during his time, since it includes a section on "preventive action," which Levi ultimately elim-

inated. Another, slightly different (probably earlier) version, appears in an appendix to John Elliff, *The Reform of FBI Intelligence Operations* 196–219 (Princeton University Press 1979).

The guidelines went into effect within the Department of Justice and the FBI as they reached a settled point in their development, but even then they continued to be revised based on experience and rethinking. Evidence of this can be found in the Domestic Security Guidelines, which include elements that were clearly left tentative. The text also includes a number of apparent typographical errors, which I have corrected and noted. Inconsistencies in paragraph numbering I have retained for fear of creating confusion.

2. Here and elsewhere, the original text is inconsistent in the way it marks paragraphs and subparagraphs.

3. Printed as "or" in the text of the congressional hearing document, an obvious typographical error.

4. "Mail covers" pertain to the examination of the outside of a piece of mail before its delivery to the addressee.

5. This was singular in the original. I have made it plural to be consistent with the treatment of preliminary and limited investigations.

6. This was written as "are" in the original text, clearly in error.

7. "The committee" refers to the Department of Justice's FBI Guidelines Committee.

8. "Inquiries made under 'pretext'" are those in which the inquirer impersonates another.

9. "Trash covers" pertain to the examination of the contents of garbage containers left in non-private areas.

10. The period was inside the closing parenthesis in the text printed in the official report of the hearings.

11. The hyphen in 30-day was missing in the original text.

12. In the report the items under IV(C) were all enclosed in hand-written brackets, with the exception of item 4, suggesting that they were more tentative than the other parts of the guidelines.

13. As published in the official report of the hearings the text reads "service," which makes no sense.

14. Referring to the Department of Justice FBI Guidelines Committee.

Index

208

INDEX

Fourth Amendment (*continued*)
and, 116; reasonableness and, 103–4,
106, 108, 109, 110–11; searches of per-
sons and vehicles and, 107; seized prop-
erty and, 106–7; warrantless surveillance
and, 116, 136; warrants and, 104–5, 108–9,
110–11, 113; writing of, 98–99
France, 48
Frank, Jerome, 99
Frankfurter, Felix, 100, 105, 142
Franklin, Benjamin, 47, 48, 68–69, 74–75
Frank v. Maryland, 104–5
freedom. *See* liberty
Freedom of Information Act, 131, 138, 161,
164
French Revolution, 42–43
Freund, Paul, xxi, 53–54
Front Page, The (play), 35
Fulbright, J. William, 95
Fuller, Jack, 187n18

George III (England), 142
Germany, 134. *See also* West Germany
Gibbon, Edward, 141
Goldman v. United States, 102, 103
Gordon, George, 67–68
government: as automaton versus human institution, 130; checks and balances and,
44; confidentiality in, 125–39; cycles in,
46; by discussion, xx, 12, 49, 51–52, 73,
82–83, 85, 156; human nature and, 46–47;
legal system and, 38–39; parliamentary,
148–50; popular knowledge about, 48;
public service and, 70–71; qualities necessary for, 71; representative bodies and,
73; science of, 48–49, 61–62, 66; theory of
delegation and, 7. *See also* branches of
government
Gravel v. United States, 132, 151
Gray, L. Patrick, xxiv, 187n31
Great Britain. *See* England
great seal of the United States, 73
Greenberg, Jack, 62
groupism, 6–7
gun control, 24, 189n11
Gunther, Gerald, xxi

Halifax, Lord, 98
Hamilton, Alexander, 61–62, 81, 144, 145, 146
Harlan, John M., 102, 103

Harris, Jeffrey, 201n187
Hart, H. L. A., 39
Hayek, Friedrich, 84
Hecht, Ben, 35
Hecht, Kate Sulzberger, xxiii
Henry, Jacob, 68
heroism, 9
Hirsch, Emil, xxii
history: investigatory abuses and, 47–48;
knowledge of, 47; law and, 41; as ongo-
ing, 83; value of study of, 81–82
Hoar, George F., 167
Hobbes, Thomas, 147
Holmes, Oliver Wendell, 41, 79
Hoover, J. Edgar: accountability and, xxvi;
appointment of, 171; death of, xxvi; elec-
tronic surveillance and, 91–92; secret
files of, xxv, 173
House Judiciary Committee, xxiii, 188n4
humanism, 52–54
humility, xiv, 39

immigration, 107
industrial revolution, 148
innovation, versus excellence, 10
In re Debs, 151, 154
institutions, societal, 8–9
Internal Security Act of 1950, 152
internet, incivility and, xvi

Jackson, Robert: as Attorney General, 164;
on branches of government, 147; electronic surveillance and, 89–90; on executive privilege, 137; on government confidentiality, 133; on political and economic
democracy, 167; Sherman Act and, 162,
163; on warrants and reasonableness,
110–11
James I (England), 57
Jay, John, 49, 73, 81, 83, 145
Jay Treaty, 48, 134
Jefferson, Thomas: Constitutional Convention and, 48; on integrity, 67; on law and
language, 53; Louisiana Purchase and,
151; on race, 68; as religious, 66–67; Robert Penn Warren and, 54; separation of
powers and, 49–50, 143–44
Jefferson Lecture, 52–54
Jews and Judaism, 68, 69–70
Johnson, Hugh, 162–63

NRA (National Recovery Administration).
   See National Recovery Administration
   (NRA)
NSA (National Security Agency), xxv,
   xxviii, 96
nursing homes, minimum standards of care
   in, 22

Olmstead v. United States, 88, 99, 101–2, 103,
   104
Omnibus Crime Control and Safe Streets
   Act (1968): minimization requirement
   of, 109; national security and, 113–14;
   other countries' practices and, 118;
   passage of, 94; presidential powers and,
   125; procedures dictated by, 94, 111–12,
   116
open society, requirements of, 71
opinion, public. *See* public opinion
originalism, xiv
Ortiz case. See *United States v. Ortiz*
Otis, James, 98
O. V. W. Hawkins Lecture (Bucknell University), 70–78

Paine, Tom, 142
Paper Chase, The (film), x
Pentagon Papers, 132, 151
Pericles, 71–73
polarization, xvii
Pound, Roscoe, 40, 44
Powell, Louis F., Jr.: on area warrants, 113;
   Branzburg v. Hayes and, 26; on electronic surveillance, 94–95, 100, 111, 114;
   on standing requirements, 155
power, 7–9, 76–77
pragmatism, 10–11
president of the United States: diplomatic
   role of, 134–35; executive privilege and,
   135; FBI and, 170; government confidentiality and, 129; imperial presidency
   and, 140; misuse of FBI by, 173; powers
   of, 150–52; warrantless surveillance and,
   xxiv, xxviii, 120–21, 123–25. *See also* executive branch
privacy, right to: Bill of Rights and, 128;
   communications abroad and, 117; First
   Amendment and, 128; Fourth Amendment and, 99–103, 110–11, 128; govern-

ment confidentiality and, 127–28, 129–30;
   housing inspections and, 104–5; for individuals and organizations, 130; probable
   cause and, 106; reasonable expectations
   and, 103–4. *See also* confidentiality
probable cause. *See* Fourth Amendment
public opinion, 11–15
public service, 70–73

Rabelais, François, 52–53
Ramsay, David, 60–61
Reagan, Ronald, 187n31
reason: artificial, 55, 57; government by,
   51–52; United States as empire of, 49
Reed, Justice, 127
Rehnquist, William, 31
religion, in founding of United States, 66–67
Revolution, American. *See* American
   Revolution
Richardson, Elliot, 16, 95
rights: minimum standards and, 7–8; toler-
   ance and, 67
Rogers, William P., 28, 30
Roman Empire, 141
Romantic idealism, 148
Roosevelt, Franklin, xxii, 89–90, 160–61
Rousseau, Jean-Jacques, 7, 141, 147

Sargent, John G., 88
Saxbe, William, 173
Schlesinger, Arthur, 159
Scowcroft, Brent, 187n32
search and seizure. *See* Fourth Amendment
Securities and Exchange Commission, xxii
security: domestic versus international, 5–6;
   international pressures and, 8; planning
   of U.S. Constitution and, 48
See v. City of Seattle, 105
Senate Judiciary Committee, xxiii, 95
Senate Select Committee on Intelligence,
   xii, xxviii, 119–25
Senate Select Committee on Intelligence
   Activities, 169–76
Senate Select Committee to Study Govern-
   mental Relations with Respect to Intelligence Activities, 86–119
Senate Select Committee v. Nixon, 158
separation of powers: allocation of power
   and, 154–55; benefits of, 141; bills of

separation of powers (*continued*)
attainder and, 153; as bulwark against
tyranny, 160; confidentiality and, 136–37,
156–59; in early United States, 49–50,
139–40; effects of power on those who
hold it and, 64–65; executive privilege
and, 127; federalism and, 145, 146; foreign policy and, 135; government confidentiality and, 127–28; Levi's December
1975 Columbia Law School lecture and,
139–60; national scandal and, 140; origins of, 140–47; as political doctrine, 159;
relationship among branches of government and, 76–77, 81; skeptical optimism and, 147–48; Speech and Debate
Clause of Constitution and, 151–52; tension among branches of government
and, 159–60; as too extreme, 149; versus tyranny, 144; war and, 140. *See also*
branches of government
September 11, 2001, attacks, xxviii, 120
Sherman Act, 160–69, 186n7
Silberman, Laurence, 173
Silverman v. United States, 102
Smith, Adam, 141, 165
Smith, Chesterfield, 16
social change, group action and, 7
Socialist Workers' Party, xxv, xxvii, 169–70
Society of Friends of Touro Synagogue,
66–70
Socrates, 72
Soviet Union, xxv, 91
Stanford University Law School, xxix
Steel Seizure case, 151, 155
Stevens, John Paul, xxiii, xxx
Stewart, Potter, 25
Stiles, Ezra, 66
Stone, Harlan F., 160, 170–71, 173
Sulzbacher Menorial Lecture (Columbia
Law School), 139–60
Supreme Court, U.S.: on electronic surveil-
lance, xxiv, xxviii; John Paul Stevens on,
xxiii; reverse discrimination and, 22;
self-restraint of, 160; William O. Doug-
las on, xxiii
Sweden, 138

Taft, William Howard, 101, 149, 163
technology, as panacea, 4
terrorism, preventive action and, xxvii

Terry v. Ohio, 107, 111
Texas Law Center, 60–66
Title III. *See* Omnibus Crime Control and
Safe Streets Act (1968)
Tocqueville, Alexis de: on Americans' liti-
gious spirit, 6; on moral principal and
political process, 63, 191n46; on public
opinion, 11; on questions for the courts,
62; on salaries for public office, 72
Touro, Judah, 69
Touro Synagogue, 66–70
Tower, John, 96
Truman, Harry S., 89–90, 149
trust, xiii, 2, 16, 126

United States v. Brignoni-Ponce, 107
United States v. Brown, 115, 124, 153
United States v. Burr, 158
United States v. Butenko, 115, 124
United States v. Calandra, 195–96n27
United States v. Curtiss-Wright, 134
*United States v. E. I. DuPont de Nemours &
Co. See DuPont–General Motors* case
United States v. Johnson, 152
United States v. Klein, 152
United States v. Lanza, 27
United States v. Lovett, 152–53
United States v. Nixon, 135, 136–37, 158
United States v. Ortiz, 107
United States v. Reynolds, 133–34
United States v. Richardson, 155
United States v. U.S. Dist. Court (1972). See
Keith case
University of Chicago, xxii–xxiv, xxix, 12,
38, 40
University of Chicago Law School, 37–42
University of Chicago Law School Alumni
Association, 33
University of Nebraska–Lincoln College of
Law, 54–60
utopianism, 4–5

values: common, 71; conflict in, 18; higher
education and, 77–78; justice and law
and, 60
Vietnam War, xi–xii, 5, 59
Voltaire, xvi, 83, 141

Walpole, Robert, 75
Warden v. Hayden, 107